Jobscape:

Career Survival in the New Global Economy

Colin Campbell

jist

Jobscape:

Career Survival in the New Global Economy

Colin Campbell

Published by JIST Works, Inc.
720 N. Park Avenue
Indianapolis, IN 46202-3490
Phone: 317-264-3720 Fax: 317-264-3709
E-mail: jistworks@aol.com
World Wide Web Address: http://www.jist.com

See the back of this book for additional JIST titles and ordering information. Quantity discounts are available.

Library of Congress Cataloging-in-Publication Data

Campbell, Colin, 1948-
Jobscape : career survival in the new global economy / Colin Campbell.
p. cm.
Includes bibliographical references.
ISBN 1-56370-316-5
1. Career development. 2. Self-evaluation. 3. Success in business. I. Title
HF5381.C2538 1997
650.14--dc21 97-28978
CIP

Printed the United States of America

1 2 3 4 5 6 7 8 9 02 01 00 99 98 97

We have been careful to provide accurate information throughout this book, but it is possible that errors and omissions have been introduced. Please consider this in making any important decisions. Trust your own judgment above all else and in all things.

ISBN 1-56370-316-5

To my partner, Carole Hood,
and my mother, Hazel Jean Tomlinson

PREFACE

The inspiration for this book came from noticing the unmistakable mirroring of trends and changes taking place simultaneously at all levels of our existence. While, on the one hand, it was reassuring to see that there is a kind of overall shared pattern in the way most events are unfolding, it was nonetheless daunting to realize that an increasing amount of risk and uncertainty is also accompanying these changes. We are in the midst of a restructuring and reengineering process that is shaping the entire world as we know it. The world has always changed and evolved over time; however, this time around we get to watch and participate in the kind of far-reaching changes that usually take at least 100 to 1000 years to make their presence fully felt. Before, changes took place in a kind of slow, sequential fashion that you could see coming far enough ahead of time to make the necessary adjustments. Today, all kinds of changes are happening simultaneously and over an ever-shortening time horizon.

Technology is transforming just about everything with its Midas touch—and even the technology itself is undergoing what seems like an accelerated evolutionary process by rendering each of its inventions obsolete almost as soon as it is created. For many, it must seem like being trapped inside a computer game where the rules and the challenges keep changing in a never-ending battle. Just when something begins to make sense, the playing field changes once again. Yet despite all of the change and fatigue that is wearing down many people and the full-warp-speed-ahead lives we find ourselves having to embrace, we are moving into an era of incredible opportunity and high reward.

This book was written to give people a better overall sense of how they can minimize the uncertainty and risk with respect to making career and life decisions, yet maximize their upside potential and improve their quality of life. By understanding how the rules of the game are evolving you have a much better chance of anticipating and preparing for the inevitable changes heading your way. But even more importantly, by the end of the book you should also have a better understanding of how to take advantage of these change factors by creating the kind of personal infrastructure and by adopting appropriate self-monitoring, learning, and opportunity-creating strategies that you can leverage enormously in your favor. The trick is to realistically create a positive or virtuous feedback loop built around a powerful personal vision you can commit yourself to fully as opposed to allowing yourself to become trapped in a negative or vicious circle—which is something many people find themselves in by default. You are never lost so long as you have a realistic direction you want to head in and a compass that continually steers you in the direction you want to go.

Obviously, the more you know about the landscape or obstacles you are likely to encounter, the better you can chart a course that minimizes frustration. For only by minimizing stress and uncertainty as much as possible are we able to clear our heads enough to believe that aspiring toward a vision or developing a strategic set of plans or options is even worth while. By the end of the book, you should have a clear understanding of the kind of mind-set, the evolving playing field, and the strategies you will need to thrive in the whitewater world of the 1990s and the twenty-first century.

I would like to especially thank Carole Hood who not only steadfastly believed in the worthwhileness of writing this book, but offered every kind of support possibly needed to spur the project on and bring it to completion, and who was completely unstinting in the amount of time she was willing to devote to the project. She is also responsible for making up all of the charts in the book. In addition, I would like to thank Andrew Hoffer and Greg Iaonnou for their editorial assistance and advice. Lastly, I would like to thank my mother for her heartfelt support and encouragement.

CONTENTS

INTRODUCTION:

The Age of Mass Customization

When someone asked the former President of Poland, Lech Walesa, what had caused the collapse of the Soviet empire in Eastern Europe, he pointed at the television and said, "It came from there." In a broad sense he was referring to the technology that is joining us all together in a global electronic village.

Although daily newspapers cover innovations in virtual reality, the Internet, and multimedia, they rarely mention how these developments are likely to alter the way we work. Yet the technology is completely changing the skills needed by employees, transforming what it means to have a career or to be employed. The scariest part is that many people still assume that the employment situation will return to normal if they just wait long enough.

Despite the effects of technology and the global restructuring of economic forces, many people assume that all they need is a few software skills under their belts in order to get their careers back on track. They think they have to make only minor adjustments to accommodate the role of the computers that now inhabit the workplace. In the 1980s, that notion would have been reasonable. The next decade, however, is going to be one of transition on a scale unparalleled since the Industrial Revolution. The new electronic infrastructure will completely transcend the geographical infrastructure that was the backbone of the industrial era.

People who lose their jobs are having to make career changes more than ever before. In fact, 50 percent of the jobs that will exist by the year 2008 do not exist at the moment. Moreover, the amount of knowledge in the world will have more than doubled by then.

What this tells us is that we must be willing to change our way of thinking and relating to the world and the changes taking place in it. As Einstein once said, "The world will not evolve past its current state of crisis by using the same thinking that created the situation."

To build a career within the new infrastructure, you will have to understand not only the changes that are taking place, but yourself as well. Only when both of these pieces are in place will you be able to thrive in the new economy. This book is designed to help you build that understanding and base career decisions on it.

What exactly are the changes to which we must all adapt?

The End of the Mass-Production Era

The mass-production era, in which everything was uniform, stable, predictable, and a simple extension and refinement of the past, is coming to an end, as is the command-and-control hierarchy that was used to manage it.

Henry Ford's claim that his customers could buy a Model-T Ford in any color so long as it was black neatly summarizes the philosophy of the mass-production era. Obviously the more uniform a society, the larger the economies of scale possible.

The metaphor that best describes such a system is the well-oiled machine. In other words, if America were run like a machine in which every part performed its assigned and coordinated role, it would be an incredibly powerful country capable of accomplishing any mass-market task it decided to take on.

In the 1950s, attempts socially to optimize this strategy promoted conformity in the form of the nuclear family, the home in the suburbs, church on Sunday, two or more children, and membership in country clubs and other community organizations. The social mores of the 1950s reflected a dogmatic belief in the inherent rightness of society's social structures and traditions. Alternatives to marriage were frowned upon since they called into question one's commitment to the greater social good and undermined the notion that there was only one right path in life to follow. This monolithic view of society was unable to contain the diversity that eventually demanded expression and legitimacy.

Although the 1960s saw the rise of alternative lifestyles, the business world was steadfast in its focus on improving the existing system, which had made the U.S. the world economic leader. Because alternative lifestyles were seen as idiosyncrasies that did not disturb the sanctity of the nine-to-five world, they were tolerated as phases people were going through. Although the erosion of family values was constantly lamented, the complaints were only half-hearted so long as the economy was growing and the future looked bright.

The economic underpinnings of society seemed unchallenged, so most problems that emerged were viewed as merely matters in need of reform. The equilibrium of the past could easily be restored, and superficial differences accommodated; all the system needed was a little tinkering.

That equilibrium is now as outdated as Henry Ford's Model T. An age characterized by ongoing innovation demands equally innovative solutions to the problems it generates. Thus the business focus has shifted from management to leadership. For many people, the world as they know it is at risk and in transition, so the need for leadership in all situations has escalated dramatically.

The Age of Mass Customization

The mass-production era is giving way to an age characterized by mass customization now that technology is capable of tailoring products and services to meet the needs of each customer. Sameness was promoted when it made the most economic sense; economies of scale are now proving to be less desirable than unlimited choice at reasonable prices. The new possibilities have naturally created rising consumer expectations, which have become a very powerful economic force.

Whether it is Levi Strauss offering to make your jeans to measure, a bicycle factory offering you a choice of over 12 million bicycle styles, or a software programmer designing a program to meet the particular needs of a company, the one-style-fits-all approach introduced by Henry Ford no longer works.

In a world of 500 or more television channels, no company can afford to advertise on all of them, so we are rapidly witnessing the disappearance of the economies of scale possible when everyone more or less watched the same shows or purchased the same limited range of products.

The bureaucratic corporate and government structures that worked smoothly in the mass-production era were never designed to deal with complex problems or markets that change frequently. Our social institutions and customs were not meant to accommodate the complicated family relationships that have emerged.

Because they cling to a cherished past, most people have not come to terms with the end of job security and the pronounced rise of alternative forms of employment (working out of your house, for instance) and less-permanent employment arrangements such as contract work. This need to customize their careers is bound to present a challenge to those who were looking for an "off-the-shelf" career that they could easily pick and depend on over the long term.

Technology Complicates Our Lives

Instead of making our lives simpler, technology complicates things and accelerates the pace of change. A secretary today is required to know word processing, scheduling, e-mail, database and spreadsheet programs as well as fax modems, laser printers, photocopiers, and scanners. Technology complicates our lives by extending the range of activities we can perform by making each task easier.

The rate at which information technology has allowed us to exchange and manipulate information has revealed the vital role information is capable of playing in all aspects of the economy. We are only beginning to realize how inefficient most of our previous means of obtaining information were. The technological and telecommunication revolution we are experiencing is allowing the information and communication processes so essential to all commerce to transcend geography, encouraging rapid product development to the point where many products have a shelf life of only three months.

When you consider that the service sector creates and distributes wealth largely in the form of information and that 90 percent of all new jobs created over the past ten years were in the service sector, you can begin to glimpse the magnitude of the economic upheaval that will make itself felt throughout the world once this constantly improving information technology becomes widespread. Just as the Red Queen in *Through the Looking-Glass* said that Alice needed to run as fast as she could just in order to stand still, you can see that incredible entrepreneurial zeal and resilience will be needed just to keep up with the pace of change.

New Ways of Thinking

To understand the paradoxical challenges we face, we must develop new ways of thinking to replace the linear, analytical model, that breaks everything down into component parts. Originally popularized by William Taylor in *The Principles of Scientific Management,* the time, function, and motion view of jobs reduced people to identical, replaceable entities. The key to managerial success was to break each function down to its smallest parts to the point where even a low-skilled worker could easily be trained to carry out a few predetermined, simple, repetitive functions. According to this view, all change is incremental and controllable, with computers refining past development, but otherwise leaving the world of work largely intact. Although such reasoning seemed naturally to complement the mass-production era's bureaucratic structure, it was actually an extremely inefficient method of production, as the Japanese have convincingly demonstrated.

This view of the world rested on a belief that all of life's problems can be scientifically scrutinized if you use linear, analytical logic to break down the world into its component parts. Once the basic units are understood and the parts properly arranged and assembled, the assumption is that you can put Humpty Dumpty (the economy) back together, and his mechanical (or economic) functions will be fully restored. Progress consists in continuously improving the parts over time—substituting computers for paper records or calculators, for instance.

Unfortunately, this mechanistic, Newtonian view of life as a closed system has long since been eclipsed by Einstein's theory of relativity and virtually all modern advances in physics, astronomy, computer technology, and biology.

One of the reassuring things we have come to learn recently is that there really is no such thing as chaos in the sense of something completely out of control. Instead, science has revealed to us that the world must be viewed as an ongoing, holistic process.

Most people have always known intuitively that the complexity of human nature and human potential cannot be reduced to a simple schematic explanation. All such attempts are dehumanizing in the end and underestimate the capacity of human beings to change, grow, learn, create, solve problems, and innovate. In other words, it is a rather impoverished view of mankind, as most people who have worked on an assembly line can attest. We have come to learn that the world is a complex place that defies our desire for simple "either-or" explanations or truths.

Open Systems

We cannot afford to see America or our own lives as closed systems. With over 80 percent of U.S. products now subject to foreign competition, those companies still dependent on economies of scale must seek out global markets to survive, let alone thrive. The same will be equally true for many job seekers.

What happens at home has always affected what happens at work, and vice-versa, as shown by the growing number of employee-assistance programs. Nowadays, with people working out of their homes, there is a blurring of boundaries, borders, and barriers. In a world of trade agreements, partnerships, joint ventures, alliances, and teamwork, it is often hard to distinguish where one system begins and another ends. The global village we are beginning to create and inhabit is forcing systems to become more integrated than they were in the past.

Much like the Internet, all parts of our lives are becoming "networked" together in more interdependent ways. Unlike the days of wide-open, undiscovered geographic frontiers, the world is becoming a rather crowded place where nations continually jostle each other in trade disputes. Indeed, the Iron Curtain—the quintessential closed system—ended up as a form of economic solitary confinement with the expected results.

At the same time that the world is becoming more complicated through this fascinating interweaving of diverse open systems, control has shifted to the outer edge of each system where they interact (for example, with customers or suppliers). Decentralization, autonomous teams, and empowered workers are evidence of this transfer of power to the peripheral "linking" points where most interaction takes place.

In the past, mass production was a noninteractive means of doing business. Manufacturers produced products, and marketers were expected to push them through mass-media advertising. What was good for General Motors was good for America. Customers bought what they were told to buy. Now, consumers can tell manufacturers what to produce. In other words, consumers are now democratizing or decentralizing what was a highly centralized and paternalistic process. Likewise, highly skilled workers vital to the information economy now have more choices as to where to work.

Knowledge is the new means of production. The lean-and-mean downsized company of today survives by being flexible and highly responsive to the needs of other open systems wanting to join forces. Much the same applies to those carving out their career destinies: they need to find companies they would like to join forces with for as long as there is some mutual benefit. In the nanosecond 1990s, no one can afford to be asleep at the competitive career wheel.

The merging of open systems is now such that we no longer see one company competing against another so much as one supply chain competing against another. This is clearly evident among the telecommunication giants that have joined forces with program providers and broadcasters or the North American Free Trade Agreement or Euromarket nations. Your company's success now depends on the success of your customers and suppliers, just as your career success may depend on the success of your subordinates, boss, team, division, company, city, state, country, or even continent.

When systems become interlocked, they become codependent, sharing a common destiny. Choosing the systems you want to become a part of, something that even includes where you live and your social network, increasingly will decide your career fate. With so much riding on such decisions, you will constantly want to be revising them to make sure the original reasons—or new, equally valid ones—still apply.

Balancing Opposing Forces

These opposing trends (such as decentralization and integration) need to be balanced or reconciled in order to take advantage of the best of both forces. Despite their apparently contradictory nature, each trend is paradoxically part of mutually interdependent systems that function similarly at all levels. By examining events at the various larger levels, I will try to show how it is possible to learn valuable lessons that apply equally well to each of us in our individual lives.

Transferable Knowledge

By studying the changes taking place at any one level, we can learn lessons that likely apply equally well at other levels. It is becoming increasingly clear that all aspects of life and nature are mirrored at every level of existence—that is, the changes we witness are occurring simultaneously at the world, continent, country, city, company, family, and individual levels. Just as a kind of monolithic societal unity at all levels supported the mass-production era, a decentralizing process is now causing the breakdown or reconfiguration of countries, companies, and even families.

For instance, we are simultaneously witnessing the former Soviet Union disintegrate, large multinational firms downsize into smaller business units, and two-career families strain to coordinate and juggle family responsibilities and career options. On the other hand, there is also an opposing tendency for the world, countries, small and large companies, and individuals to become networked together through a proliferation of joint ventures, business alliances, trade agreements, home business networks, and Internet links.

Regaining Control

We must understand the change process so that we can regain a sense of control and direction in our lives—and careers.

The ultimate purpose of this book is to help you understand the various forces and dynamics that are shaping world events and transforming companies and the workplace, and to show clearly how these dynamics can be applied to career planning. You will be glad to hear that the technologies and organizational strategies transforming hiring practices around the world will solve as many problems as they create.

You can discover most of what you need to know by simply noticing the nature of the changes taking place. The trick then lies in learning how to take advantage of these changes that are transforming the world around us. As we will see, building a career in this environment involves entirely rethinking such concepts as job security in today's "high-risk, high-return" society. The long-term "tried and true" career-building strategies that worked in the past will virtually guarantee frustration today and in the future.

But there is no need to panic in the face of so much of the change that is rearranging the world of work. For if there is one thing that characterizes Americans, it is their irrepressible resiliency. As Joel Garreau declares in *Edge City*:

> For the one thing Americans demonstrably have done better than any other culture in history—for centuries—is handle chaos and change, and invent the future. Americans are part of a wildly individualistic, determined culture that may or

> not know how to resolve dilemmas, but does attack obstacles—compulsively and reflexively. Americans believe, endearingly and in spite of all evidence, that for every problem, there is a solution. Responding to a challenge by doing nothing is not our long suit.... Fatalism is outside our repertoire. Once Americans have chosen a future, it is open to being molded and shaped, but anyone merely standing in its way is inviting a trampling. Sooner or later Americans usually clean up their new order and get it somewhere quite close to right—no matter how terrifying it appears at the beginning.

The plan of the book is to begin by examining what works well for high-performing companies, countries, and cultures and to use this larger context to frame our discussion in the last half of the book of how you might translate these trends into strategies that will work for you in your career and life planning. The reason for adopting such an approach stems from the realization that in the evolutionary process both the individual and the surrounding environment coevolve together. Understanding how the sand is shifting under your feet now requires taking a larger view of the surrounding environment. In order for Americans to "attack obstacles" and "mold and shape their future," it is now necessary to do so within the expanded realm of the global village. We are now playing in a "World Series" where the level of worldwide interactivity continues to increase daily. In other words, what is happening in Singapore can have a profound effect on your career options in America. In a whitewater world that never sleeps, the only way to avoid career vertigo or dizziness is by finding a powerful compass or vision and developing an awareness of a few dependable insights, patterns, or trends that will help you navigate amidst the shoals and undertows of the rather bumpy or discontinuous and irreversible change process in which we are all finding ourselves immersed.

It is my hope that by the end of the book, you will feel less overwhelmed by the seemingly endless number of nagging job-related problems that can be extremely anxiety provoking, if not depressing, when added together. Instead, I believe that there is no reason that you should not become energized by the possibilities and opportunities that lie in front of you once you can better grasp the way the world is "wobbling." All you need to do is choose the future and try to avoid trampling others as you forge ahead.

PART I

The Grand Experiment

CHAPTER 1

The Vision Thing

If an organization is to meet the challenges of a changing world, it must be prepared to change everything about itself except [its] beliefs as it moves through corporate life.... The only sacred cow in an organization should be its basic Philosophy of doing business.

—TOM WATSON, THE FOUNDER OF IBM

Some companies that have been around for many decades have outperformed the stock market by fifteen times the average stock growth. They have managed to renew themselves during every phase of their growth. Unlike companies that go through the traditional corporate life cycle, which eventually leads to mature stability and the slow decline of market share, these firms have gone from one success to another.

What distinguishes these firms from the many also-rans and short-term wonders? Charismatic leaders? Competitiveness? Focus on profits? Brilliant strategies? Great ideas? As it happens, though each is worthy of consideration, none of these factors proved essential to their continued success.

The driving force behind these successful companies is a set of core values that translates into a compelling vision. Since the values are more important than any individual within the organization, the company becomes the living embodiment of these core beliefs. Thus charismatic leaders are not necessary—the values themselves generate a sense of mission and common purpose.

Since it takes time to build a powerful vision, these long-lasting companies do not enjoy early entrepreneurial success. While entrepreneurs typically try to come up with a great idea and ride the product or economic cycle, visionary companies are more concerned with becoming the kind of company employees can continue to believe in. They are willing to give up on any particular product—but not on the company itself.

By developing a powerful vision, these companies have the persistence to follow through completely in their efforts to make their vision a reality. They are too committed to give up, and therein lies the secret of renewal and prolonged growth. Ideas and products become obsolete with time, but values never do. Making products that reflect highly worthwhile values never goes out of fashion.

Continuity and Consistency

Building an organization that can provide products and services that reflect the corporate vision requires an emphasis on continuity. Spending time and energy developing employees and then promoting from within are the easiest ways to ensure that highly prized values will be passed to those equally devoted to maintaining the ideals and integrity fundamental to the company's identity.

According to James Collins and Jerry Porras, authors of *Built to Last,* "In seventeen hundred years of combined life spans across the visionary companies, we found only four individual incidents of going outside for a CEO—and those only in two companies." Internal promotion ends up being one of the values espoused—the just reward for dedication to the organization's mission. Not surprisingly, there is relatively little turnover in visionary companies.

Once consistency is assured as part of the organizational design, it is easy for companies to experiment with ways to act on the core ideology.

Sam Walton, the founder of Wal-Mart, believed very strongly in experimentation, continuous improvement, and change. His concept of "a store within a store" encouraged department managers to run their sections like separate businesses. Freedom of this kind is characteristic of visionary companies.

Motorola even welcomes open disagreement about its products—but not about its core values. It is assumed that once the values are fully instilled, employees will always make decisions that are in keeping with these values.

Nordstrom's notorious one-page employee handbook baldly states: "Rule #1: Use your good judgment in all situations. There will be no other rules." Assuming that employees have bought into the notion of providing outstanding customer service, of asking anyone in the organization "any question at any time," and of "set[ting] both your personal and professional goals high," each employee is expected to rely on initiative and judgment since Nordstrom has "great confidence in [each employee's] ability" without direct supervision.

The Profit Paradox

A core ideology even takes precedence over the profit motive. Ironically, those companies that place their primary emphasis on maximizing profit tend to perform poorly compared to those with loftier ambitions, such as achieving high levels of innovation, product quality, customer service, or value.

Hewlett-Packard, which stresses high-quality products that must make a technical contribution to the industry, has easily outperformed Texas Instruments, which stresses sales and financial goals. Ford, which usually outperforms GM, eventually decided that people come first, products second, and profits third, according to former CEO Don Petersen. During the 1980s, when Ford was hit with a $3.3 billion net loss over three years, it managed to get back on track by refashioning its core values.

As John Kotter and James Heskett noted in *Corporate Culture and Performance*,

> Firms with cultures that strongly emphasized all the key management constituencies (customers, shareholders, and employees) and leadership from managers at all levels outperformed firms that did not by a huge margin. Over an eleven year period, the former increased revenues by an average of 682 percent vs. 166 percent for the latter, expanded their workforces by 282 percent vs. 36 percent, grew their stock prices by 901 percent vs. 74 percent, and improved their net incomes by 756 percent vs. 1 percent.

How Successful Are Visionary Companies?

To see how important vision is, just compare Procter & Gamble to Colgate-Palmolive, Motorola to Zenith, Nordstrom to Sears, Ford to GM, Boeing to McDonnell-Douglas, or Disney to Columbia Pictures.

In most cases, the comparison companies are usually left contemplating the vapor trail of the visionary companies and wondering what happened. By 1985, Marriott had come from behind and surpassed Howard Johnson seven times over.

Why are they so successful? By concentrating on building a powerful organization rather than merely chasing after an exciting idea or depending on a charismatic leader, visionary companies build a permanent structure capable of weathering all changes. In today's rapid-paced world, great ideas quickly become obsolete, and today's leader may be tomorrow's millstone. Visionary companies, with their strongly held values, sense of purpose, and profound commitment to whatever helps them realize their goals, usually shape the future. Their competitors are left reacting to the changes initiated by the visionary companies in the equivalent of playing by their opponents' rules. Whereas the comparison companies are having to downsize, which destroys morale and causes confusion, the visionary companies are usually positioning themselves for further growth.

In a world where people can work out of their homes, cars, or customers' locations, employees of visionary companies more than ever need to share a common purpose to compensate for the natural isolation such possibilities promote. Something must remain constant throughout the change process.

As C. K. Prahalad and Gary Hamel stressed in their book *Competing for the Future,* getting to the future first puts you in the driver's seat, whereas your competitors are forced to become passengers sitting in the back. Changing the metaphor slightly, during an age in which the road to the future always seems to be under construction, deciding where the road is going to go is much better than trying to figure out where someone else's road is likely to lead.

How It Works

By embodying both change and consistency, visionary companies are able to take on paradoxical challenges. They manage to prepare well for their long-term success by insisting on high standards even in the short run. By focusing on short-term quality, they guarantee long-term success. They invest in training, technology, and innovative practices, laying the groundwork for long-term accomplishments. By stressing the importance of the customer, they reap abundant profits.

They improve both incrementally and globally by taking larger risks. And they succeed in being both idealistic and practical at the same time.

Success comes not from choosing between polarities, but from embracing and reconciling both. The tension created becomes the creative challenge visionary companies welcome. In fact, resolving such conflicts energizes them by allowing them to get the best of both worlds. Thus vision is by its very nature inclusive. It brings together a large number of elements into a picture or whole that makes obvious sense.

As Collins and Porras summarize in *Built to Last*:

> The essence of a visionary company comes in the translation of its core ideology and its own unique drive for progress into the very fabric of the organization—into goals, strategies, tactics, policies, processes, cultural practices, management behaviors, building layouts, pay systems, accounting systems, job design—into everything that the company does. A visionary company creates a total environment that envelops employees, bombarding them with a set of signals so consistent and mutually reinforcing that it's virtually impossible to misunderstand the company's ideology and ambitions.... Visionary companies do not rely on any one program, strategy, tactic, mechanism, cultural norm, symbolic gesture, or CEO speech to preserve the core and stimulate progress. It's the whole ball of wax.... A visionary company is like a great work of art.

The core ideologies of all successful companies have naturally embedded visionary beliefs into their everyday operations. As Johnson & Johnson, an industry leader, stresses in its credo, its customers come first; its employees, second; management, third; the community in "support of good works and charity," fourth; and the stockholders, last.

During the Tylenol crisis, all product was immediately recalled, new tamper-proof packaging was quickly engineered and designed, and network videos were distributed—a clear demonstration of placing the customer before financial concerns.

Merck, in its *Internal Management Guide* (1989) proclaims, "We are in the business of preserving and improving human life. All of our actions must be measured by our success in achieving this goal." These words are more than just platitudes since Merck gave Mectizan away to Third World countries suffering from onchocerciasis, or river blindness, and provided the Japanese with free streptomycin after World War II to help eradicate tuberculosis. That Merck is now the biggest American pharmaceutical company in Japan should not come as a surprise.

In contrast to Johnson & Johnson's response to a serious public relations challenge, Intel tried to ignore complaints about defective Pentium chips. It was only when customers on the Internet became so vociferous in their displeasure that a replacement offer was made. In the age of customer responsiveness, it does not pay to place profits ahead of consumer concerns.

Vision and ideology need to be highly motivating if they are to rally the staff around a common purpose for many generations. Andy Grove, CEO of Intel, believes that "only the paranoid survive." While some inherent wisdom is beyond dispute in this statement, such a philosophy is not likely to provide for motivation over the long term. Fear is never as engaging as a worthwhile cause.

Hot Groups

The 3M Company illustrates how visionary companies align their goals, organizational design, reward system, and strategies around their vision of continuous innovation. At 3M, employees are expected to spend 15 percent of their time working on new products of their own choosing, because 30 percent of the company's annual sales must be based on products developed within the past four years. The company grants technology-sharing awards to people who develop new products and share it with other divisions. New product forums share all new product developments with other divisions. At technical forums, papers, ideas, and findings are exchanged. Dual-ladder career tracks exist for technical people who wish to continue their research without being penalized for not taking a managerial track.

Most innovations stem from "hot groups," which usually operate beyond the normal confines of bureaucratic control. They reveal the creative power of working for something important or relevant. Apple in its early years was a hotbed of innovation, with everyone working there eager to take on IBM and invent a truly user-friendly computer. Steve Jobs managed to lure John Sculley away from a brilliant career at Pepsico by asking if he would rather be part of changing the world instead of just selling sugar water. For Sculley, moving to Apple was a career demotion, yet the challenge of being part of something exciting, new, and on the leading edge proved irresistible.

Harold Leavitt and Jean Lipman-Blumen observe that hot groups feel that they "are embarking on a journey that will make the world a better place.... [and] feel that they are stretching themselves, surpassing themselves, moving beyond their own prior performance limits.... In contrast to traditional committees and task forces ... hot group members volunteer for extra work and even create it for themselves."

Expressing the Vision

For most visionary companies, believing in the organization's vision usually takes on a cultlike status. In other words, it is not so much the nature of the belief, as how deeply the vision is believed. Thus in order to gain the kind of authenticity necessary to inspire total commitment, the vision must be represented by words something an individual can live by. A timeless quality is required if a vision is to be continually inspiring and renewing.

The vision must be in language that a large number of people can easily relate to and ideally share, for it must express a common purpose that creates a sense of bonding and belonging.

Thomas Watson, Jr. declared in a 1963 IBM booklet entitled *A Business and Its Beliefs* that a corporation's success "can very often be traced to the question of how well the organization brings out the great energies and talents of its people. What does it do to help these people find common cause with each other?" To withstand the test of time, visions must even transcend the contexts they operate in, because the environment will undoubtedly change over the years. Thus these beliefs must pass crucial evolutionary challenges in order to provide inspiration. The best visions actually change the world in the process of seeking their fulfillment. Indeed, the best way to predict the future is to invent it.

Perpetual Change

Visions must embody the notion of progress and act as a spur to initiate the change process itself. As Sam Walton claimed, "You can't just keep doing what works one time, because everything around you is always changing. To succeed, you have to stay out in front." By shaping the future, visionary companies both renew themselves and ensure their continued success.

Robert Galvin, son of the founder of Motorola, echoes this belief when he claims that "Renewal is the driving thrust of this company.... Only those incultured with an elusive idea of renewal, which obliges the proliferation of new, creative ideas ... and an unstinting dedication to committing to the risk and promise of those unchartable ideas, will thrive."

Collins and Porras in their book *Built to Last* quote a Hewlett-Packard marketing manager who nicely captures both the need for renewal and ongoing challenge:

> We're proud of our successes, and we celebrate them. But the real excitement comes in figuring out how we can do even better in the future. It's a never-ending process of seeing how far we can go. There's no ultimate finish line where we can say "We've arrived." I never want us to be satisfied with our success, for that's when we'll begin to decline.

The inspiration for such change is usually a vision that is extremely bold and demanding. Conquering a mountain is a much more rewarding and inspiring ambition than merely hiking up some foothills. Walt Disney's desire to shape the imagination of children around the world is clearly an all-encompassing mission limited only by the organization's creativity. As Disney said in his Disneyland opening speech, "Disneyland will never be completed as long as there is imagination left in the world."

Turning the Vision into Action

Fundamental beliefs usually lead to the adoption of practices that reinforce both the vision and its realization. The actual strategies and tactics employed are always subject to change so long as they fulfill their intended purpose. Those companies that mistake specific practices adopted at any point in time for the actual mission tend to eventually run into serious trouble once the environment alters. Thus a distinction must be made between values, purpose, and implementation strategies. The values and purposes of an organization rarely change, but the strategies are judged solely upon their instrumentality or ability to facilitate the realization of the vision.

The difference between the vision and reality reveals the immense scope for improvement. The tension created by this difference leads to constant self-monitoring and suggestions on how to achieve the vision. Companies that fail rarely have an inspiring vision to give them such a self-critical perspective. Moreover, self-awareness is minimized if the vision is not very ambitious. By being cautious, companies tend to accomplish little and adapt to change only incrementally. With challenging goals, the contrast between the present and what is sought is striking, and the imperative to act and change is unavoidable.

For the sake of measuring progress and adopting appropriate strategies, corporate goals need to be relatively clear and straightforward. Ambitious goals stand out boldly. If someone claims he is going to quit smoking today, there is little confusion regarding what is meant. When companies want to be the technological leader in some industry, it is an equally tangible or concrete goal. Henry Ford's mission to "democratize the automobile" by making it affordable for everyone was both ambitious and easily assessable. As a vision to believe in, it was inspiring and rewarding—something that is essential if sufficient commitment is to be generated to achieve what may seem impossible.

Interestingly, the stronger the belief in the vision, the less daunting the challenges that lie ahead—which explains why most entrepreneurs do not consider themselves risk takers. At Sony or Boeing, for instance, once a commitment is made to a formidable goal, there is no going back. So long as the goal is in keeping with the company's overall vision, it is easy to translate the belief in the vision into a commitment towards the intimidating goal.

Sony bet everything on being the first to use transistors and to miniaturize consumer electronic products. This was in line with its vision of advancing technology to enhance the public's enjoyment of entertainment. Boeing committed almost all of its resources to developing the 747 when there was no perceived demand for it. But the plane was part of the company's vision of itself as a pioneer in aeronautical development. By taking a larger view of what was possible and by dedicating themselves to achieving it, both companies now largely dominate their respective industries.

As Motorola's Robert Galvin suggests, "At times [you] must engage in an act of faith that key things are doable that are not provable." Motorola is currently backing this claim by spending $3.4 billion on its Iridium worldwide satellite system, which will be capable of connecting everyone electronically to and from anywhere on the planet.

How Visionary Companies Select Their Employees

To cultivate the kind of dedication necessary to achieving such startling goals, most visionary companies select employees extremely carefully and promote extensively from within. Most workers are expected to start at the bottom and work their way up as part of the natural initiation process into the values and rituals of the organization. People who do not fit into the mold are asked to leave quickly, but once it becomes obvious that they aren't a very good fit, they usually choose to go elsewhere. The extraordinarily high level of commitment needed to achieve the ambitious goals undertaken requires that everyone be similarly aligned in his or her beliefs and dedication.

Thus the visionary company devotes what might seem like excessive time and energy in orienting new recruits to the company's way of doing business. Nordstrom, Marriott, McDonald's, Procter & Gamble, and particularly Disney are well known for their recruiting expertise, exhaustive training programs, and "universities." Joining such organizations is akin to joining a cult or a clan of sorts; however, unlike the bureaucracies that demand an all-consuming devotion, these organizations require that energies be aimed at the vision and not the company. In other words, the company exists only to serve the vision.

Shared values and beliefs are the glue that holds visionary companies together—helping the parts naturally integrate into a larger whole. As Robert Galvin states, "One responsibility [we] considered paramount is seeing to the continuity of capable senior leadership. We have always striven to have proven backup candidates available, employed transition programs to best prepare the prime candidates.... We believe that continuity is immensely invaluable." Porras and Collins found visionary companies "six times more likely to promote insiders to chief executive than comparison companies."

Sharing values does not lead to "group-think," in which everyone strives for a kind of artificial consensus in order to maintain harmony at the expense of exposing genuine conflict that needs addressing. Hot groups avoid getting stuck in the trap of trying to please one another. The gap that exists between the vision and the current reality prevents a prevailing sense of complacency.

Procter & Gamble instituted internal product competitions to stimulate change and growth. Hewlett-Packard ranks employees continually to reward merit; not surprisingly, new recruits are subject to a minimum of eight interviews prior to hiring. Similarly, Marriott interviews over 1,000 employees for 100 positions. In other words, competition is endemic in visionary companies, but it is competition for a common cause. Losers are not penalized so much as encouraged to learn from the best practices of their internal competitors.

Why the internal competition? Visionary companies essentially mirror the external market conditions inside their companies so that they can control their evolutionary development better and learn more in the process. By trying a number of experiments and retaining only the successful initiatives, the organizations maintain both their high standards and sense of direction. The natural selection process is a friendly one since everyone is seen as playing on the same team in support of a worthwhile cause. Such competition is meant to be healthy and part of the pioneering spirit of adventure. Since all lessons learned are shared throughout the organization, the playing field is a level one.

The low turnover rate lets visionary companies spend more on training; they also spend more on newer technology and on getting closer to customers or providing them with new, exciting options.

Visionary companies embrace the challenge and change that accompany all attempts to make the world a better place in some way. Their employees share in the missionary zeal of being a part of such a worthy undertaking. Individuals, like the companies mentioned, also need to have compelling visions of their future that they can immerse themselves in fully.

No one can navigate in turbulent water without a rudder and at least a fairly good idea of what direction he or she would like to go. Without a goal, there is no way of deciding which direction to take. Perhaps this is why visionary companies and individuals are so successful in life. Everything they do has a purpose and is part of a plan. In fact, it is all a labor of love. Viewed in this way, challenge and change serve as new opportunities to explore other dimensions of what is already a fascinating subject. No wonder turnover rates are so low and profits so high at visionary companies.

But what is the common direction most visionary companies are headed? And what or who is setting the direction? As we will see in the next chapter, technological innovation focused on better serving the customer is constantly reconfiguring the world and the workplace. The reengineering revolution and the emphasis on continual quality improvement offer the promise of ongoing renewal and instant customer satisfaction. But as we will see, the main bottleneck in realizing this promised land is often not the technology, but our inability to keep up with advancing technology and accept a faster rate of change.

CHAPTER 2

The Reengineering Revolution

A human is the cheapest, lightest, most flexible and reprogrammable machine money can buy.

—Tom Blunt
Manufacturing Consultant

The reengineering revolution has its roots in the "quality movement" of the 1980s. Edward Deming studied quality control in Japan and concluded that the main objective was to train everyone to "optimize for the whole system." The quality approach, according to Deming, required democratic cooperation, trust, and job security for employees. It was assumed that if employees were happy, they would willingly work to improve quality. So large American auto firms jumped on the quality bandwagon during the 1980s.

However, by the end of the Bush administration, many companies had become impatient with the high employee training costs and the slow change that characterize any incremental approach. As downsizing began in earnest during the recession, most of the high-morale preconditions associated with the quality movement evaporated rather suddenly. In its place rose the notion of reengineering corporate structures to better serve customers.

Reengineering, which is championed by Michael Hammer and James Champy, does not require employee involvement in the change adjustment process, even though cross-function collaboration is a recommended design feature. Reengineering is a top-down approved process using information experts to reconfigure the work flow to serve the customer better and to reduce cycle time or production costs by taking full advantage of the technologies available. It is a "slash-and-burn" approach that takes no prisoners. It is quick, painful, and complete. Needless to say, it requires considerable corporate resolve to fully carry out this uncompromising process to its end.

Does Reengineering Work?

Reengineering has had mixed success. According to a 1994 survey conducted by the CSC Index entitled *State of Reengineering Report*, 16 percent achieved extraordinary results, 17 percent had favorable outcomes, 42 percent reported average to marginal results, and 25 percent were no further ahead. Not surprisingly, 43 percent of the North American firms and 31 percent of the European companies reported "serious difficulties in changing the corporate culture" to be the number-one problem encountered.

Those firms that set high reengineering goals, use strategic ambitions to drive the process, and follow through step-by-step are enjoying the greatest rewards. These companies combined some aspects of the quality approach with the total transformation goal of reengineering. They used an incremental approach, orchestrated managerial and behavioral change by involving people and intensifying communication, and made sure that everyone clearly understood the milestones to be achieved along the way and the strategic importance of the overall initiative. You can be sure that managing the human component in the change process was essential for all companies that enjoyed significant benefits.

Becoming Specialists

As part of the reengineering process, companies are reevaluating how they will try to achieve market leadership.

According to Michael Treacy and Fred Wiersema in *The Discipline of Market Leaders,* Henry Ford founded his company on the theory and practice of vertical integration, which led to a single-threaded manufacturing process:

> More recently, however, companies have found ways to achieve greater efficiency—not by vertically integrating, but by virtually integrating. Today, operationally excellent companies view themselves and their suppliers and distributors not as discrete, allied entities, but as members of a single product supply team.

Developing a competitive strategy, in other words, is no longer just something that is done in isolation; it takes into account and tries to leverage all of the relationships developed among other interconnected companies.

As automobile manufacturers eventually came to realize, it is virtually impossible to be the best at all vertical aspects of the auto industry. It is much smarter to focus on key competitive advantages at which you excel, and partner with companies that are the best in their specialty area of the value-added chain. Thus companies are having to become specialists in their competitive focus. Some set their goal at becoming the price leader; others, at becoming the best in customer service, quality, value, or speed of delivery. The companies that will come to dominate in the twenty-first century will manage to combine all of these attributes through partnerships with other internal or external firms.

What is changing is the very meaning of the word *specialization.* In most people's minds, specialization conjures up an image of narrowing to some obscure area of study—a logical or analytical process leading to ever-greater separateness and exclusion. The boundaries among companies or different areas of knowledge are beginning to disappear because of the increasing integration that is taking place at all levels. Specialization now refers to a focus on one or more aspects of the integration process and not the endless pursuit of finer distinctions in isolation.

Only by working in an integrative fashion can companies and individuals who specialize mesh seamlessly with one another to achieve the virtual integration that opens up the possibilities of making products or delivering services that combine more than one leadership focus.

The Japanese were the first to show that this was possible with their cars that were high in quality, value, performance, and customer service. More recently the Lexus by Toyota redefined the standards possible in a luxury car at an unheard of low price—even with the soaring value of the yen.

The View from the Top

It sounds unlikely, but Stephen Hawking's description of the physical properties of time applies to corporate change:

> Another prediction of general relativity is that time should appear to run slower nearer a massive body like the earth.... To someone high up, it would appear that everything down below was taking longer to happen.

Corporate change seems to take longer from a management perspective, and the view from thirty thousand feet up obscures the richness and complexity below. To counteract this problem, multinationals have radically restructured their companies to get closer to their customers. Asea Brown Boveri, an extremely big Swedish-Swiss engineering multinational, has subdivided into 1,300 independent companies and 5,000 profit centers.

Obviously a school of small fish—that is, many companies within a larger company—can change direction more easily than a whale (large multinational). Within companies, restructuring has revolved around creating teams and empowering front-line workers (minnows, if we extend the analogy). In addition, the front-line workers or teams are backed up with complex information technology systems and experts to call upon when problems arise. Thus the need for a closer relationship with the customer is transforming all business relationships, both inside and outside companies.

A company full of minnows swimming as a school has not only incredible responsiveness but also the power of a much larger fish. If the company is similarly networked with other such companies, they gain the power of a whale while retaining their nimbleness. It would then seem that both multinationals and smaller companies are trying to take on similar shapes: groups within groups within groups—a coherent yet flexible form of complexity. By putting most of the decision making and complexity inside each team or business unit, it is possible to achieve a greater amount of responsiveness, accountability, and simplicity within a complex system.

Reengineering and Technology

In some form, reengineering is as unavoidable as change itself. The driving factor behind most of the changes we are encountering is technological innovation. Technology is still only beginning to show us what it is capable of, so we are in for many waves of change. The capability of computers to talk to one another and the eventual interactive world (which gets closer every day) represent innovation at a quantum level at which some threshold of accumulated incremental improvement is reached. Corporate structures will evolve to take advantage of each new major innovation. Only those companies that involve their employees extensively in the change process are likely to succeed.

Despite job loss, which is an inevitable part of reengineering, the pink-slip numbers pale in comparison to downsizing and restructuring efforts not involving reengineering. Having said that, it must be remembered that reengineering is not a one-time process. As newer, improved technology comes along, reengineering turns into an evolutionary process.

The quality movement, unfortunately, was unable to keep pace with the speed of technological development. Thus the Japanese are now visiting the United States in an attempt to learn all about reengineering. On the other hand, the reengineering revolution won't succeed unless a culture of change management, at both the incremental and quantum level, flourishes. As is often the case with competing models, companies need to strive for the best of both approaches.

The first connection between reengineering and customer service has to do with a company's workforce or its internal customers. Indeed, as consultant Robert Desatnick's research has found, effective management of the workforce is the key to success. Superior management skills account for 80 percent of the opportunity for productivity and profitability improvement. For as Nobel Laureate Gary Baker observes, "Economists estimate that human capital accounts for much more than half of all wealth in the United States and other economically advanced nations."

Reengineering Customer Service

Customer service has become a collaborative negotiation and education process between the customer and the entire workings of the organization. As the McKinsey Consulting Group is fond of proclaiming, "When you've hired the services of a representative, you have hired the entire company."

The same applies inside an organization. With experts or professional staff assisting customer service representatives and one representative possibly passing on customers to other service staff, seamless coordination is necessary, and a unified image of the company must be presented to the customer. An important ingredient in the success of McDonald's restaurants is consistency.

The people inside an organization need a clear understanding of how what they do meshes with the activities of everyone else, especially if they are working in cross-functional teams. With compensation increasingly dependent on profit sharing, a clear understanding of the various business subject areas is unavoidable. Everyone must possess, in a sense, a major in general business so that a common negotiating language can be used to resolve disputes. At Krueger International, a furniture company, an entry-level forklift driver must be able to read and understand balance sheets and financial statements, use a computer, act as a team leader when required, interview prospective employees, and understand basic statistical control information. Other companies require entry-level workers to make presentations to senior management; conduct company tours; give evidence of creative decision making, negotiation, and problem-solving techniques; demonstrate excellent interpersonal skills; display rapid and broad learning abilities; communicate effectively in writing; and demonstrate excellent listening skills—especially since each internal and external customer operates in a different context.

The list could go on, but the main point is clear. Just at the time that companies have become far more specialized, the need for entrepreneurial specialists/generalists with excellent communication abilities and business understanding has arrived. All employees are expected to be customer service representatives who operate their parts of the business as though they were in business for themselves, yet in partnership with everyone else inside the firm. Are there any weaknesses in your generic skills (for example, communication, math, computer literacy, broad-based business skills, learning ability)? If so, what do you plan to do about them? For remember, whatever your area of specialization, you will need to manage and coordinate your roles and responsibilities up, down, horizontally within your organization, as well as integrate the foregoing with suppliers' and customers' agendas.

What Is a Customer?

The definition of *customer* has effectively shifted to mean anyone with whom you have a flexible, adaptable, or continually negotiated relationship. As the world becomes more complex, companies are reducing the number of relationships, and solidifying, the ones that remain. Consequently, Motorola has reduced the number of its suppliers by 70 percent, 3M by 64 percent, and Ford by 45 percent. The suppliers (customers) are now being asked to take on many of the purchasing company's problems; help with design (both GM and BMW allow their suppliers to assist in car design); and even assist in financing, logistics (Procter & Gamble and Wal-Mart invested in a mutually beneficial information system that facilitate continuous stock replenishment), and R&D. Even retail customers are playing a much larger role in what is now a "co-design or creation" sales process given the mass customization possibilities inherent in flexible manufacturing. Within companies, workers are customizing their benefit packages and continually negotiating and redesigning their job descriptions and remuneration.

Just how close can close get? Digital Equipment applies the same internal performance-evaluation system to its suppliers; Sears is involved in the hiring of people at Sherwin-Williams who will be responsible for handling Sears' paint purchases; GE and Xerox have their people go to one another's in-house training sessions; and Eastman Kodak allows suppliers to run its supply shops.

The general direction toward which all this is headed is "systems integration." If each supplier can provide for the full range of needs in a particular area, then complex purchasing decisions become much simpler. For instance, Baxter Healthcare supplies American hospitals with whatever they need, even if it is made by a competitor. Baxter also provides hospitals with the computer systems that allow them to reorder instantly upon consumption. Big computer companies such as Unisys and IBM now call themselves system integrators since they want to provide one-stop information technology shopping for large corporate, governmental, and institutional customers regardless of the product sold.

Fortunately for the average customer like you and me, the same kind of system integration is now entering all aspects of customer service and staff training. When you call customer service, you do not want to be passed from person to person or endure a long wait while files are checked. But how is it possible to empower a single customer representative to answer all of your questions and summon up any information you might require quickly?

Restructuring "Customer Relations"

Employee relations and customer relations are inseparable. As Sam Walton once said, "The way management treats the associates is exactly the way the associates will then treat the customers. And if the associates treat the customers well, the customers will return again and again, and that is where the real profit in this business lies." The Japanese emphasize this outlook by placing employees first, customers second, and shareholders third.

The entire image conveyed by the company to customers is a result of their experience with the firm's representatives. This has always been true, but why is it more important now than in the past?

Previously, most products and services were simpler in nature and so was the concept of selling. Understanding a product or service used to be fairly easy, as was getting something fixed if you had a problem with your purchase or service. Harvard's Theodore Levitt describes the sales process that governed this era as "transaction marketing." The emphasis was on the single sale, there was a modest service component, the product was described according to features, and there was minimal commitment to the buyer. Such simple products or services were more like commodities, so the main selling feature was price. Employers also viewed workers as replaceable commodities, so the hiring focus was on wages. Sales representatives did not need to know much more than the price and some obvious product features, since customers were not faced with complicated decisions.

Today products and services are multifaceted and potentially endless in number. Once interactive shopping arrives in full force, the number of goods available to consumers will not be limited by shelf space. Most products nowadays are very complex, and if they don't work, chances are you won't be able to fix them yourself. People who make their first computer purchase need their hand held throughout the process and for many months afterwards. Every new piece of software is accompanied by what seems like a ten-pound manual. Technical support services, unlike the Maytag repairman, always have their phones ringing. The products themselves are upgradable, so that when you are making an initial purchase, you are in effect signing up for subsequent purchases to keep your product current. So the sales process has been fundamentally transformed.

Continuous Sales

The focus is now on continuous sales. The products have become "systems" that require considerable explanation. After-market service has become essential to assuring customers that they will be able to figure out how it works or how to get it repaired. To gain the trust of the purchaser in making a complex purchasing decision, a high commitment to understanding and acknowledgment of the buyer's needs must be clearly evident. Welcome to the world of "relationship marketing," now that each customer represents a potential long-term stream of purchases. Every good car salesperson knows that each customer represents at least a dozen potential sales. Now everyone else is beginning to figure this out.

Since customers are being seduced into long-term relationships with vendors, it now costs five times more to obtain a customer than to keep one. The cost of losing customers is five times the annual value of their accounts. On the upside, a 5 percent increase in customer retention can raise profitability by 25 percent to 85 percent.

The time it takes to learn about a customer's individual preferences and needs is an investment in the customer as a future purchaser. It saves the customer from having to educate another company about what it is he or she would like. In an era when time is precious, most customers prefer one-stop shopping at a place that knows them well.

Hiring, training, and motivating sales staff are no longer simple tasks. To complicate matters further, virtually everyone in the organization is now expected to assume a sales or marketing role. By reengineering corporate structures to serve customers better, everyone in the organization has been thrust into a customer service role. Large corporations have downsized and restructured because too many people in the company were too far from the customers and as a result were making inappropriate decisions.

Companies now have more respect for the increasing importance and complexity of the modern sales relationship and the need to remain close to the customer. When messages are passed from person to person, they are diluted in the process, so people further from the customer do not understand the complexities now challenging sales staff. Ideally, corporate reengineering is meant to improve customer relations by using technology to simplify processes and give everyone inside the company access to the same customer service information in "real time." By doing so, everyone can act as a customer service representative.

IPS. The Customer Takes Over

In the past our computer hardware capability has always surpassed our software's ability and the software's capability has usually outstripped the abilities of most human beings. The focus has been on making the machines more powerful, smarter, and faster; but the user has had to try to keep pace with the computer and not the other way around. Happily, we have finally crossed that bridge to the user-friendly side. Information systems can now help in the delivery of comprehensive, seamless customer service in a manner easily understood and carried out by customer service representatives.

By using what is called Integrated Performance Support (IPS), it is possible to focus at the level of knowledge of worker performance, support that performance on demand, and integrate the performance support facilities. As described by Charles Winslow and William Bramer in their book *Future Work:*

> The benefits of Integrated Performance Support [are] more satisfied workers; more productive and efficient workers; workers who take a fraction of the time to reach basic proficiency levels and then higher proficiency levels; workers who can exceed customer expectations because the support they require to respond to a customer's needs is right there at the workstation; workers who, above all, meet and exceed the performance requirements of their jobs continuously. And the overall result: satisfied customers.

By giving employees the means to easily serve customers well, everyone ends up satisfied. The IPS system is not just a concept; it has been used since 1993 by McCaw Cellular Communications, Rogers Cantel Mobile Communications, Connecticut Natural Gas, North West Water, and Guided Social Simulation.

Already the system is moving on to its next evolutionary phase, which is where the customer takes over the entire process. Hallmark has installed touch-screen kiosks that give customers the ability to design and create customized greeting cards. Lufthansa's self-service kiosks give customers immediate flight information, reservation and ticket pickup capability, seat assignment and flight check-in, and boarding passes. If kiosk systems can be made user-friendly for customers, then the capabilities of the IPS systems for customer service representatives are even more remarkable.

Supporting the Troops at the Front

With so much emphasis being placed on the front-line worker, the rest of the organization must support the customer service employees as much as possible. Whatever is needed to serve customers better dictates how the rest of the organization must be reengineered. Information must flow from the bottom up if the rest of the company is going to keep in step with changing customer needs or ever hope to anticipate them. For as Sam Walton found, "Ninety-nine percent of the best ideas we ever had came from our customers and employees."

If companies hope to obtain useful information and suggestions from front-line workers, they will need to keep them happy and motivated. Two particularly effective ways to do this are the following:

- If the customer service delivery is localized, turn front-line workers or teams into independent businesses or profit centers.
- If individuals require customer service that extends across a number of company teams or individuals, adopt profit sharing and stock option programs.

People working in independent profit centers must have broad business skills, because everyone must be entrepreneurial and able to make key business decisions affecting profitability. This includes not just decisions about whether to offer a discount to a customer but also whether to have unsatisfactory back-office support replaced or outsourced. These people must be able to choose their "suppliers." The staff who provide the technological and specialized support vital to the support function must view the front-line workers as their customers who can get these services performed by others if necessary. The role of upper management is to act as venture capitalists who want to help the front-line workers make a substantial profit so that the shareholders are happy. Thus accountability is shared throughout the organization, and the customer service imperative applies to everyone.

Where a customer has many points of contact throughout a company (for example, a hotel, school, or bank), workers need to be involved in a wide range of decision-making areas, because their activities are affected by what happens elsewhere. In complex systems, information sharing is absolutely critical if optimal trade-offs between efficiency and effectiveness are to be realized. Everyone must share a common vision and an agreed-upon set of priorities so that decisions can be decentralized to the most knowledgeable or involved people with little fear of their working at cross-purposes.

Reengineering Information and Communication

Information and communication are the key ingredients driving all customer service these days. Without information, no complex operation can run smoothly or even know what the customer wants or needs. Information is so important that it can exceed the value of the service being provided. American Airlines' Sabre reservation system is worth more than the airline service itself. Information is the fuel on which knowledge runs. And it is knowledge that makes customization possible.

Building more knowledge into a service or product makes it more user-friendly. For instance, some phone cards let operators know which language you speak.

Communication is of equal importance, because no one is in control of the entire process in any formal sense. In the past, marketing was characterized by "push," or promoting the virtues of a product or service to a customer with the hope they would buy it. Today, marketing is driven more by "pull," or designing the product or service around the needs and preferences of the customer and anticipating his or her future needs if the relationship is going to extend beyond a one-time sale. A mutual education process is required so that misunderstandings are minimized and easily corrected.

The Changing Workforce

The number of technical workers has grown by three times the workforce since 1950, accounting for one out of every four new jobs. According to Bureau of Labor Statistics economist Kristina Shelley, technical field jobs for new graduates are expected to grow by 75 percent over the next ten years and will become the largest segment of the workforce (20 percent according to the Bureau of Labor Statistics). Since 1960, scientific knowledge has been doubling every six to ten years, and the division of labor into subspecialty areas has been proceeding apace.

In addition, Professors Erik Brynjolisson and Thomas Malone of MIT's Sloan School found that the average number of employees per company peaked in the 1970s. In the last ten years, 20 percent of the employees have been eliminated, yet the investment in information technology has tripled. Typically, the investment in new technology precedes a downsizing. Technical jobs of one kind or another, however, are created in the process. How technically competent are you in your field? Are you aware of the latest technology being developed that could affect your field? What role do you play in the information and knowledge processes? Is there a specialization area likely to open up in the near future that will likely play a key role in information processing that you could develop some expertise in?

The challenge for technical workers is to remain experts in their fields. Although everyone in a organization needs to be a generalist in order to maintain an overview and to coordinate with others in the network, the technical or expert workers are the true specialists in an organization. They must be willing to answer the questions that the front-line workers are incapable of handling, or to direct their expertise into user-friendly software for those workers. Much like outside consultants, they can be replaced if they are not providing the best technical support or expert advice available. Whereas the front-line workers need to know how to deal with a wide range of customers, products, and services and respond to a rapidly broadening spectrum of customer expectations, the back-office specialist must figure out ways of making complex systems and problems both simple and integrated so that the front-line workers can easily carry out their many diverse functions.

Software now takes the place of bureaucracy and the clerical and administrative jobs associated with most bureaucracies. The easier the software is to use—that is, the less bureaucracy or the fewer complex rules and procedures required to make the software functional—, the easier it is to serve customers. The role of specialists is not to make decisions for front-line workers. Rather, specialists act as information processing providers who help the front-line workers make appropriate customized decisions in collaboration with the customers. Since intake is no longer separated from processing, front-line workers have become case managers who help the customer through a wide range of services much as primary-care nurses follow patients throughout their hospital stay. As Sam Walton once said, "If you're not serving the customer, or supporting the folks that do, then we don't need you."

Although there is a distinction between technical workers and experts, that line is beginning to blur. Experts are the people who specialize at a high level in marketing, accounting, finance, etc., yet they too are having to develop technical expertise. Almost every subject area you might care to mention is now strongly supported by complex software packages that include some measurement and evaluation tools. Information technology insinuates itself into almost every discipline or function because of the need for a consolidated picture of the customer base. In the past customers would deal with people from each department separately (for example, billing, order placing, address change), and there would be no coordination of the information regarding each customer. With the shift to the integrated service window approach (one-stop service), the customer is able to gain access to a broad range of services delivered by a wide variety of business units or partnered organizations. Both experts and technical workers need to work closely together in order to provide the flexibly designed and coordinated processes essential to the creation of a seamless operation and to anticipate future customer service delivery needs. Which specialist skill areas relevant to your work are seeing their standards rise fastest? Are you keeping ahead of everyone else in these areas?

Reengineering Training

Both Apple and Hewlett-Packard are abandoning classroom training altogether because they have found that interactive computerized learning takes half the time, costs less, and leads to 80 percent greater learning retention. The IPS system customizes training on the job so that whatever is needed can be learned when desired, in the learning style desired, at the appropriate level of difficulty, and with active assessment of mastery or proficiency. While at the workstation, it will remind the service representatives during quiet times of where they were in various learning assignments. The era of just-in-time learning and customer service has finally arrived. As far as learning is concerned, the sales representative has now become the customer whose learning needs are completely customized. The focus has shifted from the computer to doing the job or learning it in the most effective ways possible. With the kiosk system, the customer becomes empowered as well.

Not only are the concepts of training and customer service altering in response to these new exciting possibilities, but companies are becoming reengineered to an unprecedented extent to accommodate these new developments.

Upper Management

What about upper management? Aside from acting as venture capitalists, coordinators, and strategists, how are they best described, and what other roles do they engage in?

High-level executives tend to be a strong blend of both generalist and specialist. An MBA combined with a particular area of expertise and appropriate experience is often the price of admission. Increasingly, knowledge, competence, and experience are the requirements for entry into these ranks.

Modern leaders are having to devote their energies to managing their information and knowledge assets (for example, the technical and expert workers). According to Arthur Andersen's Edmund Jensen, chair of the American Institute of Certified Chartered Accountants task force on nonfinancial corporate performance measures, "The components of cost in a product today are largely R&D, intellectual assets, and services. The old accounting system, which tells us the cost of material and labor, isn't applicable."

For instance, at Union Pacific, anyone trying for a management position must first become a "data integrity analyst." Now that work flow systems, groupware, document management systems, voice systems, and interactive workstations are the structural basis for knowledge accumulation inside organizations, a good command of information technology fundamentals is essential. As Valery Kanevsky, two-time winner of the Math Olympics and expert in complexity, notes, "Knowledge is the genome of a company. If you could write down all the knowledge, you could clone the company."

According to David Ulrich, a University of Michigan business professor, "Learning capability is *g* times *g*," the ability of a company to generate ideas times its skill at generalizing the ideas throughout the company. Thus the role of upper management is to ensure both the generating and sharing of knowledge throughout an organization. Fortunately, the "Balanced Scoreboard" approach, developed by David Norton and Harvard Professor Robert Kaplan, tries to capture some of this information by focusing on customer satisfaction, organizational efficiency, and intellectual capital, and not just financial results.

Leading the Reengineered Corporation

The sharing of real-time information and knowledge eliminates the need for bureaucracy and many of the problems caused by delayed reactions. Today's leaders must create learning organizations that can map the skills of their employees to focus on the core competencies of the organizations. In addition, they must broaden any individual company's reach to include other firms in the sharing of learning. Just as multinationals use their various subsidiaries to gain competitive advantage by coordinating learning on a global scale, smaller companies must also maximize their learning opportunities.

Leaders must help companies develop competitive strategies but in a more focused way and in a much larger context than in the past—something that must be encompassed in the corporate vision. Previously, large companies often felt they could be equally good at a number of very different but interrelated activities—in other words, that they could be generalists. It seemed to make sense to buy and control as many of the vertical companies in one's industry as possible, starting from the raw-materials supplier and ending with the eventual retailer.

Not any more, however. With things changing so quickly in complex ways, companies simply can't be good at everything. There are more than enough diverse challenges within one company without taking on the headaches associated with running a conglomerate.

Even CEOs can't master everything the way they used to. As Kenan Shanin suggested in *Fortune* magazine, the complexity of today's markets and technologies has forced leaders to rely on experts for information rather than absorb it themselves. Everyone must be willing to assume leadership responsibilities.

As Rosabeth Moss Kanter wrote in the *Harvard Business Review,* "[Managers] must learn to operate without the crutch of hierarchy. Positions, title, and authority are no longer adequate tools, not in a world where subordinates are encouraged to think for themselves and where managers have to work synergistically with other departments and even other companies."

Leadership, in other words, consists of orchestrating learning and career opportunities in the service of the corporate vision.

Technology or Jobs?

> *If men have the talent to invent new machines that put men out of work, they have the talent to put those men back to work.*
>
> —President John F. Kennedy

But what about technological advances and the growing number of technical workers? Is technology going to eliminate almost everyone's job and leave us with a self-serve world in which only technical workers have jobs? These are very real concerns that are creating a profound sense of hopelessness or cynicism among many, especially those who are unemployed or reengineered out of a job. Books such as Jeremy Rifkin's *The End of Work* only serve to fuel despair with claims that the developed countries will need fewer workers within the next hundred years.

Over the past two centuries, machines have certainly replaced millions of workers, yet there has been constant job creation throughout that time period. Remember, Japan is the country with by far the most robots and the lowest unemployment rate (3 percent). Economist Robert Solow won his Nobel Prize for proving that the main difference between fast- and slow-growing countries was the accumulation of technology and not capital. Indeed, as it turns out, the key to job creation is *more* technology, not less.

Technology has been largely responsible for the job growth over the past two hundred years because it always increases productivity when properly implemented, and it is enhanced productivity that is the equivalent to the creation of wealth.

For instance, imagine that you were able to reduce the cost of producing or delivering a product or service by half. You would be faced with three options. One, lower the price of the item or service so that you could capture more market share and possibly expand the demand for the product. In either case, those who purchase the product now have more money left over to purchase other products—something that creates jobs somewhere else. The second option is to pay your workers more so they can then go out and buy more products and services elsewhere—once again stimulating growth in some other area of the economy. Third, you might let the stockholders benefit or raise the pay of management, but the end result is the same: the net beneficiary goes out and spends the money, thereby creating jobs wherever the money gets spent.

Most companies are forced into the first option fairly quickly because their competitors are not going to allow you to keep your productivity advantage for long; in other words, consumers end up with more money they can spend on other things. In this fashion, more jobs are created, and the standard of living rises.

Former presidential economic advisor Paul Zane Pilzer in his book *Unlimited Wealth* clearly explains the connection between technology and economic and employment growth by showing how:

- technology is the major determinant of wealth because it determines the nature and supply of physical resources;
- the advance of technology is determined mainly by our ability to process information; and
- the backlog of unimplemented technological advances—that is, the technology gap, is the true predictor of economic growth for both the individual and society.

In the past, most countries concerned themselves with physical resources and often fought wars over them. Nowadays, however, such resources are not as important. If they were, Russia and China would be the wealthiest countries in the world. Japan, a country with no physical resources worth mentioning, has the highest GNP per person in the world. Clearly the emphasis has shifted to technology.

The quantity of physical resources available is less important than how much use can be had from the available quantity. As technology improves efficiency, the need for large quantities diminishes. Technological advancements have rendered the Club of Rome's pronouncements about the imminent shortage of natural resources premature, to say the least. In 1988, a U.S. Office of Technology Assessment study noted that "[America's] future has probably never been less constrained by the cost of natural resources … [and that the] optimal use of new technology could result in a forty to sixty percent decline in the [demand for] natural resources, even when there is rapid economic growth."

At the moment, the potential for economic growth is enormous. Why? Because our technology has evolved well beyond our ability actually to utilize the advancements fully. The newspaper each day is filled with tantalizing tidbits regarding new developments coming our way soon. If anything, most of us are overwhelmed by what technology is capable of doing. All of those VCRs with the flashing 12:00 rarely have their sophisticated features used. This gap between what is possible and our current usage level represents the growth potential that awaits us.

The obstacle to economic growth is the sharing of information on how to make the best use of technology and the price of the technology itself. Technology is adopted once it becomes user-friendly and affordable. Through this process, technology actually changes our culture, since it continually redefines what we perceive to be our needs. At various points in time, cars, washing machines, telephones, fax machines, VCRs, and computers were considered luxuries but not necessities. Once their price came down and their use became widespread, they completely altered the society of their time and became essentials.

The big challenge in staying competitive and creating jobs and wealth involves increasing the amount of technology available, bringing down its price, making it user-friendly, and letting the world know that it exists. Although automation is bringing down the price of making things, manufacturing costs account for only about 20 percent of an item's price. R&D, design, marketing, and distribution account for the lion's share of the costs. For instance, it costs less than $1,500 to manufacture a car. So most of the newly created jobs will come in the areas that account for 80 percent of the consumer price of our purchases.

The key area for future innovation is the information processing or sharing side of the equation, which is part of the 80 percent cost factor. Since there are no physical resource constraints, and technology is running ahead of our ability to make optimal use of it, the one major growth limiting factor is our ability to gather, assimilate, and utilize the information. This shortcoming is the driving force behind the reengineering and the customer-service revolution.

What Jobs Will Be Automated?

Automation is eroding all jobs in which the activities are strictly left-brain or rational and repetitive in nature. If some task can be broken down into a series of logical steps, then you can be sure that someone will invent software capable of performing the chore (for example, reservations, ticketing). If your company decided to reengineer tomorrow, who would be most likely to lose their jobs and why? Creative right-brain functions are nonrepetitive in nature, so they are relatively safe from encroachment by automation. Tasks that are more creative will survive the reengineering musical chairs game each time it is played. What right-brain creative areas are very unlikely to be automated in your industry? Do you have these skills, or can you develop them? Can you position yourself more in that direction and make yourself indispensable?

Among the jobs that are becoming the most creative are customer service jobs since technology is putting a wealth of diverse information at the fingertips of each representative. Service personnel need to be able to handle almost any customer request, so each customer to some extent can represent a creative challenge as to which information is the most relevant and how the information should be appropriately packaged or framed. It will be the ability to handle problems that are exceptional or complex rather than simple and routine in nature that will be highly prized. Fortunately, the technology is already available to assist the front-line workers in handling complicated or interrelated service chores.

While simple tasks are relegated to user-friendly kiosks, the challenge of exceeding customer expectations and making customized adjustments that override the system will remain a human one for some time to come. In fact, customer service representatives are in the process of becoming designers or, as Tom Peters puts it, part of the "fashion" business.

Whether as individuals or as part of a team, creative customer service workers cannot become too specialized or too rule-bound, or they will be incapable of providing flexible, broad-based customer service. Their creativity stems from an ability to ignore or cross boundaries or functions and to combine the various elements in ways that satisfy each customer. Much like chefs, orchestra leaders, or creative artists, customer service representatives need to figure out how to bring out the best in the diverse raw materials or information they have to work with. With customers expecting fast response and delivery, customized service, high quality, reasonable price, and innovative value-added features, sales and service staff can use all the support they can get.

Managers as Consultants and Entrepreneurs

More good news associated with the growing importance of information in the economic and job growth process is that middle managers are not going to disappear—they will simply fill a new role. In many companies they are indispensable go-betweens helping to clarify what strategies are actually feasible on the shop floor and translating some of the rarefied corporate strategies into something that can be made workable through consultation with the front line. By turning companies into internal markets, Digital and 3M get middle managers to compete with one another in marketing projects to senior managers—so as entrepreneurs they are also improving information assimilation. In addition, they act as trainers or consultants for upper management and motivators for those who wish to rise in position. Although technology has reduced the need for many middle managers, many have gone on to manage or consult for the companies that now do the outsourcing for the company from which they were just downsized. For instance, AT&T has spent over one billion dollars on consultants since the beginning of this decade. In fact, of the 11 million jobs created since 1989, two-thirds are managerial and professional in nature.

So this growing need for entrepreneurial broad-based business skills on top of technological learning compatibility ups the customer service skills ante as well. The ideal is to have the ability to gather, process, assimilate, apply, and disseminate new information and knowledge in ways that are user-transparent, timely, and cost-effective to diverse customers whose expectations continue to rise along with what is technologically possible. Ask yourself, could you sell yourself to a prospective employer if these consulting or customer service traits applied to you? If not, why not?

Coupled with the foregoing is the need to be able to make intelligent decisions based on varying levels of uncertainty that accompany the many changes that are unanticipated. In a changing world, you are never given enough information or time to make a decision you can be sure is correct; you can only give it your best shot at the time—and learn as fast as you can from your mistakes and successes. By doing so, you reduce the mean time to customer satisfaction, which is even more important than economies of speed alone. After all, there is no point in making or providing the wrong product or service (or career decision!) quickly unless you can learn fast enough to readjust as required.

Customer Satisfaction, Reengineering, and Career Planning in a Postmodern World

As technology makes it increasingly possible to customize products and services, we move away from commoditization to the fashion or design business. Instead of their being one fashion or design, however, there are as many possible products and services as there are customers. Moreover, with each new technology altering the landscape of what products and services are available, customers get to change their minds about what they deem fashionable or desirable as more possibilities emerge. In a world where the number of possibilities and combinations continues to multiply at an accelerating rate, how can any company keep up with changing customer demand? With reengineering often focusing on serving the customer better, how can the reengineering ever stop if the customer keeps changing? By the same token, how can anyone plan or aspire toward a stable career if roles and responsibilities are being continually reengineered?

Since 1990, the $2.4 billion dollar marketing research industry has been in decline. Yet since 1993, information technology, which generates new products and distribution possibilities daily, has become by far and away the major driving force in the American economy. While it is not too difficult to ask customers about modifications they might like to existing products they are familiar with, it is rather difficult to ask them about products that don't exist yet and they have no immediate need for—or their interest in new unfamiliar distribution methods. In order to stay in business, however, companies need to create—at a rate faster than that of their competitors—new products or services that appeal to customers. However, their competitors now often come from other industries with entirely new conceptual approaches to the nature of the product and service and how the customer can be reached and better served.

The focus on the customer now determines strategy and destroys industry boundaries. As James Brian Quinn notes in *The Intelligent Enterprise,* "accounting companies no longer compete just with accounting companies, or computer companies just with computer hardware companies. Instead, the software and computer divisions of accounting companies compete with software and service divisions of computer companies, as well as those of user companies. Their executive recruitment activities compete with headhunters and personnel organizations, their consulting groups compete with independent consulting firms as well as staff arms of manufacturers, and their merger and acquisition groups compete with specialists in banking. And so on."

Keeping up with and staying ahead of the customer has become a high-risk, high-return proposition, but then so is reengineering and strategic career planning. Everyone needs to keep up with latest trends and scenario plan around them. In addition, companies need to work as closely as is possible with their customers so as to cocreate a common future where the risk and the return are shared by both. Not doing so can be very costly, for as Dorothy Leonard-Barton explains in *The Wellsprings of Knowledge,* "On average, as much as 46% of all resources devoted to product development and commercialization is spent on products that are canceled or fail to yield adequate financial returns. One report estimates that for every one hundred projects that enter development, sixty-three are canceled, twenty-five become commercial successes, and twelve are commercial failures. At the same time, some companies boast a success rate of 70 to 80 percent in new product launches." The difference? Successful product launches are associated with becoming as intimately involved as possible with customers and the external environment. Given the amount of uncertainty that accompanies all change and open-ended possibilities, the only way of reducing risk and maximizing success is by getting everyone as much involved as possible with the change process and by exploring together various ways to better meet the demands of an evolving external environment.

Reengineering efforts fail because they do not maintain an intimate relationship with employees and others in the value-adding chain throughout the change process. They forget that the employees, suppliers, and customers are sharing in the risk as well as the return. Also forgotten is the fact that people have become the biggest bottleneck in the change process. Technology is changing faster than people can adapt to it—even the customers in many instances. Only by having everyone involved in the learning process can companies, employees, suppliers, distributors, and customers move up the never-ending customer satisfaction learning curve at a faster rate.

With customers' choices proliferating rapidly as part of the endless technological cornucopia, companies will need to continually restructure or reengineer themselves as fast as possible in ways that lead to greater "real-time" customer satisfaction. Considering the unpredictability of many of the changes that continually bombard us, the only enduring advantage comes through resilience and the ability to respond quickly and economically. Without everyone involved in the learning curve equally sharing in the vital "real-time" information needed for timely and appropriate responses and without everyone sharing in the risk in some ways so as to reduce everyone's natural risk aversion, gridlock is bound to set in. Customers resist new products, services and alternative distribution methods; employees resist change; and suppliers and distributors become less flexible and less willing to enter into joint ventures or assume design responsibilities.

Why the big resistance to change? Because, as psychologists Daniel Kahneman and Amos Tversky found, perceived losses are more painful than forgone gains—that is, most people are usually twice as fearful of the downside risk than they are attracted by the upside gain. Thus only by minimizing the negative consequences associated with change will people seriously entertain new ideas, methods, and creative possibilities.

So what are the implications for career decision making and planning?

In a world filled with uncertainty and new possibilities emerging daily, you can't plan anything careerwise with utmost certainty. We are forced into using a kind of "fuzzy logic" that roughly optimizes for a number of acceptable options. Career planning essentially becomes an emerging design process or a series of successive approximations—that is, get the general vision and direction right and through a resume-building process migrate toward progressively more attractive learning opportunities over time. There really is no point in setting job specific career goals in a world where roles and responsibilities are being reconfigured constantly. More important is staying within the ballpark of where you would roughly like to be. As in baseball, you may end up playing a number of positions, but eventually you gravitate toward certain positions and teams that can make the best use of your talents. For instance, at one point Babe Ruth was a pitcher.

If you can both try to understand and treat yourself as the most important customer in your life, you will likely make decisions you can live with and be willing to go the extra mile to obtain what you would like. But an important factor to remember is that career decisions are best made when you are willing to take reasonable risks—especially in the high-risk, high-return world we now inhabit. While the 1950s and 1960s were blessed with low-risk, high-return career and business opportunities, in the competitive 1990s, globalization and technological advances are even eliminating the low-risk, low-return jobs in many instances. In other words, you need to take much bigger risks (e.g., obtaining post-graduate degrees, moving to where the jobs are, starting your own business) in order to succeed, or you end up competing with a growing number of people for whatever low-paying jobs remain at the bottom of the ladder.

But how you can minimize unnecessary risk taking? Like companies that stay close to their customers and have high rates of successful product launches, you must constantly monitor the environment for the latest technological and global trends and their likely impact. You need to invest in strategically developing and maintaining leading-edge technological literacy (e.g., anything less than a solid grounding in Microsoft Office Pro 97 or its equivalent plus knowing your way around the Internet, and you won't even get to first base). In addition, you need to strategically create a large powerful network of contacts who will keep you informed of all of the important changes taking place and the opportunities emerging, plus provide you with the means to take advantage of them (the leveraging of this value-adding chain is the subject of a later chapter).

Two other ways of increasing your choices and improving your ability to respond quickly involve your family and your personal finances. As with successful businesses, your family life may require a certain amount of reengineering or continuous improvement so that you can take better advantage of opportunities. And as with all successful reengineering efforts, everyone must be a full participant in the change process. But equally important is your financial situation. People who are running short of money usually make poor career decisions out of desperation and have few upgrading options available to them. The old rule of thumb—always keep on hand at least six months worth of income—applies more today than it ever did before.

Despite the need to seriously address the risky realities we have to contend with, it is absolutely essentially that we never forget that there are high returns associated with taking risks. For instance, some engineers and computer programmers, according to the *Wall Street Journal* in December 1995, "earn more money by moving from project to project—50 percent more in many cases—than their counterparts in steady jobs."

Coupled with an inspiring vision and a solid sense of direction, resilience and the ability to respond effectively and quickly to change (and the need to change) will always get you where you want to go eventually. For those high-risk takers in a hurry, however, becoming an entrepreneur may allow you to become a shaper of the changes taking place (the topic of a later chapter). But whether you want to be in the entrepreneurial driver's seat or a participant in another company's "excellent customer service," get prepared for many customer- and technology-driven change adventures.

CHAPTER 3

Welcome to Constant Change

Until the early 1970s, Americans felt themselves to be by far and away the world's undisputed world leader in almost every area of life. The United States was the first nation to put a man on the moon and had even made the Russians back down in the Cuban missile crisis in a clear battle of wills. Most Olympic medals and Nobel prizes were won by Americans, and world foreign policy and trade were largely determined by U.S. interests. Poor nations looked to the United States for guidance and assistance, and wealthy industrial nations depended on America to act as the worldwide peacekeeper and the defender of democracy and free market capitalism. Even on a local level, there was much to be proud about as Americans made great strides in establishing equality of opportunity for everyone.

To top things off, it was truly an age of abundance. You could quit your job one day and find another the next. Even high school dropouts were able to find high-paying factory jobs that came with both job security and significant benefit packages. Hippies were the natural products of such a wealthy era; since when in history has a generation of young people ever had the luxury of trying to find themselves over a long period of time or of insisting on not accepting work that might in any way compromise their values?

Clouds were forming on the horizon. Although America had played a decisive role in winning the two great world wars of the century and could even claim to having never lost a war of any significance, Vietnam became the Waterloo for such a Napoleonic nation. It became the first unwinnable war using conventional weapons and tactics. Ironically, the Vietnamese won their war much the same way the Americans had defeated the British during the American Revolution.

No one at the time realized that such guerrilla warfare would eventually also find its economic equivalent in the years to come when nations such as Japan and other smaller Asian Pacific Rim countries could outmaneuver many larger American companies in markets they had dominated from their inception.

Just about this time, the first oil shortage crisis arose as the OPEC nations chose to take advantage of rising oil consumption used to fuel the American war economy, especially after the Yom Kippur War in 1973. As oil prices continued to rise and inflation began to take hold, the Japanese took advantage of this change by introducing smaller, more compact cars that were inexpensive and very fuel-efficient.

The Big Three laughed at these innovations since they knew that Americans had always wanted to drive robust cars that were spacious and luxurious. One of GM's chief executives even went so far as to declare that the customers had to be at fault to some extent because there was "something wrong" with people who purchased small cars.

After the customary period of denial surrounding the changes that were taking place eventually gave way to the frightening realization that the American car industry was in peril, many Americans reacted with extreme anger over people driving foreign cars. The larger irony lay, however, in the fact that the world had changed so drastically by this time that it was really difficult actually to find a car that was 100 percent made in America. Chrysler, GM, and Ford naturally solicited the help of politicians in ending what clearly had to be some sort of abuse of the free market system. If Americans did not dominate the car industry on their own turf, then something subversive and unfair had to be taking place.

After all, this was the industry that Henry Ford enabled the United States to lay claim to. Indeed, the idea that a foreign nation could actually beat America's largest companies on their own playing field had to be preposterous. It just could not happen unless the foreign companies were cheating in some manner, or so it seemed. Naturally, after much bargaining, Congress came to the rescue of the American car industry by slapping quotas and tariffs on imported cars.

Short-term tactics such as these only managed to buy time before the awareness set in that not only were the foreign cars cheaper and more fuel-efficient, but they lasted longer, with fewer product defects. Eventually, American car engineering design associations admitted that Japanese cars were five years ahead of American-designed vehicles. What a painful realization that must have been, yet it eventually fueled the determination for companies like Ford to restructure their company around the slogan "Quality is Job One."

Fortunately, this car industry's story ending is a happy one. After realizing that Americans would not blithely continue to accept high product defect rates and autos that did not meet the current needs of car buyers, American car companies have recaptured the lead in many areas of the car industry.

However, only after the reality of foreign competition was fully accepted was it possible for the American car industry to get back in the game after the rules had changed.

What rules have changed? Or better yet, what assumptions underlying the rules must we now be prepared to discard?

The Shock of Change

For most people, it must seem a long time since they felt that the world actually made some kind of sense. Indeed, if you are not confused, it is as though you haven't been paying attention. Nowadays, the world seems out of control, rudderless, with no one at the helm. The lack of leadership is so frustrating to voters that they keep throwing out incumbents at election time in the forlorn hope that a new politician or party will be able to assume control over what seems like a worsening situation. Everyone appears to be looking for a magic solution that will restore America to its former glory days and bring back an unquestioned confidence and pride in the American dream. Movies such as *Forrest Gump* serve as a painful reminder of just how nostalgic many of us have become.

A profound sense of sadness and betrayal seems to lie just below the surface in what is clearly becoming for many an age of diminished expectations. Emotionally and mentally, America as a nation is having to come to terms with changes that are often heartrending. Entire ways of life are disappearing permanently, and it is no wonder that we are seeing people going through various stages of adjustment (shock, denial, anger, bargaining, depression, and acceptance) in coming to terms with the passing away of familiar, secure, and comfortable lifestyles.

Denial

The real challenge is accepting change and making the best of it. At first, most of us naturally deny that change has occurred. Why? As we have already suggested, all change involves some kind of loss.

Sometimes it is a loss of status, as occurs in mergers, acquisitions, downsizing, and restructuring into teams. The trend toward minimizing status in the interest of fostering a more open team environment has often eliminated parking privileges, fancy offices, and even a desk you can call your own. If the position disappeared, all of the self-esteem associated with the need for and importance of the position can be called into question. The position may have given not just a strong sense of purpose, but also a clearly defined career path.

Any desirable personal benefits associated with an older way of doing things can evaporate as well. Sometimes relocation is necessary, and longtime friends and associates are bound to be missed along with the comfortable network of relationships in which our lives were nicely organized. Mergers and acquisitions wreak havoc in companies, since even corporate culture is affected in any subsequent restructuring of the smaller or taken-over firm.

We like a routine because it is so much easier not to make decisions all the time. In a complicated world, we tend to welcome anything that allows us to coast. The prospect of having to learn new skills and solve new problems can be exasperating.

Many people are tired of changes that didn't work in the past yet required a lot of effort. There is a natural weary resentment to having once again to comply with what may seem like the latest fad applied cookie-cutterlike without any appreciation for the context. Undoubtedly, many times in the past people have been cheated by change—more was lost than was gained. The "Oh, here we go again" or "Here come the change weenies" attitude betrays how much one can become dispirited and lethargic in the face of yet another change that doesn't seem likely to live up to its promise.

Particularly when the change process is spread out over a number of years, there is always the enormous temptation to deny that any change is actually transpiring. During what were once seen as better, more stable and predictable times, it was largely true that one only had to wait out the cyclical recession, the latest management fad, or the term of office of a political party and then opportunity, common sense, and the good times would return. Change was merely an aberration, a fashion, or a short period of time when things were slightly out of balance. If you waited long enough, the world would eventually come to its senses—or so it was assumed. After all, wisdom consists of not letting momentary events distract one from deeper, more abiding truths.

Anger and Bargaining

When the formerly "tried and true" solutions to problems no longer seem to serve so well anymore, a kind of righteous anger usually rises up in us in response to what is clearly an injustice or an unfair altering of the rules. We assume that we only need to bring the world back to the previous sensible arrangement and then the old solutions will work just fine. Many parents believe that if schools only concentrated more on restoring the three R's to the school curriculum, a lot of society's employment problems would likely disappear. Yet even the staunchest supporter of educational fundamentalism has a sneaking suspicion that what seems to be so obvious a solution is not likely going to put the lid permanently back on this Pandora's box.

Although we naturally feel betrayed that someone changed the rules without consulting us, our anger or bargaining or pleading for a return to the old ways will not help us when the rules have changed permanently. Even though a company may have once paid $45,000 to someone with a certain set of qualifications and experience, that does not mean that the company will do so today. It is sad to see so many people not getting jobs because their salary or position expectations are so inflated in relation to the current job market.

Depression

As the awareness sets in that we are now operating under new rules that seem to keep changing daily, it is only natural that many give up in despair. This is especially true of older workers who, once unemployed, find that the educational requirements for jobs of equivalent pay far exceed their own qualifications. Having been out of school for so long, they assume that they are too old to return to school for the number of years needed to meet the new job posting requirements. This belief can be so contagious that even people who are in their twenties can be seduced into such thinking. I remember a twenty-six-year-old telling me that although he agreed that it was important to get more training or education, it was too late for him. But he might see it for his two kids.

Remember, in *Forrest Gump,* the personality transformation that overtakes Gump's lieutenant who loses his legs in Vietnam? His bitterness and despair poison him spiritually to the point at which he becomes a suicidal alcoholic who pursues his self-destruction with a vengeance because he has been cheated out of what he believes was his heroic destiny. By wantonly trying to destroy himself, he is perversely asserting the one choice most commonly exercised by children during their terrible two's—the willful right to say no to assert their sense of independence and control.

Acceptance

Fortunately, the change adjustment process doesn't end there, or we would all be in deep trouble. The light at the end of the tunnel is not an oncoming train but the simple acceptance that the rules have changed and a genuine commitment to try and make the best of things under the new circumstances.

If the solution is so simple, why is it that we resist change with such passion and determination? Why does the lieutenant in *Forrest Gump* pursue his self-destruction so ferociously?

Obviously, we are afraid of losing something we feel is so essential to our identity or our values that we may even feel it worth defending with our lives. For many, a lifetime has been invested in a set of beliefs or a way of life, and no one is going to take that away from them.

Change and the Corporate Bureaucracy

Charles Heckscher, in *White-Collar Blues,* found that most of the companies he studied failed in their efforts to change successfully, despite assuming all of the trappings of decentralization, teamwork, empowerment, mission statements, and continuous change. Ironically, these strategies typically led to incredibly low levels of demoralization and performance and to higher levels of formal bureaucracy.

Downsizing or restructuring invariably involves decentralizing operations, which disrupt the previous networks. The context for cooperation suddenly disappears, and the sense of community vanishes along with it. Middle managers respond either by following bureaucratic rules or by withdrawing. The resulting layoffs encourage workers to narrow their focus on their own area and ignore the rest of the organization, since all the old ways of doing things no longer work. Most people are completely unable to function beyond sticking to the bureaucratic rules, which have now actually multiplied. More rules are usually put in place to counteract the increased decentralization.

Although everyone who remains usually works hard, the spirit of cooperation disappears, so everything tends to get worse rather than better. With the layoffs, spans of control increase to a point at which it is hard to form relationships with anyone. Most employees usually hope the changes are temporary and that the company will eventually return to its senses.

Surprisingly, loyalty to the company as a whole remains largely unshaken since there is a tendency to assume that the changes must be in the best interests of the company or it would not head down this road. Some will think that upper management is momentarily misguided. The biggest shock, however, comes from the realization that middle management is actually viewed as a variable cost, just as blue-collar workers always have been. The pervasive fear that results from the realization that anyone is expendable turns the organization more inward than is even typical of most bureaucracies. This trend is accompanied by a kind of paralysis. Mistrust of others begins to grow, and a desire for stronger leadership is a much-hoped-for solution.

The formal shift to team-based approaches and the encouragement of empowerment are usually resisted. Almost everyone finds the new arrangements too confusing and dislikes having to arrive at a consensus before acting. Middle managers feel that the need for consensus is both extremely inefficient and ridiculous, since most employees are not sufficiently trained to understand the issues involved or to work cohesively as a team within the confines of typical business deadlines. Most are more comfortable with consulting with others in the organization but prefer to reserve the decision-making power for the appropriate hierarchical level.

Although people in organizations are naturally resistant to change, middle managers, who have the most power to lose in a teamwork environment, resist the most. For, as James Brian Quinn notes in *The Intelligent Enterprise,* "Just as Gorbachev could change the top level of the U.S.S.R. and establish grassroots support for change quickly—but not move the middle layers of bureaucracy—western mid-level managers resist radical changes endlessly. Jan Carlzon found it easy to change the top and motivate point people at SAS, but devilishly difficult to move the huge mid-level bureaucracies that past practices had built up."

Yet in almost every instance, each company spends a great deal of money and time promoting the virtues of the new economic approach. Upper management makes many speeches, videos are created, team training is purchased, and lower-level decision-making is encouraged. Ironically, most people in the organization feel that upper management is simply abdicating its responsibility regarding setting direction and designing implementation strategies. It seems as if no one is at the helm.

Upper management is often convinced that it has done all that is reasonably possible to convey the new message and is greatly shocked to find out that no one understands what is supposed to be happening. All kinds of cross-organizational forums and teams are set up to solicit feedback from everyone at all levels, yet very little feedback is likely to be forthcoming. Although there is a lot of grumbling and complaining, few are willing to voice their views in public. Keeping one's head down seems to be a better survival technique.

Even executives who promote open-door policies, such as breakfasts with the troops, do not succeed in learning what is the matter. Most employees do not feel that it is their place to criticize. The unspoken rule in bureaucracies is that either you solve a problem yourself or you pass it on to someone else. Talking about problems openly is a sign of weakness or an invasion of someone else's area of responsibility. People brought in from the outside rarely last long. How could they possibly know anything about how the company should be run? Their advice is simply ignored.

Now that most relationships have effectively been severed and the bunker mentality is more entrenched, rigid thinking and negative politics increase. It is hard to create new informal relationships, because a sense of impermanence undermines implicit deal making. If you do someone a favor, he or she might be moved to some other team or area before you have a chance to call in your IOU.

The new emphasis on customer satisfaction encourages moving people around too much. Bosses, peers, and subordinates are hard to keep track of because everyone is so busy carrying out a greater number of responsibilities left behind by those who are laid off.

Given this breakdown in communication and the narrowing of focus to tasks alone, it is only natural that more infighting breaks out and the sense of community falters. So despite all of the efforts to free up the bureaucracy, many companies are becoming more rigidly bureaucratic than they had ever been in the first place.

Participatory management does not overcome bureaucratic barriers because almost no one wants it. Why? Everyone is used to the paternalistic parent-child relationship inherent in hierarchical structures and wants a return to clear orders or direction. It seems as though the parents have simply abdicated their responsibilities.

Even attempts to involve staff in the planning process can fail miserably—they do not see this as their job, nor do they feel competent enough to contribute. The reason the focus shifts quickly to doing only what is required is that at least this is something that is clearly understood. When the traditional laws of cause and effect no longer make sense, many stick to the little that do—the narrow bureaucratic confines of their own roles. By doing so, most people lose touch with the organization as a whole, with the expected economic results.

How have many of the companies reacted to the failure of the company to embrace the new ways? Many flounder, changing structures a number of times, hoping to get them right eventually, but these efforts were usually in vain.

So what are some of the underlying causes for these failures to bring about change successfully? Aside from some of the reasons already mentioned, it is necessary to understand the true meaning of loyalty in the contexts of the needs and values of those involved and the corresponding expectations of bureaucratic organizations.

Bureaucracies often demand complete loyalty or allegiance to the point where everything else is excluded. As it turns out, most people in such firms do not belong to industry or professional associations and have few community commitments aside from their work for the company. These employees are often viewed as lacking in corporate commitment and as unlikely to succeed. In exchange for making these life sacrifices, most companies implicitly had promised a stable "identity" and a safe "family" environment in which workers are well taken care of. In this context, a strong sense of affiliation or belonging flourishes. Superiors are expected to nurture and coach their subordinates. Everyone is expected to be devoted to the company as a whole.

The level of dependence fostered generates a desire to protect the family at all costs—the main strategy being to hide from the rest of the world. Most individuals in such companies, such as GM, have next to no idea what other companies are doing. Benchmarking is virtually unheard of—something that GM steadfastly refused to do throughout the 1970s and 1980s. All standards are internal. So even though GM's customers deserted in the latter part of the 1980s, the company firmly believed it was doing an excellent job in meeting its customers' needs. Because employees had few connections with the outside world, that world, for all practical purposes, didn't exist.

Under the bureaucratic structure, fewer informal teams exist, but they are fairly large in scope. Once restructuring takes effect, everyone is placed on many teams and rotated frequently so no strong relationships develop. What remains of the informal relationships are large numbers of fragmented small teams that no longer have any meaningful connection with how work is being carried out. Lacking any real power or accurate information, the remaining small coteries can serve only as forums for complaints and rumor-mongering.

Bureaucracies require very explicit role descriptions to function well. People who take on clearly defined responsibilities are granted autonomy to carry out the prescribed functions, but the functions themselves must be clearly demarcated. Attempts to encourage cross-functional teams break down any traditional understanding of who is expected to do what. The notion of negotiating one's role is utterly foreign. Accountability, which is the backbone of bureaucracy, has always been built into the hierarchical structure. In team settings, accountability becomes too diffuse and confusing.

The shock (of being treated as a variable cost), denial (that you will be personally affected by the prospect of layoff), anger (over the disruption of what were highly efficient informal groups and the lack of clear instructions), and bargaining (that things will return to normal if you wait long enough or work hard enough) associated with those childlike wishes of hoping that someone would just make the changes go away eventually lead to a sense of depression. If continuous improvement strategies are adopted, they seem like the final nail in the coffin. How can things ever return to normal if the changes are never going to stop? Early retirement begins to look awfully attractive to people with this viewpoint.

The price paid for loyalty is often the sacrifice of flexibility. Normally, loyalty requires stability so that a mutual long-term commitment can be produced. If the organization is continually changing, there must be something that one can remain loyal to, but it cannot be a rigid structuring of bureaucratic relationships.

What is needed is a common purpose to bring people in an organization together regardless of the structures and strategies of the moment. For a purpose to be shared, it must allow all of its employees to play a vital role in the establishing and maintaining of any overarching vision or purpose. In the companies that fared poorly in their restructuring efforts, the loyalty was to the familiar structure and its clearly defined relationships and not to something of more lasting importance. In other words, the loyalty was to the company as a whole, but only in terms of the status quo.

Part of the problem associated with bureaucracies lies in the very informal nature of the loyalty contract itself. Because such an agreement is tacitly understood or implied, there is no means of negotiating what is already taken for granted. When it is no longer possible for upper management to keep its end of the bargain during a downsizing, there is a natural tendency to avoid telling the truth in the interests of "protecting" the morale of everyone. Decisions and strategies are carried out covertly because they go against the grain of what has been promoted over the years. Sooner or later, however, the rumor mill guarantees that the information gets out, and before long most employees develop a cynical attitude to any pronouncements from on high. Once the trust is gone, so are all of the sources of accurate information that are essential to the operating of any complex organization. When reliable information about a changing external environment is no longer forthcoming, the organization heads into an economic tailspin, after which, more than likely, a number of turnaround specialists are imported to try to bring the organization to its senses by shaking everything up completely and realigning structures and processes. Unless trust and morale are restored and a true sense of urgency manages to create a sense of common purpose, these efforts are usually in vain.

Successful Corporate Change

The key qualities missing in the loyalty trap are accurate information both internal and external to the corporation. By trying to limit the number of external connections of its employees, the company forgoes valuable sources of information and influential contacts. By not communicating honestly with employees, upper management ends up contaminating and politicizing the entire information, cooperation, and coordination process. The solution to these problems is thus the encouragement of their opposites: more loyalties or commitments outside the organization and complete openness, honesty, and negotiation regarding all developments within.

Those companies that do manage the downsizing and restructuring process reasonably well are less dependent on loyalty as a form of security. Instead, truly participatory management is used at all levels so that any sense of loyalty stems from taking ownership in the decision-making process. People are involved in all aspects of the change process. Upper managers are intimately involved in change at every level of the organization. Implementation is not something that is simply assigned to others.

Instead of just having videos, speeches, and change management training, open forums are attended by people from every level in the organization. Information is not withheld, and everyone who is likely to be adversely affected is clearly apprised of the situation and the reasons for it. Aside from the open and continuing dialogue process so essential to the functioning of complex organizations operating in complex environments, the glue that holds the companies together during the restructuring is often the sense of a common purpose. Invariably a powerfully held vision or ideology transcends both the environment and the current strategies being implemented. It is this cement or glue that is vital to maintaining consistency in the face of constant change.

If we put this into the context of restructuring and the customer-service revolution, a clearer picture emerges about what is missing. When Philips NV decided to develop an on-line product for children, cognitive psychologists, anthropologists, industrial designers, and sociologists were sent out in vans to various places in France, Italy, and the Netherlands to brainstorm with children and adults about what new electronic products might be attractive. By bringing the children into the design process, Philips managed to identify potential customers, create interest in the products before they were released, and win the support or loyalty of those asked to participate.

This interactive process is increasingly vital to success in a marketplace filled with countless products and advertising overload. The key to surviving is not time to market, but "time to acceptance." As Regis McKenna notes, "To build customer loyalty—to build brand—companies need to keep their customers engaged in continuous dialogue.... Companies must keep the dialogue flowing and also maintain conversations with suppliers, distributors, and others in the marketplace."

For instance, Wal-Mart has always had Saturday morning meetings to combine computerized data with customer responses to sort out what is actually going on and what changes need to be made. Even regional managers on the road have weekly virtual meetings on Wal-Mart's own television network. Motorola uses its own "university" to bring together distributors and suppliers into the organization's information loop.

Downsizing

If we now apply similar logic to a company's downsizing, we can see that considerable consultation is needed with employees if it is to be carried out successfully. The key is not the speed taken in implementing the restructuring process but the time necessary for its acceptance. The companies that failed miserably in their downsizing efforts used the old broadcast marketing or one-way techniques and not an interactive one. That is, they showed videos, gave speeches, sent memos, provided training, and passed out literature, but they never tried to engage people as individuals for their ideas or support, nor did they customize the implementation process. Any attempt at dialogue with the employees was usually a one-time event, so the process was not treated seriously—a corporate reality aptly captured in Dilbert cartoons. Had an ongoing information-sharing process been part of the corporate structure, perhaps considerable support for the process would have been forthcoming. In a changing world, people need honest, real-time information, feedback, and support and not just a glitzy campaign.

For instance, when Virgin Atlantic Airways found itself with 400 too many people during the last recession, it asked its employees for creative suggestions for solving the problem. The winning suggestion was 3- to 6-month sabbaticals, for which employees applied. Turns out many wanted some time off but had been worried about appearing less committed to the organization. This solution gave them time off plus a vote of appreciation from everyone in the company.

At Springfield ReManufacturing Corp., their "open-book" management system involves shutting down the entire plant for half an hour each week—a time when every employee is then taken line by line through the most recent financial statement as a basis for continuous, participative, quality improvement.

Employees and consumers want more control over the ways in which they are approached or asked to change. Loyalty to a brand or company has now become loyalty to a clearly understood developing relationship, with both sides providing the kind of information valuable to one another. Thrusting information or change upon people almost always backfires. As it is, everyone is overwhelmed by information and change. The solution lies in creating trust and responsiveness to the process of change and in providing the kind of information that restores some sense of predictability and control. Without predictability, most people become frozen with fear. Without trust, no one even bothers to care anymore, and cynicism engenders a self-fulfilling vicious circle.

Rigid hierarchies are vestiges of a feudal era. Shakespeare greatly admired a world in which everyone had a predestined place in the grand scheme of things. It harkens back to when the sun, moon, and stars were thought to revolve around the earth as though the entire universe were loyally bound by the earth's right of sovereignty. So long as each country or company could operate as a world unto itself, the inward focus made sense.

Economic growth dictates that new customers be found regardless of where they live. The interpenetration of markets on a global basis is also a natural outgrowth of an increasing world population where immigration becomes the natural spill-over effect. The barriers of time and space have disappeared now that the information highway is capable of linking each individual and company to the rest of the world instantaneously. In a sense, the mountain has come to Mohammed.

Thriving on Change

No country, company, or individual can survive any longer by ignoring the larger context, which is beginning to overwhelm the formerly self-contained, cozy, and country club-like local environment. People have to play in the big leagues whether they like it or not. Change is not a choice any more than breathing is. Individuals who have not traded their souls for the false sense of security that loyalty to and dependence on a single organization encourages adopt more of a portfolio-diversification strategy toward change. The companies that tend to profit best from downsizing and outsourcing also are more outward looking and don't necessarily demand slavish loyalty from their employees.

Resistance to change is the natural product of all states of dependence since all control has been abdicated to an external agency. Attraction to change comes from having a wide variety of choices and a clear sense of a mission in life so that appropriate options are explored.

Denial, bargaining, and depression are strategies we use when we cannot face up to unpleasant truths. Although each of these tactics is a natural part of the adjustment process, the more they are indulged in as a means of clinging to a vanished past, the greater the amount of pain and suffering that must be endured. The hardest part of all change is the inevitable pain and suffering that is unavoidable regardless of one's predisposition toward the process.

Those companies and individuals who learn to welcome the transition always have something more promising that lies ahead than whatever it is they are leaving behind. Developing a powerful vision or mission regarding the future helps bring it into clearer focus. All strategies require a clear target if we are truly to believe they are likely to work. Those who don't know what it is they are aiming for are like hunters lost in the woods on a stormy winter night without a compass. Under such circumstances it is all too easy to just sit down, give up, take shelter, and hope the storm passes by and some solution eventually emerges in time to save one's life. It is far better to carry around an internal compass, a helpful map of future possibilities, survival skills, and an emergency communication device capable of connecting you to the outside world at all times. Then you are never lost and without hope.

The remainder of this chapter is devoted to helping you explore the various factors that are capable of fostering a powerful attraction to change.

How the Rules Have Changed

One of the assumptions that has fallen by the wayside is that being in first place or highly competitive today is a guarantee that you will enjoy the same status tomorrow. Many large countries, major companies, and important individuals have learned this lesson the hard way and are still trying to recover. Who would have thought that Russia could fall from its superpower status so drastically in such a short period of time? IBM and GM are still smarting from their respective industry comeuppances. Even company presidents and politicians can be heroes one day and outcasts the next. Just think of Steve Jobs, John Sculley, and almost any politician you might care to name. Recent history has become the stuff of Shakespearean tragedy as larger-than-life people, companies, or nations learn that excessive pride or complacency can lead to near-fatal consequences.

One of the key qualities of masters in the martial arts is their ability to monitor their environment. Their powers of concentration regarding their surroundings appear to be almost unlimited by all accounts of those involved in these disciplines. Supposedly, no one is ever capable of sneaking up on a master without his knowledge. While I certainly cannot lay claim to this kind of prescience, I nevertheless agree that during times of confusion and uncertainty, it is crucial for players to be aware of what is going on around them.

So it would seem that one of the new rules of the game is that we always pay attention to changes taking place at the moment, seek to understand the forces underlying the changes, and see where such changes are likely to lead.

Surfing the Technology Wave

The previous chapter discussed the extent to which technology has insinuated itself into almost all areas of our lives. As already mentioned, this technology gap represents the potential for economic growth and job creation once we learn how to take advantage of the features that go unused. It is these unused features that hold the key to the next changes.

You might stumble upon the fact that language-translation and voice-recognition software are slowly becoming more serviceable. But how do you make use of this information? Although you could get a sense of when any individual development is likely to become more useful by reading feature articles and more widespread by noticing how fast the price is dropping, the most important consideration is not any single innovation in isolation but how each innovation fits together with others taking place simultaneously. Are they part of a system, or could they be in the near future? In short, it is the combination of changes taking place and not any one new exciting invention that will clearly reveal what is likely to happen.

Everything in life is part of one or more systems. So if one part of a system is changed, there is bound to be a ripple effect of some kind throughout the system. However, if there are a number of changes taking places at once or in close succession, it may be possible for the entire system to become transformed in some evolutionary sense.

When IBM pays $3.5 billion for Lotus Notes, you can be sure that it wasn't just because management happened to think Lotus Notes is good groupware (software that allows everyone in an organization to share information, knowledge, schedules, plans). It is a clue that something much larger and more profound is shaping up and that somehow groupware is an important piece in the puzzle.

The questions to ask are: what existing technology, industries, companies, and individuals are likely to be affected? As the new technology makes possible new competitive relationships and advantages, what kinds of reengineering or restructuring become attractive or inevitable? Who is likely to win, and who is likely to lose?

Predicting Where Change Will Come

A crucial question to consider is: what other factors could have an important bearing on the speed of change in this area? This can be recast as: what are the other change-limiting obstacles—either technical or regulatory—and what would happen if each was somehow overcome? Since almost any obstacle can be overcome, the question becomes how important is the overcoming of some limiting factor?

For instance, when President Kennedy announced that the United States was going to put a man on the moon, it seemed like a technical impossibility. When oil prices went through the roof, a computerized fuel-efficient carburetor was invented that cost only $25, compared to $300 for a regular carburetor. People in the old industry lost their jobs. Put simply, whatever needs to get invented gets invented. If it doesn't, the need is probably not perceived as great enough. This is why reengineering is successful: it forces people to tackle seemingly impossible goals that they normally would never consider, in ways never dreamt of. They end up thinking along completely different lines than they did formerly since the obvious methods of improvement are not going to make a major difference. Just think of how many disaster and science-fiction movies have scenes where technical people are asked to repair something well beyond fixing, yet somehow they manage to fulfill their orders to "make it so."

A good way of assessing where any change is likely to end is to ask yourself, "If every company had whatever it is, and all customers could easily take advantage of it at a reasonable cost, how would the industry be different?" For instance, one of Wal-Mart's keys to retailing success is its electronic data-exchange system, which has given it the edge over its competitors in continuous stock replenishment and pricing. Suppose that all of its competitors now have the same system. At this point there needs to be some other means of competing that benefits the customer other than low price.

Just ask the other economic growth question: how can shopping be made easier for the consumer? You would probably find that a new innovative form of on-line database marketing would be combined with virtual shopping.

Remember that one part of an integrated economic chain can expand to take over important functions performed by other companies. For instance, many people might think that Microsoft is a computer-world juggernaut that cannot be toppled. Nonetheless, it is extremely vulnerable to pincerlike attacks on three fronts, any of which could undermine its dominance in the industry. Intel, the maker of the chips found in most PCs, is designing software capabilities into the chips themselves, eliminating the need for some software. Oracle is interested in providing the interactive database service necessary for the delivery of fully interactive services. Users would use Oracle's proprietary software to take advantage of the on-line services. But perhaps the biggest threat of all comes from the inventors of Java software for the Internet. Java allows you to use the software on other computers of the Internet: you do not even need to own the software you are using, since you are just using someone else's on his or her machine. This eliminates the need for most software, large hard drives, and many peripheral devices on most computers. Notice how everything is made simpler and ultimately cheaper for the user at the same time. Indeed, IBM plans to exploit this opportunity with its "global netcentric" computing system, which requires users to purchase only a $500 computer system or "toaster" to make full use of the remote hardware and software. Sun Microsystems now has a similar product with remote computing access on the Internet built right into a computer chip.

Any new product or service that can exploit the existing culture in new problem-solving ways stands the chance of catching fire. Remember that the VCR all of a sudden made movies and films of all kinds available to everyone. This points to another important consideration: any new innovation should solve some problem or meet a pressing need—the more mundane, the better. One problem facing many people is a shortage of time, so timesaving conveniences are bound to do well. Point-of-sale terminals that allow customers to have the money electronically withdrawn from their bank account has become an appreciated convenience, much like automatic teller machines. E-mail became popular because it combined the thoroughness of written communication with the speed of the telephone and the convenience of voice mail at a negligible cost.

Another good question to ask is: what part of the entire process is the most expensive? You can be sure opportunity for improvement exists in this area. At the moment, distribution is often the most expensive cost factor, which is why so much money is being poured into the information highway—it is dirt cheap. Imagine buying software or having your personalized daily newspaper downloaded on the net. If you purchased software on the Internet, you would not need any physical product of any kind since the software would be directly installed on your computer. Need a backup? Just call for a reinstallation. What about that customized daily newspaper? If you could be provided with a lightweight computer tablet with a screen that was easy on the eyes and had access to as much or as little news on any topic you were interested in (such as PointCast offers), would you buy it?

In areas where high performance is required, often the most expensive parts are the control mechanisms or information systems. Consequently, in many cars today the electronics under the hood exceed the price of all of the steel in the car. Mechanical devices will become equipped with transmitters to indicate low volumes (vending machines) or mechanical or electronic difficulties (which are already used in Xerox's more expensive photocopying machines).

Undoubtedly, new control or information features that add to the convenience of driving or minimize breakdowns will sell well. Satellite cellular phones that allow for voice, fax, data, paging, and location positioning will become popular for the same reasons once the infrastructure is in place and the cost comes down. Try to think of novel applications of wireless technology, and you probably can't go wrong as long as many of the other conditions mentioned are also being met.

Other aspects of time and space convenience extend the one-stop shopping notion to an all-in-one-box concept. Home-office machines such as telephones, faxes, scanners, printers, answering machines, and copiers, are being combined into a single device. Roughly 2.2 million such units are expected to sell by 1998.

Buyer habits are also critical to the success of any innovation. As a rule, do not expect buyers to change their habits. Any new invention that is not compatible with previous technology is always going to have trouble getting off the ground. One of the reasons it took so long for PCs to become common household items was the amount of time necessary to master the intricacies of DOS. No previous life experience prepared you for this challenge. It was like going out and buying a car before you knew how to drive one. Web TV, on the other hand, stands a chance because you need to know only how to use a remote control.

The question of whether you would buy something is another telltale sign. Just ask yourself under which conditions you would likely purchase any particular good or service, and chances are these conditions will be met sooner rather than later if the benefits are attractive.

Chance and the Growth Cycle

Before most products or services are widely accepted, they go through various growth phases. In the beginning, prices are typically high, and few people know about or understand the new offering. Digital cameras are currently at the beginning of their growth cycle. Sales will stay low until prices drop and consumers understand the product or service, and then sales will take off. Computers are an example of a product at the take-off stage of the growth cycle. Eventually, most people will have purchased the product or service, at which point sales will taper off. Televisions have been at this "mature" stage for a few years. Finally, the product is replaced by something else, and sales collapse. Turntable sales virtually ended with the advent of the CD.

The growth cycle is tied in with the larger economic climate. Normally, innovations occur when there are obstacles to economic growth. However, it takes time for new technological innovations to reach the take-off stage. Once these innovations take off, the economy picks up with a concomitant rise in productivity. At the moment, computers are paving the way for the next period of economic growth since their use will reduce the cost of energy and improve productivity at the same time.

Some applications of the growth-curve method of predicting future trends include anticipating:

- Imitation growth (where catch-up companies adopt a new process introduced by the industry leader);
- Adoption growth (where a single new technology is adopted in the marketplace);
- Substitution or takeover growth (where a second technology displaces an older first one); and
- Multivariate or successive takeover growth (where a third technology might displace a second one that has already displaced a first one).

This same concept applies broadly to entire economic sectors. An examination of an agricultural growth curve shows that during the late 1880s and early 1890s, farm equipment became mechanized and more labor-efficient, causing the agricultural work force to diminish from 40 percent to 4 percent of the overall workforce by 1975. (This is a reduction in the percentage of employed workers in agriculture, not a measure of the number of workers employed in the industry.) Between 1900 and 1930, the number of workers employed in agriculture remained the same, but the total workforce increased from 30 to 50 million. Thus, the increase in productivity allowed output to increase without needing extra workers. Eventually, productivity so increased that the number of workers declined after 1930, until in 1970 the industry employed only 25 percent as many workers as it did before 1930.

This phenomenon is now occurring with blue-collar workers, whose numbers peaked in the 1940s as a percentage of the workforce. Although the decline in jobs in this sector has been gradual (46 percent in the 1940s to 38 percent in the 1980s), the curve is now sloping progressively downward. By 2020, blue-collar workers will represent far less than 20 percent of the workforce. Blue-collar workers of the future will be highly skilled college graduates trained in the use of sophisticated technology. By then, they will be considered white-collar workers.

In 1900, only 20 percent of the workforce were white-collar workers; yet by 1965, approximately 50 percent were white-collar workers. By 2020, over 75 percent of the workforce will be white-collar. This trend mirrors the growth in the service industries, although white-collar jobs now take up an even larger share of the manufacturing industries. The increasing efficiency of high-tech in manufacturing is having the equivalent effect of farm machinery on the number of farmers in the agricultural industry. Indeed, Jean-Claude Paye, secretary-general of the Organization for Economic Cooperation and Development (OECD), predicts that eventually only 2 percent of those employed in developed nations will be working in manufacturing and just one percent will be employed in agriculture. The move to the service industry reflects a worldwide trend. As Paye suggests, "By 2000, it is expected that the number of paraprofessionals and professionals will exceed 20 percent of the workforce, making these knowledge workers the most prominent segment of the workforce as more traditional manufacturing and laboring jobs continue to disappear."

Demographic Change and the Job Market

It is also possible to predict that almost one-third of the workforce will retire by the year 2010, although some may continue as part-timers. The job opportunities in a particular industry will then depend on the number of people already employed in it and its rate of growth or decline.

By 2010, jobs in the health care sector will likely account for 20 percent of all the jobs in the service sector. Other areas that will experience high growth rates include electronic equipment maintenance, quality control, information systems, employee training, toxic-waste management, technology consulting, and technology service. Almost all these professions will require a college diploma as a minimum qualification.

For career-planning purposes, a general understanding of where economic growth will come is of great long-term benefit. Job seekers are better equipped to plan their forays into the job market if they know the long-run prospects of their careers rather than the prospects for a specific year.

Today's Major Growth Curve

We are always being told we are in the information age, but where in it are we? Presently, we are nearing the end of the infrastructure stage of development, where we need the various technological components necessary for creating the information highway. This stage typically favors smaller companies that come up with the most innovative ways to solve technical problems (for example, network switches, cable modems) that slow down the developmental process.

The next phase we are on the verge of entering is the enabling era, which consists of the development of the technology to take advantage of the infrastructure that is being developed (Windows NT falls in this category). Expect this phase to last for at least five years and to favor medium-to-large companies. Last comes the content phase, which will last indefinitely though it will undergo a prolonged growth spurt (something has to fill up the 500-plus channels other than reruns) and will come courtesy of some large multinational firms in partnership with one another.

The further along the process we travel, the greater the number of partnerships, mergers, and acquisitions we will see. Why? Because as we climb the economic food chain, everything tends to get more interconnected and therefore more complex, necessitating bigger "wholes," so to speak.

As we will see in the next chapter, we need to develop an appreciation of the nonlinear nature of time and change when many systems begin to overlap and interact simultaneously. Most likely the reason we find ourselves confused is that so many changes are occurring at once. What we need is a new way of looking at time that frees us from the "ratchet effect" of having to work at an increasingly stressful pace.

PART II

Laws of the Jungle

CHAPTER 4

Time: The Hot Commodity

If you are a manager sitting in a meeting with your colleagues and you conceive of the long-term future as far away, you are not going to take it very seriously. Instead, you will do in the present what is most profitable and practicable so as to face the future in a strong position. But if you conceive of the future as being already here in your midst in the shape of assumptions, plans, visions, technologies, and expectations, and if you see it interacting with your past and present in an eternal now, then you are going to take it more seriously.

—CHARLES HAMPDEN-TURNER AND ALFONS TROMPENAARS
THE SEVEN CULTURES OF CAPITALISM

Time can be viewed according to a culture's orientation to the past, present, and future. Cultures that focus primarily on the past are mostly concerned with maintaining historical consistency or precedence in the present. Those stressing the present are assumed to be somewhat traditionless and unpreoccupied with future developments. Cultures emphasizing the future tend to plan ahead strategically.

Some cultures view time as sequential, with one event following on the heels of another. Other cultures are synchronic in their view of time, meaning that both the past and the future play a major role in current decision making, as though the past, present, and future were happening concurrently in a kind of telescoping of time.

Serial time can be conceived of as throwing a number of balls at a target one at a time. Synchronous time allows for many events to occur simultaneously—much like a juggler keeping numerous balls in the air and constantly deciding which ball to throw at any one moment. With serial time, the order in which the balls are passed or thrown is scheduled in advance. With synchronous time, the order in which the balls are thrown can be altered at any point in time. In other words, carrying out tasks in sequential time tends to be rigid, but activities performed in synchronous time are extremely flexible.

Time and Economic Success

These contrasting views of time determine how cultures experience time and how they think about it. To a large extent, economic success is partially owing to one's view of time. Those cultures, companies, or individuals that are more future-oriented and synchronous in their time orientation tend to enjoy greater prosperity.

Cultures that favor a sequential view of time place great emphasis on punctuality. These cultures believe in the very strict scheduling of events and are somewhat averse to spontaneity and long-term planning. Although sequential cultures, such as ours, are concerned with planning, most of the focus is on the short term since it is the only time period where events can be rigidly planned in advance with any degree of predictability. Longer time periods tend to defy such planning efforts because too many unforeseen events can intervene. Thus there is big stress on shortening cycle times, speeding up production, and meeting deadlines or quarterly profit projections. The present and the immediate future assume critical importance. Time is an enemy that must be mastered.

What is wrong with this view? After all, isn't it vital to get things done on time or get products to market before one's competitors? As we shall see, the logically sequential view of time is very shortsighted and lacking in creativity. We need to see time as a creative challenge rather than something to be mastered once and for all.

Imagine a large number of people lining up to purchase lumber in a stockyard in the United States. Typically everyone would be given a number or take a place in a line to have his or her order filled. The stock clerk would try to go and get the materials as fast as possible for each customer, then offer to serve the next in line in a typical sequential manner. Most people, I would assume, have had more than a passing acquaintance with lines of this nature.

Suppose the clerk decided to adopt a slightly different approach to the long line of customers anxious to purchase their materials. Let us assume that the first customer in line requires some two-by-fours and some three-inch nails. The clerk now asks everyone in the line who wants two-by-fours and three-inch nails and quickly jots down the total number of each requested by everyone in the line. She then hurries off to get enough of each for everyone in the line and asks everyone to take as many as required from the retrieved piles of items. The process is then repeated with the next customer in line and so on.

Not only is this a significantly faster way of serving everyone, but the longer the line, the faster customers' orders can be handled.

Synchronous service or production thus tries to do more than one thing at a time, coordinating the various activities to speed up the overall process. While some customers will definitely end up waiting slightly longer under this system, most of the customers will be served much quicker than if the purely sequential approach is used. Although such a system can play havoc with some schedules, it nonetheless is faster overall and has the advantage of being completely flexible so that any surprises can be accommodated relatively easily.

The Japanese used this view of time to help them quickly undermine the American auto industry and has led to an enormous research-and-development productivity advantage. Since most of Detroit's Big Three car designers conceived of the car design process sequentially, there was no major attempt made to coordinate the design of many cars at once. Consequently, most cars that came off the line had few interchangeable parts when compared with Japanese cars. Having to design and make a wider variety of parts for each car meant that it took much longer both to design and to manufacture each car.

The Japanese, on the other hand, insisted that their car designers use common parts in order to cut design, overhead, and assembly costs and to cut down significantly the amount of time needed to get the car to market. Other activities were synchronously coordinated as well.

According to Gary Hamel and C. K. Prahalad in *Competing for the Future:*

> In the early 1990s it was estimated that Detroit's Big Three require an average of 8.0 years to develop an entirely new model line; the figure for Japan was 4.5 years, with individual model variants developed in about half the time. This allowed Japanese car makers to recoup their investments more quickly, have more up-to-date products, and give customers more opportunities to switch allegiances. A disciplined approach to agreeing on product development priorities (focusing), seamless functional integration (blending), and tight integration with a network of capable suppliers (borrowing and co-opting) also means that Japanese car companies were capable of developing a new model with 1.7

million person-hours of effort rather than the 3.0 million person-hours typical of U.S. manufacturers. Not only do Japanese auto firms get a much quicker payback, they need a much smaller payback to reach the black on a particular model.

Making Synchronicity Work

Networking and integration of functions are key aspects of a synchronous view of time. The notion of a number of events simultaneously taking place at once in a kind of interweaving pattern leads to an extremely flexible and adaptable system.

The Japanese have had a long-standing practice of allowing any worker on an auto assembly line to bring the line to a halt if a problem develops. This policy stems from an awareness that much more useful information will be learned over the long run from stopping to identify and correct significant problems than is saved by letting the odd defect pass unnoticed. Thus an assembly line for the Japanese involves much more than simply moving as many car chassis along as quickly as possible.

In countries that are more oriented to a synchronous view of time, arriving late for an appointment allows the person waiting to get on with other activities in progress. When punctuality assumes less importance, other arrangements are made to accommodate the potential lateness or other contingent occurrences. Such cultures will cook up food that keeps well in case other unexpected guests arrive at any point in time. Exactness is less important than the overall goal of friendship or maintaining a business relationship.

Building Long-Term Relationships

Many U.S. companies trying to do business abroad are continually frustrated by such inexact and nonpunctual business dealings. It is not unusual for an American company to fly into such a country and meet with prospective business partners with the expectation that a deal can be concluded in a couple of days. When the prospective customers refuse to be rushed or tied to any particular negotiating schedule, frustration begins to mount. In many cases the deal is lost to a competitor with a vastly inferior product simply because the other company was willing to spend more time getting to know the customer.

Why is so much time required prior to what may seem like a simple purchase? In many Asian and Latin American countries the focus is on establishing long-term business relationships. If a company sells you a product, you want to be assured that it will honor any warranty should the product prove defective and that customer assistance will be available as required, especially with foreign companies.

According to a recent survey carried out by the International Semiconductor Cooperation Center, Japanese companies expected foreign suppliers to focus on technical support services; however, U.S. suppliers reported that building their sales organization was their highest priority. Interestingly, 93 percent of Japanese purchasers felt inconvenienced by foreign suppliers, yet only 43 percent of the suppliers believed they had at any time inconvenienced the purchasers.

In Asia in particular, you are judged by the people you do business with. Suppose that an Asian company decides to do business with a foreign company locally and it turns out that this same company has taken unfair advantage of another local company and word gets out. Most of the other local companies will now refuse to do business with the Asian company that had previous dealings with the foreign company since it is obvious that this Asian company must be involved in shady dealings as well or they never would have done business with the foreigners in the first place. All of a sudden, a lifetime of building up a reputation has been destroyed despite no wrongdoing on the part of the Asian company. No wonder considerable emphasis is placed on getting to know one another prior to doing business.

Dealing With Delays

Product delivery delays is another area where the sequential versus the synchronous view of time causes problems. Although you might expect that synchronous cultures are less concerned with broken deadlines, the reality is somewhat counterintuitive. Delays—but only short delays—are acceptable in synchronous cultures.

Why only short delays? If you remember our lumber-store-line example, some people would end up waiting a little longer for their purchased items, but most people would actually be served sooner than under the sequential model. There would only be a slight delay for those who waited longer; otherwise, such a system would break down. After all, if you were in line and people behind you were getting their orders filled before you were, you would be willing to accept only a very slight delay. The same is true in Japan.

Delivery schedules in Japan are much tighter, yet last-minute changes are expected to be accommodated. When all companies in a country are involved in synchronous activities, both goals can be met. Consequently, it should not come as a surprise to learn that 92 percent of the Japanese purchasers of foreign products were willing to accept delivery delays ranging from a half day to one week, yet 74 percent of foreign supplying companies felt that two-to-four-week delays in delivery were acceptable. Delays, however, are extremely costly. According to one study, although 75 percent of a product's cost is tied to the conceptual design stage, a 50 percent cost overrun on development cuts profitability by only 3.5 percent, whereas a six-month delay in launching a product undermines profitability by 33 percent.

The advantage of using a synchronous approach to design lies not just in bringing down costs and shortening development time, but also in the difference in quality possible. Indeed, the serial-design method used by Cadillac clearly demonstrates the shortchanging of quality typical of the serial approach:

> Cadillac used a disastrous serial-design method. The designer of the car's body would leave a hole for the engine, then the power-train designer would try to fit the engine into the cavity, then the manufacturing engineer would try to figure out how to build the design, and finally the service engineer would struggle to invent ways of repairing the car. The results were predictable. On one model, the exhaust manifold blocked access to the air-conditioning compressor, so season[al] maintenance meant removing the exhaust system. On another model, the connection between the spark plugs and spark plug wires was so tight that mechanics tended to break the wires when they pulled them off to check the spark plugs.

Why are longer delays more acceptable in cultures bound by a sequential view of time? Ironically, since everything takes so much longer to accomplish when operating sequentially, such cultures are used to longer delays or waiting periods. The Japanese, who have been able to reap the benefits of synchronous timeframes, see no need for delays. Not only that, the Japanese feel quite free to telephone a supply company and change the specifications and still expect deadlines to be met, since changes are easily made if your company is synchronously designed. American firms that are heavily invested in sequential approaches find such specifications maddening since entire schedules are thrown out of alignment.

In a similar vein, U.S. companies doing business with such a foreign country are likely to find that legal contracts are of little importance. In Japan a company will ask you to break an agreement previously signed if circumstances have changed over time or to change specifications at a minimal cost. Moreover, contracts are often signed before the specifications have even been fully determined. Since stress is placed on the overall relationship, individual details are not expected to become a source of problems. Besides, changing specifications is much less costly in the synchronous model compared to the sequential approach.

Keiretsu

We can see in this example that permanent links join the past, present, and future. Doing business requires that several aims and objectives be synchronized since it is expected that business arrangements are more permanent in nature and that a cycle of renewal will be established over time. Since interruptions are inherent in the synchronous model, it becomes necessary to gain enough comfort with a business partner so that both parties are sufficiently confident that conflicts can be easily resolved over time and that many objectives can be met with a minimum of fuss.

Given the failure of many U.S. firms to negotiate successfully with Japanese companies, the U.S. government now insists that the Japanese break up their long-standing relationships with supplier firms *(keiretsus),* because they feel excluded. This is the equivalent to asking a country to give up its traditional proven way of doing business. Ironically, many U.S. firms are now pursuing highly networked relationships with one another, while some Japanese firms are beginning to look closely at more competitive worldwide sourcing. Perhaps we are beginning to learn from one another.

Despite having only scratched the surface of the cultural differences that exist with respect to time, it should be easier to understand why many U.S. companies have been so frustrated in their attempts to do business with the Japanese. Failure to try and understand other cultures is usually at the bottom of most trade disagreements and most cross-cultural problems. When you consider that it wasn't until 1993 that U.S. automakers actually shipped cars to Japan with the steering wheel on the right side of the car, you can begin to understand why U.S. cars sales there haven't taken off. In addition, cars in Japan are often sold door-to-door, unlike in America. Moreover, you cannot purchase a car unless you can prove you have a parking spot for it—something that is not easy to come by in Japan. Japan is a small country where space is at a premium: homes are small, streets are narrow, and as a result, most cars are small.

This is not to say that there isn't need for reform of Japan's closed distribution system, its designated bidder system in public service contracts, or its exclusionary *keiretsu* alliances; however, once more deregulation has taken place, cultural issues will still need to be addressed by Japan and its trading partners as the globalization trend increases in scope and volume.

Concurrent Engineering

Fortunately many American companies have adopted flexible manufacturing methodologies and are using concurrent engineering, which involves a simultaneous cross-functional development process that takes advantage of synchronous synergies.

The movement toward mass customization requires the kind of flexibility that can be achieved only by operating in this manner. Each customer is in a sense an interruption or distraction since the manufacturing process or service delivery mode must be altered in each instance to meet the specific requirements of each customer. As we move toward just-in-time or while-you-wait manufacturing, a completely adaptable system is absolutely essential for success.

For example, there is a manufacturer of bicycles in Japan that offers over 12 million types of bikes, which can be made while you wait. Just imagine how long you would have to wait for your bike if all of the bikes ordered on a given day had to be made and assembled one step at a time.

Cyclical Renewal

Since the synchronous model shortens product development time and allows for many different product types to be made at once, it should come as no surprise that Sony introduces four new products each day. The shelf life of each item is only ninety days, and those products that do not show any promise are removed and never heard about again. Successful products undergo continuous improvements, however. This experimentation makes it easier to determine customer preferences, ensuring that Sony always stays close to its customer. Companies not employing this strategy are usually easily eliminated from the marketplace because of their inability to keep pace with fluctuating customer demands.

Cyclical renewal processes are naturally built into the synchronous model. The Japanese tend to view the "genes" of one product as giving birth to succeeding generations of products. All too often, many U.S. firms will view products using a life-cycle model. This model typically sees products beginning as novelty items. The products then pass through a highly profitable stage, but eventually enter a mature phase of low margins, and subsequently die.

Those firms that overlook the rebirth potential in many products will often abandon a product once it is through its most profitable phase. Not only do many U.S. firms miss out on future business opportunities, but they fail to take advantage of product development as a learning process that improves a company's core competencies. Considering that core competencies determine where and how a company is able to compete in the future, much is often being sacrificed for the sake of the fast buck.

Time and Internal Customers

The concept of time has important ramifications in the area of labor relations. Employees are a company's internal customers, and their demands often fluctuate as well. Both

Japan and Germany enjoy less labor strife because there are many occasions when business and labor get together other than during contract negotiations. Since both frequently work together to help resolve mutually beneficial issues, the relationship is less adversarial and more one of partnership. It should come as no surprise that Germany, another formidable economic powerhouse, also functions on a synchronous view of time.

Companies that deal with unions only at the bargaining table probably find that unions are rather unfriendly toward management and vice versa. Striking a deal is but a small part of trying to live together, yet unfortunately the cultural differences such a practice fosters turn the entire arrangement into a "lose-lose" proposition for both management and labor. Strikes, walkouts, lockouts, and grievances serve only to undermine the competitiveness of any company, something that cannot be afforded in a highly competitive global marketplace.

By spending time together when no negotiation is taking place, both parties are better able to get a more rounded view of each other and as a result are better willing to listen to the other side's point of view once negotiations are actually begun in earnest.

The extra time Asian and Latin American firms spend on building a trusting relationship or foundation prior to conducting business usually pays off down the road and leads to contractual renewals despite any momentary conflicts that are bound to arise in the natural course of events. The American emphasis on closing the deal in order to speed up the sales or negotiation process often backfires down the road when conflicts arise and the terms of the contract favor one side disproportionately. It is better to see a particular sale as the birth of a relationship likely to bear fruit repeatedly in the future.

Given our discussion so far, it should be obvious that the synchronous versus sequential view of time has enormous business and financial implications affecting the ability of companies to compete both now and in the future. Much the same could be said of countries themselves. Those countries that have well-integrated societies and business infrastructures are able to leverage the potential latent in a synchronous view of time. It is worth taking stock of some of the implications for individuals who often feel trapped in a culture that is most likely rather sequential in its orientation.

Trapped in Time

> *Time is what we want most, but what alas! we use worst.*
>
> —William Penn

Until recently the nine-to-five business mentality prevailed. Everyone was expected to show up for work at the same time and place so that everything could be tightly scheduled and coordinated. In keeping with the hierarchical tradition, it was always wise to arrive before the boss and leave later. Supervisors were expected to keep a close watch on workers, because the work was designed so that each worker understood only a small part of the overall tasks in progress. Much like border collies herding sheep, supervisors made sure the efforts of individuals were kept in check. Originality was not appreciated because it threatened carefully designed policies, procedures, and regulations. The assumption was that without such controls there would be chaos.

Each person, including every supervisor, was assigned a limited number of chores. The span of control was minimized to provide additional checks and balances. Great pride was taken in claiming to run a tight ship. So long as everyone followed orders and met deadlines, it was assumed that the company would succeed.

Such systems usually make perfect sense to everyone inside the organization because the primary focus is on the internal workings of the organization. When you become "institutionalized," you have completely bought into the long-established practices of an organization. No doubt IBMers felt this way when they allowed the organization to wield great influence over their personal lives.

The strong inward orientation is used to create a separate culture that is somewhat removed from the outside world. As such, institutions are closed systems—that is, they do a good job of serving their own needs. Customers from the outside are required to fit into the system. The most obvious examples are governments and banks. You are required to fill out their forms, play by their rules, and even wait in long lines to receive money they owe you. Your needs are comparatively unimportant.

Because these systems are not particularly efficient, excessive stress tends to get placed on speeding up everything to increase output. Much like Charlie Chaplin in *Modern Times,* we feel the ratcheting effect of our workloads or personal responsibilities constantly being increased. On this treadmill, no matter how fast we run, it is never fast enough.

We feel pulled in so many directions at once because we are required to fit into many closed systems, each separate from one another. In the synchronous model, time is actually your friend and not a source of constant pressure. Why? Because all of the systems are open and integrated with one another, it is always possible to reschedule or juggle everything so that the unexpected can be accommodated and the most convenient arrangement taken advantage of. Given the cyclical and flexible nature of this view of time, there will always be other opportunities to solve problems should the current opportunity slip away. What is required, though, is an entirely different mind-set.

Escaping the Trap

The closed-system, purely linear nature of the sequential time model makes each moment in time precious in the sense that you will "pass this way but once." The tension and stress produced by such urgency tends to promote a compulsive preoccupation with time, perfectionism, schedules, and the present moment. Closed systems, which lend themselves to a kind of static perfection, rely on schedules and rules as a means of gaining control over time. The inherent inability of any system to contain the randomness of life events leads to a redoubling of effort to maintain control and to the designing of even more closed systems in a never-ending battle against time and life.

The Type A or highly driven character described by Douglas McGregor is the natural product of such an environment. High blood pressure, heart attacks, nervous breakdowns, and other medical ailments seem to come with the territory. The endless need to beat the clock usually results in the development of constant anxiety and barely suppressed anger, frustration, and disappointment since anyone caught up in this vicious circle is bound to lose the battle sooner or later.

Fortunately, we are beginning to evolve beyond this state of affairs, though we are far from home free. Flex-time, part-time, contract work, office daycare, and working outside the office or at home are the beginnings of the restructuring of the work world that in the long run will lead to a much more adaptable and flexible system. Currently, the main beneficiaries of these changes are the companies initiating such changes. However, despite the misgivings of many, we all stand to benefit from these changes once integrated infrastructures are fully in place to support the new ways of living and working. Unfortunately, like all transitional phases, there is still much in the way of upheaval and confusion that will accompany the change and sorting-out process. Once the dust settles, however, we should be able to settle in and feel at home in any world that is inherently more flexible.

Dealing with Flexibility

What about in the meantime? Although later chapters in the book will try to answer this question from many perspectives, let us briefly look at the kind of disposition needed for a world in the midst of a transformation process.

Before we go on to discuss the importance of a culture's views on the past, present, and future, ask yourself the following questions as a way of determining your own time preference:

Do you tend to do only one thing at a time?	Yes/No
Are you always on time generally speaking?	Yes/No
Do you find yourself running out of time frequently?	Yes/No
Do you hate being interrupted or distracted?	Yes/No
Do you insist on keeping to schedules?	Yes/No
Are you uncomfortable with growing older?	Yes/No
Do you resolve conflicts on a first come, first served basis?	Yes/No
Are you uncomfortable renegotiating former agreements?	Yes/No
Do you prefer elaborate job descriptions?	Yes/No
Do you prefer a lot of rules and regulations?	Yes/No

The more "yes" responses given, the more frustrating you are likely to find life in the future.

Past, Present, and Future: Overlapping or Separated from One Another

> *Future shock is dizzying orientation brought on by the premature arrival of the future.*
>
> —Alvin Toffler

In 1967, Tom Cottle was able to compare how nationalities value time and perceive the connection between past, present, and future by having people draw circles to represent the past, present, and future. The size of the circle was meant to determine its importance, and the relationship between the circles was determined spatially by distance or overlapping (see Fig. 4.1). In the United States, we see that the future looms large and only barely overlaps with the present. Germany, a synchronous country, shows a greater degree of overlap between the past, present, and future. Japan, not shown here, is actually three concentric circles with the future containing the present and the present containing the past. In other words, there is a complete overlapping of the past, present, and future representing a completely synchronous culture. For the French, we see that the past, rich with cultural tradition, is almost as important as the present and overlaps with the present noticeably. Russia, on the other hand, shows a meager present, a valued past, and an important future completely cut off from the past. Subsequent events in Russia have completely confirmed such a viewpoint.

Those countries that show respect for the past and integrate it with the present typically revere the elderly and value experience, qualifications, class, tradition, and culture. Obviously, this describes many people in America as well as elsewhere. Change is often resisted because great importance is placed on the continuity of the past in the present. By preserving the past, they are maintaining control over their identity. Unless the future promises to reaffirm vital aspects of their culture in some recognizable way, there will always be great reluctance to accept change.

In some ways this may become Japan's Achilles heel. By being so completely synchronous with respect to time, Japan will find it difficult to make some of the adjustments being forced on it by technology. In 1995, 160,000 college graduates in Japan were without jobs. Employment in the manufacturing sector decreased by 740,000 jobs or 5 percent. The unemployment rate, now at 3.1 percent, is expected to rise to 5 percent over the next three to five years. Such a low unemployment rate stemmed from keeping jobs in Japan instead of locating production overseas. Only 10 percent of its production is abroad, compared to 25 percent for the United States and 19 percent for Germany. With the value of yen so high, there will be no choice but to resort to foreign production, such as the numerous Japanese auto plants scheduled for construction in the United States.

Figure 4.1

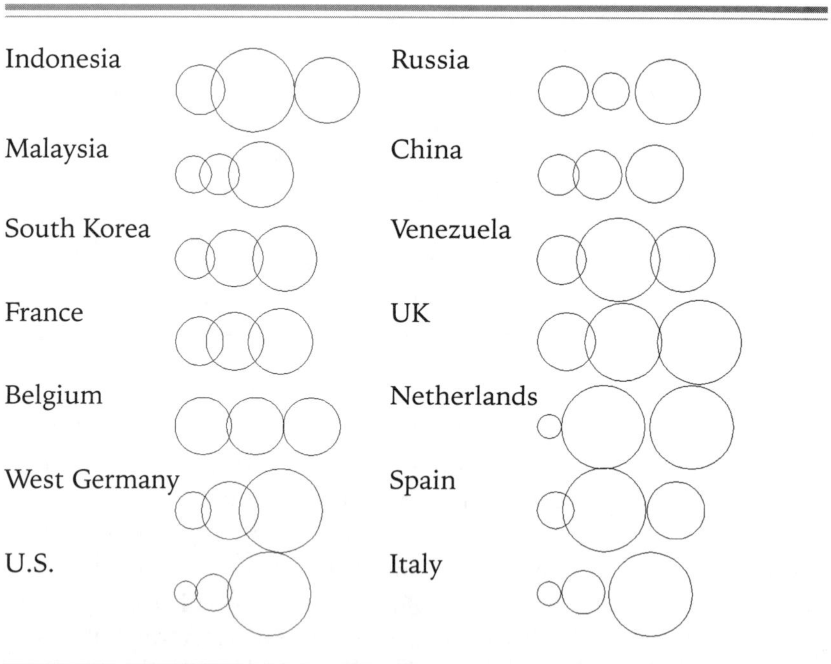

Source: Tom Cottle, "The Circles Test: An Investigation of Perception of Temporal Relatedness and Dominance," *Journal of Projective Technique and Personality Assessments*, No. 31, 1967, pp. 58-71.

According to Salomon Brothers' Tokyo economist, Robert Feldman, 6.5 million office workers in Japan could be dismissed without affecting productivity. McKinsey & Co. estimates that as computer-intensive discounters continue to steal market share from the traditional labor-intensive distribution system, they should end up with 40 percent to 60 percent market share by the year 2000—something that will displace many small retailers.

Like most other countries, change is being thrust upon Japan. Even older employees are being asked to retire earlier. The Japan Productivity Center, in 1992, found that Japanese companies will need to reduce their workforce by 39 percent to equal the productivity of American firms. Thus the tradition of a job for life is being called into question. Deregulation is inevitable, and with it will come a less-ordered society during the transitional phase.

Charles Hampden-Turner and Alfons Trompenaars, authors of *The Seven Cultures of Capitalism,* found that the Japanese view of time has more recently begun to spread out more linearly, though considerable overlapping nonetheless remains while the past no longer overlaps with the larger future (see Fig. 4.2). Thus the Japanese are already psychologically preparing to make a break, at least temporarily, with some of their past traditions. Ideally, however, a synchronous culture is likely to be more creative in making the changes once the political will or motivation exists to make the changes. The question remains as to whether the rest of the Japanese population share the viewpoint of its managers. Kenji Sato, one of Japan's younger writers, claims that "Most Japanese really don't want much deregulation" because they have so much invested in the old order.

Resistance even exists at the intercorporate level. An article in *Forbes* magazine describes a Tokyo distribution firm, Misumi, which recently tried to diversify into medical equipment. Japanese medical supply firms, leery that Misumi would use its computerized network to undercut existing wholesalers, refused to fill its orders. Unfazed by its lack of support by the medical companies, Misumi is using the Internet to search for U.S. and European suppliers. "The old Japan, capitalist with feudalistic remnants and obsessed with control and order, is simply out of date." So even synchronous cultures face challenges to their comfortable ways.

Figure 4.2.

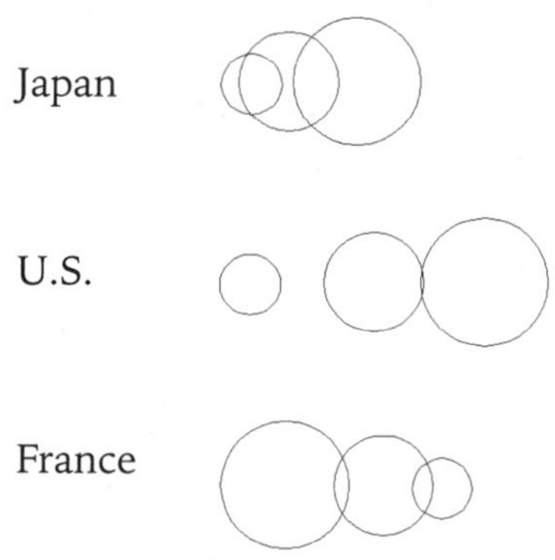

Two other changes of note to Cottle's Circle test are those of the United States and France. In the case of France (see Fig. 4.2), there has been a retrenchment toward the past and an inability to come to terms with the effects of contemporary technological realities on employment. From the beginning, France has been hesitant to join the European Union and is loath to give up the employment social taxes set at 40 percent of an employee's wage that have been a long-standing tradition in the country. Companies, as a result, are reluctant to hire any workers if they can avoid it, so unemployment levels have risen from 2.6 percent to 12.5 percent over the past twenty years. With 150,000 new job seekers entering the market place each year, drastic changes are inevitable.

In the case of the United States (see Fig. 4.2), the past is quickly receding in importance for managers. Restructuring and reengineering both suggest an abrupt rupture with past traditions as opposed to an evolutionary approach to change. Although it probably is not possible to completely evolve beyond the hierarchical business model, much can be done to make systems more integrated and responsive to those affected by them. According to Art Kleiner, author of *The Fifth Discipline Handbook* and *The Age of Heretics,* "The industrial-era model—giving orders, in military fashion, through a hierarchical chain of command—doesn't work any more ... it may be responsible for the deadening lack of quality in the world today."

Reengineering and Time

Hierarchies are perfect examples of the sequential view of time since information and decision making take place in a lock-step sequence up and down the chain of command. With cause and its effect so separated in time, it is no wonder that one loses sight of the other. Both the organization and the individuals usually end up losing touch with their original purpose and find themselves unable to respond to change in a timely, concerted way. One solution offered by reengineering is to dynamite the edifice and start all over.

Reengineering the United States, however, would essentially amount to throwing out the past and installing a kind of synchronous model designed by experts, or as Michael Hammer, the reengineering guru, puts it, "When people ask me what I do for a living, I tell them I'm reversing the Industrial Revolution." The question that undoubtedly remains for some people is whether reengineering is the best way to bring about such a profound level of change throughout society.

Unfortunately, there is not always choice in the matter. Only now that the world is shrinking, thanks to telecommunications and global trade, are we beginning to understand the complexities that characterize living systems, especially as they become disrupted. As Lewis Mumford suggests, "The ecological investigations of Darwin and the later biologists established a concept of the web of life, of that complex interplay of geological formation, climate, soil, plants, animals, protozoa, and bacteria which maintains a harmonious adjustment of species to habitat. To cut down a forest, or to introduce a new species of tree or insect, might set in motion a whole chain of remote consequences." Indeed, following such events many species end up competing to take their place in the new ecological order. Automation, downsizing, restructuring, deregulation, free trade, information technology, mass customization, and worldwide wireless communication systems now serve as the equivalent of floods, forest fires, volcanoes, or earthquakes.

To become more synchronously flexible so as to take advantage of a world in upheaval, large companies are downsizing into much smaller companies. Indeed, the analogy of large businesses versus small businesses probably nicely encapsulates the issue for the world we are heading into. As the trend toward outsourcing accelerates the pace of corporate downsizing, we are left with a world filled with smaller businesses. Even the larger multinationals are redesigning themselves around the small business motif. Small businesses have usually had to be more synchronous in nature. Job descriptions are flexible as everyone scrambles to make sure the job somehow gets done.

Thus all of us must become more entrepreneurial in our lives if we ever hope to juggle successfully the many changes coming our way. Perhaps some of us will even have to downsize our lives as part of restructuring our relationships so that everything is better aligned around a common purpose. The third part of this book is devoted to a discussion of how you can restructure your life to take advantage of the change that surrounds us.

Teamwork and Time

The true quantum leap to the synchronous mode for all business lies in the increasing networking of businesses of every size in alliances and partnerships of various sorts.

Within companies, the synchronous mode has taken hold in the form of teamwork consisting of individuals from each cross-functional area. Teams allow numerous departments to interact simultaneously so that flexibility and adaptability within an organization become possible. Teams, like small businesses, are organic in nature and completely responsive to their environment. Like chameleons that change color to fit in with their environment, teams are capable of changing their shape and function according to how roles and purposes get renegotiated in response to changing and diverse internal and external realities.

The ability to renegotiate one's purposes or roles when necessary is the quintessential quality of the synchronous model and the basis of wholeness and balance for individuals and companies. Mass customization requires the complete integration of functions within an organization in order to maximize flexibility and adaptability. When a company is integrated, all the people know the vision of the organization and how they contribute to it. When an individual is well integrated with all aspects of his or her environment, the broad range of possibilities inherent in the situation is more obvious, and the ability to take advantage of them is enhanced. By being able to move in a number of directions at once, the individual can envision a number of possible futures of which no single possibility necessarily excludes the others.

The key point to remember is that we are heading into a world that is as polychronic as is humanly possible. Multimedia convergence (which synchronously brings together all media at once, combined with content charged with global diversity) is probably going to challenge just about every comfortable assumption you have regarding virtually everything. In other words, we have moved beyond what once might have been considered manageable sequential change within a particular setting to overlapping changes coming at us from an number of directions at once.

The convergence of the world at your doorstep promises to be as exciting as it is challenging so long as you learn how thrive in a multidimensional environment. Fortunately, you will not have to take this new economy, rite-of-passage journey alone. As the next chapter will show, working in synchronous time means working in groups. Indeed the ultimate convergence involves the telescoping of space and the compression of time so that the concept of a "global village" not only begins to make sense, but also becomes relevant to us in a meaningful way.

CHAPTER 5

Exceptions to the Rules

There is nothing more difficult to take in hand, more perilous to conduct, or more uncertain in its success, than to take the lead in the introduction in the new order of things, because the innovator has for enemies all those who have done well under the old condition.

—Niccolò Machiavelli, *The Prince*

Most companies are hierarchical to greater or lesser extents—that is, some sort of chain of command, however vague, is revealed in any organizational chart. Regardless of the way it is laid out, no such chart accurately describes how business is actually conducted inside an organization—only the formal relationships are evident. If companies had to rely solely on these formal relationships to get things done, most businesses would come to a grinding halt almost immediately. Why? Because you can never make enough rules to cover every situation—which explains why unions often threaten to "work according to rule" as a sabotaging strategy.

Mindlessly following rules like a primitive robot has always been good for a laugh much the same way foreigners trying to conduct themselves in a foreign language using a translation book quickly leads to ludicrous statements and interpretations. The TV sitcom "Mork and Mindy" certainly capitalized on these shortcomings. In governments, this frequently happens when everyone follows the rules; but the individual rules, even when rational, do not add up to a coherent whole, especially if the intended purpose of each rule is not clearly understood.

Loyalty and Bureaucracy

So how do things manage to get done? Quite simply, workers must actively use all of their common sense for tasks to be completed. But what is the basis of this compliance?

Compliance comes through a commitment that requires strong, compelling reasons for doing something. Among the reasons is an implicit agreement among members of an organization.

In a bureaucracy, the agreement tends to be that each person doesn't mind doing what he or she is told to do so long as the task makes some sort of sense and a certain amount of freedom or autonomy is allowed within the established rules. Members of bureaucracies like to think of themselves as experts in each of their little niches, and they resent being told how to do their jobs. In other words, even though top-down control pervades bureaucracies, each layer wants a piece of the control in the carrying out of the orders from on high and appreciation for all of their loyal efforts. The Faustian bargain then is complete loyalty in carrying out the orders in exchange for power over the implementation process, plus explicit signs of approval from above once the tasks are expedited. With each layer of power comes a paternal sense of responsibility to the "family members" below who need guidance, pats on the back, and a strong sense of direction.

Unlike in the feudal past, when absolute loyalty was directed to a lord or master, bureaucratic loyalty is to the organization itself—something that is easier in good conscience to pledge fidelity to and also something that is easier to share with others in an organization. With everyone making this tacit pledge of allegiance much the way everyone sings the national anthem, much cooperation is naturally forthcoming, since there is a sense of common purpose. Once there is a pervasive understanding that all really want to help in getting the job done now that they are working together toward a common goal, networks of friendships develop around tasks requiring mutual coordination and cooperation, and favors are exchanged as a means of overcoming obstacles and solidifying relationships. People end up enjoying the spirit of working together and buying into the paternalistic ethic.

Loyalty becomes the motive for cooperation. And cooperation, which involves people doing more than their jobs stipulate, makes bureaucracies, which normally would not work, capable of functioning reasonably well. Transcending the desire for merely personal gain fosters considerable trust and a sense of common purpose that can actually turn bureaucracies into happy "families."

Many of the orders that come down from upper management do not make much sense in the context of what is actually possible on a day-to-day level—something upper management tends to be far removed from, caught up as it is, in grander planning and strategizing. Each management layer tends to encounter this problem in one form or another. Those who are successful inside bureaucracies quickly learn to form alliances with other key individuals at their same level of management and below, even in other divisions and departments. Indeed, roughly one-third to one-half of middle managers' time is devoted to lateral coordinating activities. By this means, which is becoming an increasingly larger part of their job, it becomes possible to alter or ignore orders in a concerted politically acceptable way or lobby for reconsideration of what may be clearly unworkable.

Having allies inside a bureaucracy is also the fastest way of getting anything done in what otherwise can be a laborious decision-making structure. So over time an extremely informal power network naturally emerges in all bureaucracies as a way of speeding up how things get done and as a way of solving problems of one kind or another. Considerable solidarity often emerges from these informal "teams," since without it little would be accomplished. The former Soviet

Union's underground economy was the equivalent informal response to bureaucracy in a highly political setting.

In other words, bureaucracies often have many of the earmarks of the new economy: people work together as members of teams, everyone is given and cherishes a certain amount of power of autonomy, and considerable coordination and cooperation can exist throughout the organization. People will often openly express how much they enjoy working in this kind of a setting, given the strong bonds of loyalty and common purpose that exist. They will even forgive the company and individuals within it for any errors of judgment because it is usually assumed that the mistakes were honest and that everyone will be fairly dealt with and rewarded with promotions and increases in salary over the long term. The internalization of these values is usually so strong that the sense of loyalty to the company is quite resilient even to extreme shocks such as downsizing and restructuring.

Loyalty is essential to the functioning of bureaucracies; without it, they would be completely unadaptable to any environmental changes. Middle management is typically the group that places the greatest emphasis on loyalty and on working as a team since the enormous coordination function it plays would become a nightmare of regulations if a network of relationships were not in place to override the limitations of the bureaucratic structure. Consequently, middle managers stress the community aspects of working in bureaucracies and put group effort and the organization above their personal gain in most cases.

What I have described to you may sound a bit idyllic. Though they often function in positive ways, there are downsides even to the beneficent forms of politics that emerge in these settings. The interpersonal informal networks that are formed are often grouped according the people who are similar and share common corporate interests.

Each group can end up excluding various individuals who don't "fit in" (for example, outsiders and minorities), particularly those from other corporate levels. The different groups can become political bottlenecks for one another at times, especially if each group fails to understand why cooperating with others is in the best interest of the organization in any particular case. And ultimately there is a slightly out-of-control or random quality to such informal groups since they are based on the chance development of one-to-one relationships within an organization, and there is no way of actually confronting each group's agenda since these groups don't exist in any formal sense.

Rules

Rules are the natural byproduct of a scientific, bureaucratic view of existence. Science tries to find nature's rules, while people try to organize societies using rules. Implicit within the search for appropriate rules is the desire for control or order. Without rules, it is assumed that chaos and anarchy will surely follow, so exceptions to rules are only grudgingly allowed. The finality of the Ten Commandments does not suggest that their applicability depends in any way on individual circumstances. Although every culture embodies rules, a key difference among cultures is how they view exceptions.

Historically, the need for rules increased as populations grew in size and life in complexity. Viewing people and events from a situational perspective has been associated with simpler societies and smaller communities. For society at large, the law of the land or the public morality is expected to prevail. Countries that place a strong emphasis on applying the same set of rules across all circumstances have been referred to as universalistic cultures, while those societies that show a preference for taking the context into account are known as particularistic cultures. Although some cultures may display a more universalistic attitude toward certain topics and more particularistic leaning in connection with others, cultures as a whole tend to have a bias one way or another.

Universalistic cultures view legal contracts with great respect. Particularistic cultures stress the importance of relationships over the wording of any legal document. For universalists, there tends to be one correct truth, reality, or perspective, while for particularists, many perspectives can act as reasonable starting points in assessing a situation, so there is more of an open-endedness regarding what is right or true. Since reason by its very nature consists of generalizations, universalists are decidedly rational in outlook and persuasion. Arguments are resolved through an appeal to logic or justice. Judgment tends to be quick and decisive. Particularists reserve judgment until more is known about a situation and the nature of the relationships involved.

Japan's Particularist Culture

It might come as a surprise to learn that the Japanese did not have a word for "objective" prior to Western influence entering the culture, and even then the phrase for objective translates into "the guest's point of view." The Japanese word for subjective translates into "the host's point of view." Thus even the translation maintains a sense of relationship or context.

The Japanese prefer that multiple perspectives be adopted, because it is assumed that it is thus possible to get a better sense of the whole. Comprehensive views are believed to lead to more harmonious perspectives, with each situation forming only part of the overall pattern. Each part, however, is assumed to play a dynamic role within a much larger context.

By focusing on a particular fact or rule, it is assumed that the surrounding facts, rules, and context are left out of focus or are lost in the background. As Magorah Maruyama suggests in his essay "New Mindscapes for Future Business Policy and Management," using the viewpoints of as many people as possible allows us to gain a larger perspective on any problem or issue.

For the Japanese, the truth is an endless process of discovery, and there is no such thing as a completed product. Thus it was the Japanese idea of the quality circle (of viewpoints) that ended up spawning the notion of *continuous improvement*. Toyota workers are always expected to be aware of five different reasons for why anything happens in the company. Each reason represents a possible area for improvement, so by constantly thinking of more reasons or perspectives, workers can multiply opportunities for improvement accordingly, especially with each employee effectively acting as a management consultant.

By stressing differences rather than singular facts or objects, Maruyama believes that more knowledge is gained. Accepting multiplicity, variety, and diversity as the basis for finding whole patterns is a variety-enhancing activity, whereas taking a number of facts and reducing them to one explanation is a variety-reducing exercise. The former represents an endless creative challenge, unlike the latter, which leads to a rather static, definitive point of view.

The Problem with Objectivity

As Hampden-Turner and Trompenaars suggest in *The Seven Cultures of Capitalism*,

> The problem of "objectivity" is that those who claim to have it believe they need to look no further, need to listen to no one else, and never alter their convictions. They have "the data," or "givens." But those pursuing polyocular knowledge will never be satisfied, never know enough. And it is nonsense to claim that the monocular or objective view is more scientific.

Most of our discoveries emanate from lateral or inductive thinking, not from deductive logic (see Table 5.1). Unusual possibilities combine together intuitively in our minds to form new patterns of recognition. In other words, our minds like to form "wholes" without our knowing or understanding all that is involved. The natural tendency to ask "what if" or toy with an idea tells us that our minds like to experiment or play with combinations.

Table 5.1 Universalistic and Particularistic Cultures

Universalist	*Particularist*
Particular situations and human relationships can be understood by fitting them into universal truths and rules.	Decisions are based not so much on hard and fast truths, but on the weighing of all competing factors.
Overarching rules apply across most circumstances.	Context determines which rules apply.
Rational, analytical bias toward objectivity.	Relational, inclusive bias open to emergent process.
Arguments resolved through appeal to logic or justice.	Multiple perspectives increase the possibility of a comprehensive solution.
Judgments are quick and decisive.	Judgment is reserved until more is known about the situation and relationships involved.
Focus is reductionist.	Many perspectives act as realistic starting points.
Differentiated	Integrated
Static, definitive	Endless, creative
Universal moral order and the law of the land have supremacy—right conduct is derived from universal principles.	Harmonious personal and particular relationships become microcosms of the larger social order.
Once the objective solution is found, the consultation process ends, and the solution is applied in cookie-cutter fashion across all contexts.	A dynamic harmony is created from myriad differences—everyone cooperates continually to increase the effectiveness of the whole.
Deductive	Inductive
Analysis	Synthesis

Inductive reasoning, which allows for everything to be included in the thinking process at once, keeps the mind churning. Deductive reasoning, which proceeds lock-step in a logically linear fashion, much like sequential time, leads to the drawing of single conclusions based on specific facts or assumptions. However, life is always creating possibilities, and reality unfolds rather unpredictably, despite our best planning efforts.

Putting It All Together

> *There is no escaping the underlying sense that the product or service can be no better, no more sensitive, subtle, aesthetic, congruent, or intelligent than are the relationships and the communication among those who created the product.*
>
> —Charles Hampden-Turner
> *Charting the Corporate Mind*

The connection between parts and wholes is the means by which we learn, think, create, and innovate. Our ability to understand this process underlies our ability to understand ourselves. It is the secret to good management, to quality, and to careers.

Quality in not one thing. It is the coming together of many attributes into a consistent, harmonious whole with each part integrating seamlessly with every other part. Even parts that are different blend together in what seems like an effortless way. No part exists in isolation. The extent to which parts are not well integrated into the overall design or function is a sign of poor quality.

We usually conceive of quality in terms of efficiency and effectiveness. Even aesthetic evaluations typically involve measures of efficiency and effectiveness. In efficient systems all the parts interact with a minimum of energy or time potential being wastefully discarded. For example, modern gas furnaces consume roughly 98 percent of the natural gas they are fed. In an effective system, a desired result may be fully realized, but how it is achieved may not be necessarily efficient. For example, using dynamite to kill a mosquito may be effective, but (unless it is an especially large mosquito) the method is not efficient.

Often we attempt to optimize the trade-offs between efficiency and effectiveness. If we are able to lead a life that is both highly efficient and effective in meeting our needs and goals, we are likely to feel that the universe is unfolding the way it should. When any aspect of our lives fails to conform to what we believe is achievable in terms of efficiency or effectiveness, we feel frustrated. Either we feel we are wasting our time and energy or we are getting nowhere fast. These are the standards by which we judge almost everything in our lives. More importantly, they are the contexts we use to determine the meaning everything has to us.

Another way of saying the same thing would be that we look at everything in life according to how each part fits together. If something seems irrelevant to us, it might as well not exist. We are always seeking our patterns, structure, order, or meaning in an attempt to make sense of ourselves and the world around us. By doing so, we are better able both to alter the external environment to suit our purposes and to influence the course of events. Since the world is constantly changing, the task is unending.

As the world becomes more complex, the various parts become increasingly interdependent and critical in importance. A failure in one part of a complicated system can often shut down the entire system, as most computer owners know. Thus quality takes on greater importance.

Unfortunately, often in America the emphasis is placed on the quality of the individual parts, not on the quality of the relationships among the various parts. This inability to see the forest for the trees was not a big problem during the mass-production era because only relatively simple, easily understood interconnections were necessary. Assembly lines were inherently simple in design, with only one link between each stage of assembly. During this era, products were both uniform and technologically unsophisticated, which was why local corner garage mechanics were able to fix most cars fairly easily.

No longer! There is more computing power under the hood of the average car than was on board the first *Apollo* mission to the moon. Sophisticated (and expensive) diagnostic technology is now needed to fully serve most vehicles, so dealership service areas are now reaping the benefits as local garages fold.

The Japanese largely dominate the world market in the design of sophisticated and complicated products—VCRs, TVs, electronic equipment, automobiles. Not surprisingly, they were also the first to champion high quality standards. In Japan, the Demming Award night, which recognizes the companies with the highest quality products, is equivalent in popularity to our Academy Awards night.

How We Lost the Competitive Edge

Although most American companies are recapturing their competitive edge in some of these areas, why did they lose the competitive lead in the first place? Why were they unable to see that the relationship of the parts to the whole greatly exceeds the importance of any given part?

In addition to being trapped by a sequential view of time and a universalistic perspective, many Americans are victims of the analytical, logical method, which characterized the simple stand-alone machine era. The pre-Einstein notion of science proclaimed objectivity as the means by which factual truth was to be gained.

By examining each physical item in isolation, investigators assumed that the secrets of its inner working would be revealed. Moreover, the knowledge learned regarding each of the parts only needed to be added to achieve a complete understanding of how the parts fit together in a rather simple cause-and-effect relationship. While simple machines lend themselves nicely to mechanistic analysis, complex systems tend to be more organic in nature, especially if they incorporate feedback loops that both monitor and adjust in response to changes in their environment.

The mechanistic or traditional scientific objective viewpoint is static, since the object under examination is supposed to remain unaffected by the examination process. Therefore all interpretation was presumed to be free from the examiner's bias or influence. Analysis was merely like a microscope that zeroed in on ever more fundamental facts and constituent parts. If something were only exhaustively analyzed, you could learn all there was to learn about it.

The pervasiveness of this viewpoint extended into business and organizational design. Alfred Sloan divided GM into separate departments by functions. The chain of command was one way. Departments did not communicate with one another, and the flow of information throughout the organization was primarily from the top down. A built-in assumption was that management was a science and that universal truths could be discovered and applied across all organizations.

Even people were considered to be largely interchangeable factors of production—human "resources." As such, they were hired or fired according to inventory needs. The relationships among the individuals in an organization were considered to be defined statically by the organization chart. The primary emphasis was on controlling relationships so that each individual's contribution could be strictly regulated. If anything, the humanness of employees has been an undesirable, if unavoidable, reality. Henry Ford once asked,

"How come when I want a pair of hands I get a human being as well?"

In America, behavioral psychology became the dominant school of thought, although it has never been popular outside North America. Like the traditional scientific method, behaviorism divides actions into parts and examines their functions with the hope of explaining how to correct behavioral dysfunctions. Individual problems are treated as if they were amenable to universal solutions. For example, individuals only need to be properly matched to appropriate job descriptions, and all problems should be solved.

Management by objectives also compartmentalizes jobs into separate entities. Measurement, which is considered key to evaluating such objectives, is typically numerical, since only numbers have the ring of indisputable authority or factual solidity. Contribution to the bottom line becomes the holy grail of such measurement objectives. More ambiguous ways of evaluating overall corporate success are sacrificed to what is easily measurable and presumable beyond dispute so far as its desirability is concerned. Cause and effect are conveniently assumed to be obvious and completely contained within fiscal time frames. The "bottom line" business-made-simple assumption is that everything must be fine so long as a company is profitable.

The Obsession with "Object-ivity"

Cultures preoccupied with measuring separate facts tend to judge everything according to size, speed, or amount. As Hampden-Turner and Trompenaars suggest,

> Those business cultures greatly dependent on analysis find it difficult to capture the imaginations of employees in superordinate goals or larger visions.... Size and volume become very important in what the Japanese regard as an

> "obvious culture."... We rapidly exhaust the possibilities and are left with only the grosser extremities, 600-pound men and 90-hour pole squatters, hailed amid superlatives: "terrific, giant, dynamic, wow!"

The basic underlying assumptions of a culture caught up in separateness or "object-ivity" are that (1) everything in nature is separate, (2) individual objects somehow influence one another across their separateness in a one-way cause-and-effect manner, (3) everything takes place in serial time, (4) truth can be discovered and measured by analyzing each part in a logical step-by-separate-step process, and (5) truths learned are universal in application.

The primary emphasis is clearly on individuality or separateness. American history is replete with the worship of "heroes" who single-handedly slay any number of historical dragons. It is naturally assumed that the contribution of any one individual clearly stands out from the other participants. America's vast spaces allowed for individuality to flourish in ways unthinkable in densely populated countries with strong older traditional cultures and no wilderness to be tamed or survived. In America, the Marlboro Man, the Lone Ranger, Rocky Balboa, and Arnold Schwarzenegger's various incarnations point to a fascination with the triumph of the individual over insuperable odds or corruption, the protection of the weak and innocent, and the importance of realizing one's individual dream. Such hero worship is reflected by sports figures and CEO's who make salaries highly disproportionate to those of the rest of society. If the individual is the most important building block in society, then the entrepreneur's fantastic success is the key to a country's property. Indeed, no other nation launches so many new businesses annually.

Nowhere else in the world is as much focus placed on individuality as is common in the United States. The wealth of services provided for individuals represents one of the reasons America leads the rest of the world in its shift from the industrial to the service economy. Almost 70 percent of the country's GDP is devoted to private consumption.

The virtues of individuality are obvious: greater flexibility and a chance to outperform everyone else. America's lead in annual patent registration, Nobel prizes, and starting new businesses shows a highly innovative spirit in action. No one would question the importance of innovation in the new economy.

Getting Ready for the Next "Last Frontier"

Although individuality will never cease to be of vital importance, the world, including the United States, is moving beyond individuality as the driving economic evolutionary force. Now that the West has been won, the wilderness tamed, and the United States densely populated, the notion of the individual as separate from the rest of society is fast becoming an anachronism. The world has become an extremely complicated place, especially for individuals.

The latest frontier is knowledge on a scale never before even imagined. Ironically, though, it is becoming available on the modern-day equivalent of the down-home place where you can just lean across your fence and have a friendly chat on just about any topic that captures your fancy. And where is this neighborly place? It is just a modem away on the Internet.

The Internet resembles the Wild West in many ways because inherent in its design is the inability to control or dismantle it. The Defense Department built these features into this communication network twenty-five years ago so that in the event of a nuclear attack that knocked out a part of the system, the rest of the system could continue to function. How did it accomplish this feat? The key was to construct a system so that the information being communicated would look for any available way of getting to its destination. In other words, a message sent from New York to Los Angeles might be bounced from Florida to Alaska before ending up in Los Angeles.

Communicating on the Internet is inexpensive because messages sent take up so little bandwidth on a telephone line that the signal essentially is akin to a hobo hopping aboard a number of freight trains in order to get to somewhere—it just piggybacks on other calls wherever telephone line space is available.

Originally, the Internet was created to allow military research scientists to communicate simultaneously as often as necessary. By connecting together the best minds available from all over, the Internet helped to speed up knowledge sharing and quicken the pace of innovation. Aside from the obvious benefits of creating an intellectual "group mind," the net started to become a less formal place where all kinds of activities having nothing to do with research began to flourish. Private messages, news groups, bulletin boards for selling things, fantasy worlds, and games of all kinds began to spring up all over the place—it became a fascinating place where any number of activities could take place. Once word of the many uses that could be made of the net became widely known, it didn't take too long before business and people outside universities wanted access to such a wealth of information that could be retrieved so easily and to the other limitless informal communication possibilities that beckoned.

One big obstacle, however, was holding back the Internet's popularization: it was very difficult to use the required knowledge of rather arcane Unix commands to make it work. Many on the Internet wanted to keep the system difficult to use so that the net would not degenerate into an extension of the CB radio—something that has happened to some extent. Despite these difficulties, the number of computer users accessing the net over the past five years have risen by a rate of 5 to 10 times faster than the number of transistors being placed on computer chips—they double every eighteen months. Though growing quickly, it still wouldn't set the world on fire at that pace. But like Prometheus bringing down fire to the common man, a group of programmers designed browsing software, Mosaic and Netscape, which made using the Internet as simple as pointing and clicking, and then they gave it away for free. Since that time, the net's growth has been exponential, and the amount of economic activity now focused on its development is truly staggering. By now, you may even be bored with yet another article hyping the Internet and its future promise.

My reasons for mentioning the Internet point to how knowledge comes about in our modern high-tech world, for such knowledge is the touchstone to where the future jobs and entrepreneurial opportunities lie. We now live in an age where we can almost invent whatever it is we would like. If there is something people want badly enough and it can be sold for a reasonable price if widely adopted, then it will be invented faster than anyone can imagine. Believe me, there are very few exceptions to this rule. The Manhattan Project, designed to build the first atomic bomb, was considered technically impossible, certainly within the time frame of the war. Putting a man on the moon by 1969 was also an impossible feat. And just coincidentally, there were four doctoral dissertations written on why interactive browsing software such as Java could not theoretically be invented.

Another rule regarding innovation and knowledge expansion can be derived from our Internet example. When any new desired invention is made so easy to use that even an eleven-year-old can use it, you can be sure that everyone will be using it in no time. Why is this so? Quite simply, because with almost everyone wired or networked together, knowledge, including gossip, travels faster. And innovation and knowledge growth are limited only by the speed by which information can be shared by people or machines working on a common or similar problem.

To give you a sense of how fast difficult problems can be solved when a number of people work together on a problem, in 1977, $100 was offered to anyone who could solve an encryption problem that was supposed to take four quadrillion years for a supercomputer to solve. The prize won by four MIT researchers in 1994 who used 1,600 rather ordinary computers on the Internet working simultaneously to solve the problem.

Developing New Ideas

Most Nobel prizes and patents are now granted to groups of individuals. Why? As Robert Reich explains in *Tales of a New America*, the "big ideas" or grand inventions of lone pioneers that set the stage for continued prosperity and wealth can no longer be sustained. When the United States was largely isolated from the rest of the world, inventions or ideas enjoyed a long life unchallenged by competing improvements from other innovators or nations.

Today, however, you are lucky if you enjoy a three-month advantage over competitive versions of your invention or idea. Besides, it is not possible any longer to hoard knowledge of any kind. Most innovation is now collective in nature with many people working together as part of a team. Even the nature of innovation has shifted away from the "big idea" to the notion of continuous improvement of existing products and processes. Indeed, 80 percent of all R&D funds are devoted to improving existing products.

In the past, individuals were able to succeed largely through willpower and determination. In the static, hierarchical world of the organization man in the past, the only way to succeed was often by bucking the system and creating your own path for success. Biographies of people like Lee Iacocca served as an inspiration to all who aspired to use their talents within large corporations despite the obstacles certain large, unresponsive corporations managed to place in their way.

The days of such talented and resourceful individuals seem limited. In 1991, *Fortune* magazine stated that companies led by "rugged individualists" were not performing well. When historical circumstances change, a new kind of hero is often required. As Charles Garfield in his book *Second to None* asserts,

> Success in today's economic environment requires not the solitary ingenuity and leadership of a lone pioneer, but the innovation, creativity, and full participation of every member of the organization.... The model employee in the new story of business whether managing or managed, must be the fully participating partner.

Ironically, as a fully participating partner, the individual is more important in a group environment than in the previous business setting. It used to be easy to replace employees because they weren't well integrated into the business as a whole. With a limited job description and few reporting relationships, the worker in a hierarchical firm did not exert much influence on the organization in general. In the new "story," full participation suggests many points of contact and influence.

Groupwork

Employees can no longer be viewed as interchangeable parts of corporate machinery, but must be understood in connection with the many roles and relationships they are being asked to assume within a groupwork-oriented job environment.

While the employee as fully participating partner may be a somewhat new concept to U.S. firms, it has been a long-standing practice in both Japan and Germany. For instance, Japanese firms spend ten years rotating new managers throughout every department so that they will learn to see the firm from many perspectives and find the area of the business they would like to become an integral part of. By employing workers over a longer period of time, Japanese firms enjoy greater continuity and stability in the face of changes in the external environment. The multiplicity of perspectives afforded by job rotation becomes the creative power needed to solve problems on a continuous basis. And it can also reduce stress. Silicon Graphics offers a six-week sabbatical to each employee every four years so that at any one moment 10 to 15 percent of the company is away. Those remaining cover for the others on sabbaticals, often in other departments. It turns out that even the employees covering for those away find that the new roles and responsibilities help them avoid burnout and allow them to dabble in new areas before asking for lateral transfers.

American firms with high turnover and burnout rates often find learning ability, accumulated knowledge, creative potential, and core competencies walking out the door as employees leave or are downsized. Even Bill Gates has suggested that Microsoft would become a mediocre company if its top 20 people left. Microsoft's challenge is to keep rotating its staff, many of whom are now millionaires owing to stock options, through interesting and challenging enough assignments or projects. The power has obviously shifted from head office to the new means of production—the knowledge worker. Unlike before, employees are not cogs in a wheel but the source of creativity, innovation, and excellent customer service. And creativity does not take orders, nor can it be closely controlled—it can only be nurtured.

In the old "story," the command-and-control model allowed for stability and control over direction. Everyone was kept on a short, tight leash.

The former stress on control derived from the scientific notion of equilibrium. Many scientists earlier in the century felt that it was important to maintain equilibrium as a means of staving off entropy or chaos. That was before they had any understanding of either chaos or the role that disequilibrium plays in growth or complexity.

Equilibrium or Stagnation?

Ironically, it is now realized that equilibrium is the final evolutionary state of an isolated system. Closed systems inevitably lose their ability to change and slowly wind down to a lifeless level of equilibrium where essentially nothing much happens. In other words, change creates life and growth, whereas constant stability results in eventual stagnation and decay once internal energy is dissipated over time. Or, as Margaret Wheatley claims in her book *Leadership and the New Science*,

> In the past, systems analysts and scientists studied open systems primarily focusing on the overall structure of the system. This route led away from observing or understanding the processes of change and growth that make the system viable over time.

Open systems are continually exchanging information and energy with the external environment. By constantly interacting with the outside world, open systems are kept perpetually off-balance to some extent. As information and energy are exchanged with the outside world, a system needs to be constantly readjusting to digest or incorporate fully whatever is new into its system. In the process, a system becomes slowly transformed by the continual reconfigurational adjustments.

However, each modification represents renewal and growth. By employing positive feedback loops, those aspects of the external environment that become part of the internal system can be amplified to the point where significant change and adaptation occur. Instead of stability, growth consists of reorganization and renewal. Stability as such loses relevance. What becomes important is resilience.

As Wheatley has discovered concerning self-renewing systems,

> Part of their viability comes from their internal capacity to create structures that fit the moment. ... The system possesses the capacity for spontaneously emerging structures, depending upon what is required.

Consistency and Coherence

Regarding the need for consistency, it turns out that systems usually change in a way consistent with their established relationship with the environment. Change does not occur randomly but in keeping with certain clear reference points within an organization, such as the organization's values, mission, or area of competence. Completely unpredictable change, however, could occur if the organization lacks a shared set of values or purposes, since these are vital guideposts necessary for establishing boundaries for the direction of change.

What is really meant by continuity and consistency is coherence. Do the parts of the organization hold together well? Are they sufficiently well integrated so that any new information reaches all levels of the organization? Corporate identity is participative in nature. It is the sum of internal perspectives regarding the organization. Obviously if enough employees do not share a clearly identifiable viewpoint regarding a company, its future direction and success are questionable. Excessive turnover rates or downsizing can jeopardize the historical memory component, the ability of the organization's structure to maintain the identity as originally conceived, and the ability to wisely interpret information from the external environment.

The weaker the internal linkages and the poorer the communication channels with the environment, the more volatile any firm may be—for example, vacillating about what kind of business it is, who its customers are, where its money should be invested, what kind of partners the firm should choose, what it should outsource, what new products or services it should develop, etc. Any sudden shift in the environment can obviously magnify the importance of one or more of these concerns while compounding the confusion. For instance, IBM's outsourcing of its operating system to Microsoft was a poor decision hastily arrived at. Their OS/2 launch was equally ill conceived, given how well entrenched the Windows environment had become with customers and software application designers. Unfortunately, IBM had lost touch with all of its external customers and suppliers. Intel, on the other hand, is deeply involved with Microsoft, software designers, multimedia firms, suppliers, and customers in a big way. As a result, Intel is poised to surpass General Electric in worldwide profitability.

The more connections there are with the outside world, the more generally stable any open system is. With many points of contact, considerable information regarding the external environment is forthcoming, and the many adjustment processes that result produce a fairly strong structure that is well adapted to the changing nature of the outside world. Ironically, by exposing ourselves to the outside forces, we end up creating a stronger sense of identity. Many countries, cultures, companies, and individuals have erected barriers and tried to isolate themselves as a means of protecting some sense of identity. But as we have indicated, creating a closed system usually marks the beginning of the end.

The Risks of Isolation

If you tried closing yourself off from the rest of the world to see how long you were able to maintain your identity, you might lose a sense of yourself fairly quickly. Others act as a reality check to let us know if we are being perceived as we would like to be. Most people need external reference points to facilitate the self-monitoring process. Without feedback, it is hard to separate illusion from reality.

As David Bohm, author of *Wholeness and the Implicate Order*, observes,

> Fragmentation is now very widespread … and this is leading to a kind of general confusion of the mind, which creates an endless series of problems and interferes with our clarity of perception so seriously as to prevent us from being able to solve most of them.

Survival obviously requires an ability to respond appropriately to our environment, so information about the changing world can give us realistic choices or freedom to choose an identity that does not conflict with external realities. In fact, information is the primary ingredient in evolution itself.

Information and Evolution

> *The part is in the whole and the whole is in the part [and] the part has access to the whole.*
>
> —Ken Wilbur

After we were conceived, we all went through a number of embryological development stages. During our development in the womb, many processes took place within us simultaneously. Organs, bones, blood, and tissue formed at the same time. How were so many processes coordinated in a continually emerging form? The secret lies in what is called *parallel processing*, which uses different parts of a system to work on various problems separately, and to share the results continuously with the other parts of the system.

In a desktop computer, all of its power is used to solve one problem at a time. Fortunately, computers are fast enough so that many problems do manage to get solved by taking them one at a time. The supercomputers you hear about, however, use parallel processing to try to solve problems synchronously. They are capable of solving many complicated problems by having various internal parts work together or in parallel.

There are many more similarities between DNA and computers than anyone would have expected. In 1993, Leonard Adleman, a mathematician and professor of computer science well known for his research in computer security and cryptography, decided to build a DNA computer. But unlike computers, which work using zeros and ones, DNA has four basic nucleotides, or building blocks. Nonetheless, Adleman was able to solve an extremely difficult problem with his DNA computer. As Thomas Bass in *Wired* magazine explains,

> Because of the massively parallel reactions involved in biochemistry ..., Adleman's computer ... was a hundred times faster than the best of today's serial supercomputers. Its energy consumption was a billion times more efficient than electronic computers, and its storage capabilities were a trillion times denser than ... videotape.

Richard Lipton, a computer scientist at Princeton, has already managed to invent a coding scheme to convert DNA's building blocks into the zeros and ones of computer language and believes that it is possible to create for less than $100,000 a DNA supercomputer with trillions of processes happening at once.

While the brain does not have as many processors as a DNA computer, it does have a trillion processors capable of a few hundred operations per second. Where is that in the scheme of things, you might ask?

Serial computers, which most of us own, are capable of solving what are called *long-thin problems*—that is, problems that have many steps, each of which can be solved one step at a time. This is why computers can calculate much faster than we can. DNA computers, on the other hand, are capable of solving *wide-short problems*—or problems with many tasks, though each task can be solved in just a few steps.

Where does that leave us? We fall somewhere in the middle. The many interconnections in the brain mean that we are capable of solving complicated problems; thank goodness, since we certainly are in the process of creating our fair share of complicated problems.

Computers are evolving from having simple machinelike qualities (serial processing) to developing lifelike qualities (parallel processing). Once we begin fully interacting with computers, we will be able to think of computers as extensions of our parallel processing abilities. The extent to which computers control us, as opposed to the other way around, indicates where they are in the evolutionary scheme of things (machines versus living organisms).

We have been slaves to machines for years because we have had to conform to the logic of efficiency and effectiveness as dictated by inherent limitations of most machines. Machines tend to be simple, dumb, unresponsive, and capable of working only one linear way. Most of us have had to learn to adapt to machines, not the other way around, since machines are incapable of adapting to change or anything else. The inability of machines as we once knew them to adapt to change is spelling the end of their era.

New Creative Challenges

Freed from the tyranny of machines, employees will face an entirely new set of creative evolutionary challenges that will engage more of our mental and emotional makeup.

The mind-numbing qualities of working on assembly lines or of operating most machines have been largely beyond dispute. The stultifying bureaucracy typical of the industrial or machine age was simply a structure that evolved to complement the mechanistic way of thinking. The Kafkaesque nightmare of being trapped in a bureaucracy that you cannot comprehend was for many a daily reality. Often people truly were cogs in an alien machine. Charlie Chaplin's frantic efforts to keep pace with the machines in *Modern Times* brings back memories of the sweatshop working conditions that once prevailed. Those who think these were the good old days should be reminded of Lewis Mumford's comment, "If you are enamored with a machine, there is something wrong with your love life. If you worship a machine, there is something wrong with your religion." Most people do not aspire to become automatons.

As computers get easier to use, they become more like extensions of us, since to a great extent they do our bidding. The power latent in information technology becomes immediately accessible to everyone. In the process, the world potentially becomes one big open system containing many subsystems within it.

Microsoft, in conjunction with McCaw cellular, is hoping to launch roughly one thousand low-earth-orbiting satellites, enough to blanket the world. Each satellite will act as a computer hooked up to all of the other satellites so that together they will act as one massive parallel processing computer. Everyone in the world will be able to have a direct linkup to a satellite for any communication, computer, or electronic purpose desired. In a sense, we will all be wired together in a wireless world. The amount of information generated and communication made possible will be truly staggering.

Organizing the Information Flood

But what about information overload? According to Marvin Minsky, a mind cannot grow very much by only accumulating more and more knowledge. It must develop new and better ways to use what it already knows. That's Papert's Principle: "Some of the most crucial steps in mental growth are based not simply on acquiring new skills but on acquiring new administrative ways to use what one already knows."

Any increase in complexity requires a corresponding reorganization so that sufficient order is maintained and the desired amount of effectiveness and efficiency is realized. Parallel processing or synchronous time requires higher levels of overall order. This is why evolution is an upward journey toward greater complexity and additional layers of coordination.

Every time you get a promotion or your job description expands as a company grows, you need to be more organized in order to coordinate a larger number of tasks and relationships. A change in one part of your life is likely to require corresponding changes in other parts of your life. Normally, such changes involve figuring out ways to organize all aspects of your life so that one area doesn't conflict much with another area. New kinds of efficiency and effectiveness are needed in order to maintain your quality of life.

Every opportunity to reorganize your life so that it is more organized overall is actually an opportunity to improve its quality. Thus change, particularly if associated with increasing complication, fosters restructuring of relationships, tasks, and life flow.

The history of life is one of expanding complexity. For instance, the cell, the atom, and the individual were originally considered to be stable systems. Before long, cells became multicellular organisms, atoms quickly became absorbed in molecules, and individuals banded together for safety and other purposes. Where once the characteristics of the individual cell, atom, or individual determined how natural selection would play itself out, natural selection now applies more to multicellular organisms, molecules, and groups.

The ordering principle is groups within groups as complexity flourishes. Life consists of organisms inside other organisms, biochemical-molecular stews, and people who can be grouped according to ever-expanding subcategories as diversity proliferates within every kind of categorization. According to Leo Buss, a Yale University biologist,

> The history of life is a history of different units of selection. The major features of evolution were shaped during periods of transition between units of selection. At each transition—at each stage in the history of life in which a new self-replicating unit arose—the rules regarding the operation of natural selection changed utterly.

The business world is undergoing just such a transition in its units of selection and in the ways the laws of natural selection behave. Formerly, the unit of selection was the individual business. All of that has now changed.

Individuals by themselves no longer fare that well in the world any more. People who run one-person operations earn less than salaried employees in most cases. Even small businesses acting alone are nor prospering at the moment. What has happened to challenge assumptions once thought to be unquestionable?

Individuals trying to run their own businesses or invent innovative ways of doing something often run into serious difficulties early on. If you try to invent something, you will find the marketplace now crowded with similar competing inventions or innovations.

Almost all patents issued end up gathering dust. Why? Because inventing something or thinking up some new wonderful idea on how to improve things is not the same as developing the notion all the way through to its full commercial potential. Rarely is one person capable of this; and, in many cases, not even one company is capable of doing it. Inventions today are extremely complicated since most of the easy ones were thought up long ago. The more complicated the invention, the greater the number of players needed to get it to market in a hurry. For instance, when Intel wanted to promote its ProShare videoconferencing software, it needed to get Compaq Computers to preinstall the necessary hardware on its computers in order to reduce the hardware costs from $1,800 to $600—which customers are more likely to spring for—and strike a deal with Bell to reduce high-speed modem ISDN line fees as part of a package deal. Welcome to the world of interdependency.

The Creativity of Groups

Even on a smaller scale, mom-and-pop operations are giving way to franchises. The new unit of natural selection is the group, whether it be among individuals or groups of companies.

British management researcher Meredith Belbin has found that if you stack one group with the most intelligent managers, the group with the most intelligent managers always comes last at solving problems, and the group with the most creative managers is far down the list. The new reality is that you need a broad cross-section of people to get things through the various phases of development—each of which tends to favor a particular personality type or set of talents. Entrepreneurs usually run into trouble once their business reaches the organizational phase, with Apple Computer being a classic example.

Even companies that create inventions often lack the expertise, skill, and financial resources to take full advantage of their discoveries. The solid state transistor was sold by Western Electric to Sony in 1953 for $25,000, and RCA needs Japanese companies to make its color televisions. Although America starts the most new businesses and often registers the most patents, it is no longer necessarily those who are quickest off the mark who are the most successful. Complicated products and services require long, sustained development. However, the process can be accelerated if more players become involved.

Not surprisingly, Japan and Germany, with their emphasis on groups, have taken over many of the areas of technological complexity—precisely the areas that have the greatest evolutionary future, the biggest profits, and the best overall competitive advantage. As Robert Reich notes,

> Color televisions evolve into digital televisions capable of showing several pictures simultaneously; videocassette recorders into camcorders. A single strand of technological evolution connects electronic sewing machines, electronic typewriters and flexible electronic workstations.

In *The Comparative Advantage of Nations*, Michael Porter builds his case for claiming that it is clusters of individuals, companies, industries, and nations that form the modern basis for competition. Integrated networks of customers, suppliers, competitors, financial institutions, and government support are seen as the linkages vital to competitive advantage. It is the winning "team" that triumphs, not the lone hero who rises from the crowd. If the group or cluster is the new fundamental unit of evolution, how does evolution take place within groups?

Innovation

> *It is not so much the organism or the species evolves, but the entire system, species plus environment. The two are inseparable.*
>
> —Alfred Lotka

Innovation is more often than not a group process. However, let us include even different internal personality aspects of a single individual working together in our definition so that we can extend the concept of innovation to our personal lives. Just as parts of society can evolve, so can we evolve psychologically.

The key ingredient in understanding the evolution of innovation is called *coevolution*. Evolution is commonly associated with individuals and their needs, whereas coevolution involves two entities meeting one another's needs as they change over time. The interaction between the two entities is not a zero-sum game where one side wins at the expense of the other but rather a system that allows both parties to win or grow by utilizing one another's strengths.

Shakespeare could not have written plays filled with such a wealth of language if he had lived during a different historical period. The confluence of languages—Romance, Anglo-Saxon, and Latin—during the fifteenth and sixteenth centuries that surrounded Shakespeare during his life in England became the raw material for the rich word tapestries he was able to create. The particular political stability that England enjoyed during that time also fostered a sense of society as unified and whole, as did the pre-Copernican notion that the universe revolved around the earth. In many ways, both he and his plays are products of their time. Much the same could probably be said about every major historical figure, whether in the arts or in other areas of life.

Innovation, change, and knowledge develop in a similar manner. What is possible is constrained by the combinations available at the moment. When IBM's Thomas Watson, Sr. assumed that the future prospects for computer sales were not promising, he was making a very practical claim since a computer that fills a room and uses eighteen thousand unreliable vacuum tubes is not likely to find a lot of customers. Later IBMers were equally right at the time in saying that the future of the PC that they themselves had invented was limited. Similarly, the patent lawyers of Bell Laboratories were originally unwilling to patent the invention of the laser because they saw in it no applications for telecommunications. Given what was true at each of these moments in time, all these assumptions were extremely reasonable.

Typically, one or more complementary inventions need to come to pass before the potential latent in any particular innovation can be realized. Life tends to show that instead of being linear or step-by-step, causality is often circular in nature. In other words, two inventions, each occurring separately in time, cannot realize their potential until both exist. What results is a kind of mutual causality—that is, invention A causes invention B to function in an entirely new way and vice-versa. The interaction of the two create an entirely new entity, just as hydrogen and oxygen combine to produce water. Looking at these kinds of events from a linear perspective, cause and effect appear to be widely separated in time.

Psychologists are quite familiar with clients whose childhood problems may have no pronounced effect until there is an important shift in the clients' environments (for example, becoming unemployed) at later stages in their lives. No doubt, environmental pollution promises to be one of those things that will come back to haunt us in ways we have yet to foresee.

In most cases, there is a long, hard road of minor improvements of various kinds that cumulatively end up making a great difference over time. Most of us are used to buying software that began with a 1.0 version and has since evolved up to 7.51. Chances are the latest version of software incorporates the developments of many other software packages with different applications. Most word processing software is now capable of performing many desktop publishing functions.

Software manufacturers are now making it cost-effective for you to buy multifunction office software that is all bundled together and all cross-functional. No single new application amounts to much, but when several are put together, you end up with something that handles almost any application. It goes without saying that no single computer programmer starting from scratch and working his or her entire life would likely be capable of writing all of the code you will find in these new programs.

The number of software programmers who worked on Windows 95 over so many years is testament to the monumental complexity of such tasks. Just to test its prerelease versions of Windows 95 with end users and programmers, over four-hundred thousand beta copies were distributed for free. Why so many tests? In complex systems, it is not possible to completely eliminate problems, nor is it cost-effective to try. It is worth while to minimize them to the point where optimal functionality is achieved. Over time, problems can be corrected as they become more obvious. Such is the essence of total quality control or continuous improvement.

The coevolutionary process suggests that improvements in one part of the system are likely to be of limited value unless there are corresponding improvements in other parts of the system at the same time. Many governments institutions, companies, and individuals fall down markedly in this department. The mechanistic model simply focuses on fixing a part when often the problem is systemic in nature. This is why so many government initiatives, corporate downsizings, and New Year's Eve resolutions fail over the long term. The same old rut that individuals and groups of any size get stuck in is the result of systems that reinforce a particular set of behaviors.

The environment we operate in is also part of the system; it is part and parcel of the rut that seems to trap us. Many people have quit their jobs and picked up and moved to another part of the country in order to make a fresh start. In a new setting with none of the old reinforcing elements in place, they are capable of changing in ways their former situation would have tried to restrain. The same is true of companies that change their location. Sometimes this move allows them to downsize painlessly, but also it enables them to recruit people more appropriate to the changes they are in the process of making.

Resisting Change

Once systems achieve an equilibrium or permanent structure of sorts, homeostasis comes into play. Equilibrium implies stability or the ability to remain unchanged, as does a fixed or rigid structure. Homeostasis is used to describe the inertial tendency of any system to return to its established equilibrium state after being subjected to any disturbance (for example, the latest management fad). Individual changes in ourselves or our environment are usually quickly assimilated in such a way that the change potential is minimized as much as possible. The past pulls on us in much this way.

Most of us are comfortable with our ingrained habits and put up considerable resistance when required to change them. The old habits feel "natural" now because they are so familiar to us that we no longer have to think about them. So we are inclined to believe that they must be inherently right. It is quite normal for most people and organizations to operate on autopilot much of the day, because it is possible to step up the pace if you don't have to make any "new" decisions.

Fighting Inertia

In this environment, since the way in which things are done is taken for granted, the question becomes: how is it possible to speed up the system? Typically, the way chosen is to continue doing whatever was done in the past but do more of it by replicating the process somehow (for example, by hiring more people just like yourself, downsizing more, dieting more).

All systems—even systems for change—like to franchise themselves. Management fads spread in a cookie-cutter-like fashion across corporate America every couple of years, yet most of the companies return to their old ways once the initial enthusiasm dies down.

Most inventions are not used in new imaginative ways; instead, they are typically used to replace existing technologies. The first forty years after the invention of electricity resulted in productivity improvements of less than 1 percent per year. Waterwheels were simply replaced with dynamos. In this way, homeostasis prevailed. The system incorporated the new invention into itself without having to make any major changes. It was not until people figured out that electricity could drive small dynamos inside factories and that factories could be located outside cities and rearranged inside to take advantage of the potential latent in electricity that productivity began to rise by 5 percent per year. Computers have suffered a similar fate. Roughly forty years after their appearance in the marketplace, we are beginning to take better advantage of what computers are capable of. For decades, they merely replaced calculators and typewriters and acted as a backup much like filing cabinets.

People were unable to see the potential latent in computer technology because they were trapped in their perception of the way everything is typically done. Even IBM, the inventor of the PC, was unable to see the long-range possibilities that its invention opened up, just as Xerox gave away its Altair computer to Steve Jobs and Stephen Woszniak, who turned it into the first Apple computer.

A long series of continuous innovations over the past forty years have made it more obvious how computers are capable of completely transforming the workplace as we know it. So the fact that the majority of all innovations are simply part of a slow continuous process stems from our inability to imagine novel possible uses for our inventions. Our failure to see how more than one invention can be combined with another (for example, replacing vacuum tubes in computers with transistors) retards the rate of innovation. Joel Barker in *Future Edge* calls this "paradigm paralysis" or the inability to see things from a perspective different from our established mind-set.

Change is viewed as an enemy, an intruder, or an unnecessary nuisance. When the Swiss invented the digital quartz movement for watches, they did not even bother to patent it, because they knew that a watch had to have springs and precision wheels inside to make it a watch. Seiko did not share this limited view of what a watch was supposed to consist of, and before long Seiko was on the verge of eliminating the Swiss from the watch market altogether. It was only a brilliant stroke of imagination on the part of one Swiss worker, Nicholas Hayek, that ended up saving the Swiss watch business. He believed that bringing more imaginative design to watch faces would give them a kind of vanity appeal, and thus the Swatch was created. Others in Switzerland considered him crazy, but he nevertheless went on to pursue the concept on his own, and the rest is history—over one-hundred million Swatches were sold by 1992.

Fostering Creativity

Since new combinations and perspectives are essential for innovation to take place, it is vital that a process be developed that allows for new idea creation and a variety of viewpoints to be generated continuously if innovation is to be optimized both from a cumulative and imaginative point of view. In addition, rigid or fixed structures need to be avoided; otherwise, a kind of paralysis that resists change is inevitable. At the same time, a group organization is more likely to survive in a competitive environment. As a group, all of the parts must be integrally related so that information or desirable change can flow freely from one part to another. Lastly, the system should be effective in both adapting to and altering its environment—that is, capable of evolution. What we have described is something clearly organic and not machinelike in nature. As physicist Fritjof Capra, in *The Turning Point* suggests:

> The first obvious difference between machines and organisms is the fact that machines are constructed, whereas organisms grow.... A machine will fail if its parts do not work in the rigorously predetermined manner, but an organism will maintain its function in a changing environment, keeping itself in running condition and repairing itself through healing and regeneration.

How can human beings become more innovative? By becoming members of teams. Teams can consist of the different sides of your personality; your family and friends; teams in the workplace or community; or teams of companies, cities, states, or countries. So teams can exist within teams. But the key for both success and survival in a rapidly changing, highly competitive world is being a part of a number of strategic teams. According to an Accounttemps survey of 150 executives, poor team skills were by far and away the biggest drawback in getting ahead, regardless of how competent a person was.

Teams, like multitasking technology, extend our reach and our parallel processing abilities. As Archimedes once said, "Give me a lever long enough and a fulcrum to rest it on, and I can move the world." With information technology as the fulcrum, teams are a means of gaining that kind of leverage.

Not all teams are alike. Unless a team is self-managed, in touch with its customers, fluid in structure and members, and diverse in composition, it is a machinelike operation. Although some kinds of team structures may be more appropriate to certain kinds of problems, industries, or levels of complexity, an overall organic fluidity is essential when continuous change or disruption characterizes the environment.

Semco, a Brazilian equipment manufacturer, manages to cover all the bases with its teams. Everyone shares all relevant information about the company, its current state of progress, and its strategies. Team members are frequently on more than one team and make decisions on everything that happens. Because of the profit-sharing structure, teams become only as large as necessary so as to maximize profits for everyone in a self-regulating manner. Overall, the company consists of three layers of teams within teams, or as their president, Ricardo Semler describes,

> Actually, they are no "layers." What we use is the image of concentric circles. We are really trying to symbolize the idea that there is a lot of interaction that goes on in a circle form because it moves throughout the organization, and decisions move that way. This is much different from the idea that decisions are made by someone above and the commands come downward. The concentric circles help to diminish the idea of a vertical hierarchy.

> Because people are rotated among teams and can be on more than one team at a time—with some teams having conflicting priorities—discussions are open, multiple perspectives explored, and problems hashed out until a workable agreement is arrived at. Since the organization is democratically run, everyone gets to vote on the competency of their superiors and to replace them—including the president—if absolutely necessary. They also decide how to handle downsizings or salary adjustments. Before these changes were instituted, the company was on the verge of bankruptcy: now it is one of Brazil's most profitable and widely respected companies.

Teams are like a marriage or any relationship that is established and maintained over a period of time. Aside from flexibility and continual negotiation, they involve a lot of work and patience. Teams have the advantages and disadvantages of democracy. But the payoffs are disproportionately positive, as history has shown us. So long as everyone works together, everyone reaps huge benefits. Even "the prisoner's dilemma" concerning whether to confess and implicate a partner is often resolved in real life by criminals picking only partners who are very unlikely to confess, so that everyone likely gets off for lack of a witness.

It is important to remember that what is possible changes when more people are involved. A single drop of water or flake of snow possesses different properties from those of a whirlpool or an avalanche. Quite simply, more is different because the number of possible permutations and combinations multiply exponentially when more people or interactions take place. The collective parallel processing power or "wholeness" needed to deal with a complicated world is to be found in groups and not individuals.

Characteristics of Creative Groups

What characteristics are shared by organically functioning groups?

- They are demographic or devoid of centralized control; removal of one member does not jeopardize the group as a whole, so the system is resilient, but somewhat unpredictable since no one is in control (for example, the Internet).
- There is a high degree of "connectivity" between members or constant sharing of information so that positive changes in one part of the system can be quickly shared and magnified throughout the system, thereby enhancing evolvability.
- Each member is autonomous in some sense so that a variety of perspectives is possible, making adaptation and innovation easier.
- The influence of each member on others in the group is not linear because so many mutual influences are occurring simultaneously, which is why the whole is greater than the sum of the parts and the possibilities achievable are virtually boundless.

What about individuals who try to go it alone? Small businesses, except in the creative fields, are now losing business to larger firms. Why? Because large companies have downsized and restructured so that they are now like a team of small businesses with more resources, technology, distribution, and marketing strength than individual small businesses. The small businesses that are winning are forming alliances with other small businesses in order to capture some of the advantages that come with being a larger company. Increasingly, if you are not part of a team, you are not likely to remain in the game for long. The same applies to yourself and your personal life.

As Paul Saffo of the Institute for the Future claims, "The organization of GM in the sixties was a complex analog of a mainframe computer." In this era, the model organization mirrors our networked information structure. It's a web, not a hierarchy. The big difference: in a hierarchy, your title determines your power; in a web, it's who you know, the more people you know in a meaningful way, the more teams you can effectively become a part of, the more mountains you will be capable of moving. Of course, the first team that you need to have working for you consists of the various sides to your nature and the people who are nearest and dearest to you.

The Internet's capability to truly act as a World Wide Web has enlarged the context of what is possible in "real time." As a result, we must become more high context, synchronous, and particularist-oriented (see Tables 5.2, 5.3, and 5.4) even in our concept of careers, jobs, opportunities, groups, teams, or personal networks. International trade agreements, joint ventures, alliances, and mergers and acquisitions are all attempts to find the synergy possible in larger, more complex "wholes," which is the very essence of growth itself. In other words, learning to think outside the "universalistic, reductionist, or low context" box now means learning to see the interconnecting, merging, and mirroring of group and category contexts simultaneously taking place in all areas of our lives and our surrounding global context. It essentially is a cross-fertilization process resulting in increasing the number of hybrid and diverse contextual possibilities; yet, at the same time, there is a profoundly enhanced overall sense that we are all in this "larger multifaceted context" together. Welcome to the pluralistic world of the global customer, career, team, group, and web of relationships.

Context refers to the entire set of facts and circumstances that surround communications and events. High- and low-context cultures have unique ways of viewing the world and consequently possess distinctly different "operating systems."

High-context functions are characterized by a relationship-focus, which has a past, present, and future. Meaning comes from the many variables surrounding the function, all of which are seen to be interconnected and interdependent.

Low-context functions are characterized by a task-focus, a precise and expeditious use of all resources—people and things. Meaning comes from an intense approach to the function itself, which is often compartmentalized.

Table 5.2 Cultural Differences Moving to a High-Context World

High Context	*Low Context*
Context is a key determining factor, and each variable is considered as part of a whole (particularist).	Context is less important than established rules and principles (universalist).
Time is required to sort out numerous implications; ambiguities must be worked through (pluralistic focus).	Quick decisions can be made once prior detailed information has been received (reductionist focus).
Situational ethics	Universal moral order
Shared information	Highly centralized, tightly controlled information
Relationships are key—subjective data important.	Information is key—objective data important.
Business and social relationships merge.	Business and social relationships are separate.
Inclusion is based on status.	Inclusion is based on competence.
Meetings can be ad hoc and key people will attend.	Meetings need fixed agendas and prior announcement.
All new information needs to be carefully analyzed for implications.	Fast-flowing and disorganized information results in overload or psychological shutdown.
All feedback is personally impactful. Nonverbal communication is important—the medium is as important as the message.	Feedback is impersonal and objective. The message is more important than the medium.
Harmony and individual validation are important.	Impersonal, objective "truths" are important.
Loyalty and cooperation	Expedience and effectiveness

Table 5.3 High/Low Context - Cultures

• Japanese	High Context ↑
• Chinese	
• Arab	
• Greek	
• Mexican	
• Spanish	
• Italian	
• French	
• English	
• Canadian	
• American	
• Scandinavian	
• German	
• Swiss	↓ Low Context

High- and low-context cultures have very different ways of viewing the world, and the further apart they are on the scale, the more pronounced the differences across numerous variables. These differences include time orientation (past/present/future, sequential/synchronous), communication patterns, relationship orientation, and resulting spatial considerations (closeness/distance).

Table 5.4 High/Low Context - Business Functions

• Human Resources	High Context ↑
• Marketing/Sales	
• Management	
• Manufacturing	
• R & D	
• Technical	
• Information Technology	
• Engineering	
• Finance	↓ Low Context

Note: These tables (Tables 5.2, 5.3, and 5.4) were derived from original work by E.T. Hall.

In the next chapter, we will see that as international boundaries become more permeable or less restrictive, the new interaction possibilities transform the entire career decision-making context. Now our skills are subject to global benchmarking, but the number of potential permutations and combinations for joining forces to exploit the new, unfolding global opportunities is growing exponentially. Like it or not, we are all now playing in the high-risk, high-reward "big leagues" where those who are fastest up this new learning curve can prosper enormously.

CHAPTER 6

The Borderless World

There was a time when people could be jacks-of-all-trades. Although division of labor existed, it was based on a diversity of tasks that needed to be performed. Nonetheless, it was possible to easily develop a working knowledge of quite a few areas. Jobs didn't exist as a set of rigidly defined job descriptions; rather, they had a do-it-yourself nature. People could roam the land looking for odd jobs here and there, perhaps specializing to a minor extent if they were so inclined. People were hired "hands." They could easily work in teams since there was a common understanding of the entire job process or task that needed to be performed. Information flowed freely and was quickly understood and applied. The people involved were easily interchangeable, except for quality-of-work considerations.

Both scientists and working people were for the longest time generalists in the broadest sense. Few boundaries existed in the world of work or knowledge, and those that did could be easily crossed if you took up an amateur's interest in the area. Aside from being statesman, Benjamin Franklin was a scientist, humorist, postmaster, and printer; and Thomas Jefferson was an inventor, planter, architect, and writer.

As knowledge grew in each field, guilds developed to act as apprenticeship stewards for their occupational area. Workers needed individual tutelage on the job to acquire an expanding skill set. Similarly, professions arose around areas of increasing complication, and professional schooling often consisted of a prolonged apprenticeship as well. Nevertheless, within each guild or profession, you were expected to learn everything there was to know in your area of endeavor. So people remained generalists but were confined to their vocation of choice. Everyone seemed to have a complete overall knowledge of the chosen occupational area. Specialists as we know them today did not exist.

The small-town atmosphere seemed to allow for a teamlike, easygoing collegiality or approachability among the inhabitants. You could get the doctor on a moment's notice, drop in on the schoolteacher, or get your horse shod while you discussed general affairs with the blacksmith. Town-hall meetings brought everyone together to sort out problems as required. A kind of equality and democratic mutual respect seemed to prevail. Boundaries between occupations never caused breakdowns in communication. Everything could be explained or understood if you were willing to take the time and explain or listen. Problems could be sorted out with common sense instead of a gun. People had grown up with one another or known one another for a long period of time, so it was always possible to appeal to someone's better nature or the bonds of the past. Indiscretions could be forgiven if the surrounding situation was fully understood, and contriteness was clearly evident. While this may sound like a nostalgic description of a past that never existed, it must have been true enough of the time to become a stereotype of sorts.

How the Boundaries Formed

So what has happened since then?

Many decried the shift to the industrial era, which was the actual creator of jobs as we have come to know them. The transition to the industrial era was quite painful in England and lasted for fifty years (1780-1830). Charles Dickens chronicled the worst abuses of life in factories. People longed for the days when there was more varied employment and no fixed schedules. It was commonly felt that relentless factory work robbed workers of not only their dignity but their humanity. For instance, Thomas Carlyle believed that as a result men had "grown mechanical in head and heart, as well as in hand." Ironically, many are now mourning the passing of this same industrial era. Perhaps it is a comment on what human beings can get used to.

The two factors responsible for placing the workforce into narrow stalls were the economies of scale possible in the mass production era and the continued branching of knowledge into further categories and subcategories.

As companies grew in size, they kept subdividing into branches, divisions, and departments, much as the military does. In a similar fashion, knowledge continued to proliferate, with each new innovation or breakthrough leading to new areas of compartmentalization and specialization.

As might be expected, communication eventually began to break down as more and more vertical layers (resulting from subdivision—for example, a small business loans department) or horizontal functions (resulting from new categories emerging—for example information services or a supplier relationship department) were added. As anyone who has played Telephone—where you whisper information into the ear of the person next to you, who then passes it on in the same way—will tell you, the message ends up as nonsense very quickly.

So long as this process continued, more walls or barriers to communication continued to be erected. Each area was well on its way to becoming an empire or fiefdom. A labyrinthine jungle of departments and divisions made just finding the right department or person you needed to deal with a chore in itself. For instance, in Los Angeles, a company needs permission from eight different agencies just to plant a tree and forty-seven more permits to chop it down.

The Boundaries Start to Crumble

Aside from reaching a point where more bureaucracy or empire building actually meant substantially less efficiency, technological development suddenly introduced a wild card. In the past, the speed of change was limited by the rate of information exchanged inside large companies. It frequently took three to six weeks for information to rise from the bottom of the corporation to the top, and the same time for information regarding a major decision to find its way back down to the front line. Like trying to steer a large ocean liner, changing directions was very slow.

Until computers were able to talk to one another, they did not really improve communication. Once networked together, however, they changed all the rules of the game. Information that used to be hoarded by upper management all of a sudden became democratically available to whoever could make the best use of it. An information explosion much like the Internet's meteoric growth rate suddenly began to transform the level of communication possible regardless of the barriers posed by rigid organizational charts or academic departments.

It was as though everyone in an organization who was previously confined to some particular office or cubicle was just invited to join a large corporate jamboree. It didn't take companies long to realize that there were much faster ways to make decisions, especially now that upper management could be provided with real-time information, undistorted by office politics and compiled in a way that facilitated decision making.

Middle managers, who in a sense predigested information for upper management and oversaw the implementation of their decisions affecting those below, were viewed as expendable now that software existed that could manipulate the information into whatever form was desired. Information from the activities of frontline workers was instantly accessible to those at the head office; similarly, frontline workers could also obtain decision-making information or assistance if it was programmed into the software.

All that remained was to reorganize the lower-level workers into teams in a way that crossed the corporate department barriers as it did at the top of the organization; and most of the decision making, other than for the harder calls, could be shared among the team members. In other words, frontline teams needed only to be a mirror or clone of upper management. Just as the vice-presidents of the various departments frequently get together to solve corporation wide issues, why couldn't a similar team of lower-level workers, each from representative departments, achieve the same goal at a more mundane level so long as they had sufficient decision-making information technology in place along with access to upper management from time to time or as emergencies arose?

And Many Jobs Crumble with Them

Before long, corporate downsizing managed to toss a large number of redundant middle managers, whose role had been usurped by technology, out onto the street. Although only 10 percent of the workforce, middle managers accounted for 20 percent of the layoffs in the United States stemming from downsizing.

Not only were management jobs in jeopardy, but so were the jobs of those who merely accumulated or conveyed transaction information within or between companies.

Between companies? Every transaction, whether inside or between companies requires order forms, billing, payment, account reconciliation, shipping, scheduling, and other related activities that set in motion and complete the transaction from one end to the other. Now that computers are capable of "talking" to one another, there are really no restrictions as to whom they talk to. All of these activities can be carried out by a computer with no human intervention necessary—even the rescheduling of operations in manufacturing. The process has become like one seamless network in which information, like feedback, flows freely between the parties involved, and all of the accompanying overhead is handled by computers.

For example, K-Mart has a Partners in Merchandise Flow program with more than two hundred of its suppliers. When an item is sold at the cash register, the supplier of the item is notified so that the supplier's computer tracks inventory for K-Mart and sends more product when supplies are getting low. The computers involved take care of everything, including invoicing and electronic payment. By not having to reenter information into another computer, intercompany order processing costs are reduced from $13 to $1.50 per order, according to the Electronic Data Interchange Association. Thus any repetitive information processing jobs will simply disappear.

Widening the Loop

The ability of information to flow freely will also bring the customer into the electronic information loop, eliminating many traditional retail jobs in the process. Once interactive television becomes a full-fledged reality and there is enough bandwidth for crystal clear videoconferencing, cities, office buildings, and retail outlets will decline drastically in importance, since many of the information functions they fulfill can be accomplished through multimedia channels much more cost-effectively.

Thom Bliscock, vice-president and chief business scientist for AT&T Global Information Solutions, told retailers at a 1994 Retail Trends and Technology Show that by the year 2000, 50 percent of today's retailers will be out of business, and by 2010, 45 percent all retail sales will be made using interactive television. There is no need to purchase a refrigerator from a standard retail outlet when the same item can be purchased directly from the manufacturer over interactive TV that allows access to all pertinent visual and factual information. Only one "tire-kicking" outlet in one's vicinity will be necessary. Helpful sales representatives well be available twenty-four hours a day on one's home interactive TV to answer any questions and to take one's order. Even the most technologically phobic person would find it hard to pass up a 50 percent cost saving on an item purchased by this means.

The Old Borders Evaporate

Like magician David Copperfield making the Statue of Liberty disappear, even the corporate office may evaporate into thin air in some instances. Verifone, a U.S. company that markets credit card authorization to retailers, consists of a sales force that works on the road with customers, a CIO who works from his New Mexico ranch, and a CEO who manages activities from his home in Seattle. Since the products are made in Thailand and India by a third-party contractor, there is no need for an office of any kind. How effective is this paperless virtual organization? It has captured 60 percent of the U.S. market and has been growing 25 percent per year since 1988. Verifone has largely escaped the concept of structure, borders, or boundaries that often define companies that are geographically anchored by their real-estate holdings or office rental space.

Link Resources, a marketing research firm, claims that there are over 16 million full-time, home-based businesses in the United States. Approximately the same number are part-time. This $500 billion industry is growing rapidly as the telecommunication and information technology revolution continues to eliminate geography as a workplace or business constraint. In 1996, 44 percent of all business startups were home-based. There are now nineteen billion 800-number calls a year in the United States. For AT&T, its thirteen billion 800-number call represents 40 percent of its entire yearly calling business. Nowadays, it can be a single mother answering the phone from home and providing the desired information or service for a larger company or for her own home-based business.

Though convenient and environmentally friendly, home-based businesses suffer from one potential drawback: home can be anywhere in the world. Satellite transmission allows for information to be transferred around the globe instantaneously.

Consequently, many U.S. firms are getting people in other countries to process information, design software, offer technical support, or act as call centers. Holiday Inn gets accounting done in India, while IBM has software developed there. Insurance companies often have claims processed in Ireland. Software consortia in India have been running multipage color ads in *Forbes* and *Fortune,* trying to drum up computer programming business. Given that there are well over 300,000 software developers in India willing to work for $400 per month, their competitive presence cannot be overlooked.

Many other countries around the world are now also benefiting from the rationalization of services based on price. With the GATT, tariff and trade barriers continue to fall, making foreign outsourcing more attractive. Other trade agreements such as NAFTA also speed up the economic integration of goods and services delivery beyond national borders.

Over the long term, wages are likely to reflect more of a global wage structure, which does not bode well for anyone with low skill levels in the United States. As MIT economist Lester Thurow asserts, "If you have Third World skills, you are going to earn a Third World wage." This skill disparity is currently accounting for the widening split in income levels for those with less marketable skills.

Shoring Up the Barricades

Many politicians, such as Ross Perot, believe that the answer to jobs being exported to other countries is to put in place high protectionist tariff barriers and become Fortress America. Russia tried this approach for the greater part of this century and reaped the rewards that such a myopic solution entails. Responses like this are no different from ethnic groups trying to close themselves off from the rest of the world in order to preserve their way of life, or from individuals trying to resist technological or cultural change for as long as they possibly can.

In all cases, it is a losing battle and one that is guaranteed to destroy the very things the protectionist measures are aimed at preserving. Not only is this approach more deadly than working with the "enemy," so to speak, but it hastens the coming of the end and ensures that the loss or damage suffered will likely be crippling. In a word, it is "suicidal" in nature since all closed systems degenerate over time. As the *Economist* puts it, "History shows that countries that use trade policies to preserve the existing structure of their economies can look forward only to a faster pace of decline. They may even be tomorrow's third-world economies."

Putting your head in the sand has never solved any problems. The chaotic and unruly economic phase Russia is now in the midst of is a direct result of trying to operate as a closed system. The impossibility of ever achieving a closed system was made abundantly clear by the huge underground economy that developed in Russia and fostered crime and corruption. The underground economy, which is an open one with the U.S. dollar serving as a stable currency, has eventually triumphed over the closed one, and the former Soviet states are currently going through their Wild West or Gangland Chicago phase.

Eventually the dust will settle in the former Soviet states, and they too will become competitors in the worldwide market economy. If we combine the former Soviet bloc along with India, China, and other developing nations, there are now close to four billion people in the process of entering the capitalist marketplace in earnest. They are an economic force to be reckoned with and surely not one that can be denied for very long without long-term adverse consequences.

The Ecology of Nationalism

The walls dividing countries will disappear despite the rear-guard efforts of politicians, so the important thing for individuals, companies, and countries is to come to a better understanding of the process that is unfolding and a sense of the time frames involved. Once this has been achieved, it will be possible to focus on developing successful strategies to take advantage of the inevitable.

If we view countries or continents as ecological or economic systems that are beginning to come in contact with one another, it will be easier to understand some of the changes taking place. In addition, we must take into account the evolutionary effects of technology, which is the means by which the various systems are being brought closer together.

In economics, the consumers always benefit if perfect competition exists among a large number of providers, since they then end up paying the lowest possible price; in nature, natural selection produces the ablest species if competition is maximized among a large number of species in the environment—that is, we rise to meet the level of competition.

If the number of competitors is reduced by isolating groups into individual environments, the evolutionary process is slowed down, weaker attributes survive longer, and customers pay higher prices for goods—that is, the quality of life is lowered. Eventually when a slow-evolving, isolated country meets up with or can no longer avoid a showdown with a rapidly evolving one, the slow-developing country is quickly humiliated or destroyed (for example, Iraq versus the United States in the Persian Gulf War, or Russia versus the United States economically). Information technology, by rapidly interconnecting nations globally, has begun to throw every country into what we might call an economic or evolutionary World Series.

Moreover, the technology is competing directly against individuals for jobs in each country as well. All of a sudden it's "show time." A lot of countries, companies, and individuals have been caught unprepared and are having to pay for their lax ways. It is a bit like the National Guard when called up during the Persian Gulf War—many men were overweight and badly out of shape and thus deemed unfit for service.

In this instance, the worldwide competition is two-fold: company (or country) pitted against company (or country), and individual versus technology. Of the two competitive challenges, the global one has been much less devastating than the technological battle faced by individuals who have been replaced by the rapidly growing power of information technology; in other words, technology has been evolving at a far faster rate than countries, companies, or human beings have.

Unfortunately, the two forces working synchronously are delivering a knockout punch to those with lower skill levels and is even beginning to encroach also on some with higher skills.

Why does the global competition pale in comparison with the technological one? The main reason is that global competition (for all of its hype) is still in its infancy in some ways and ironically will be America's savior in the long run. Only 12 percent of America's GDP comes from foreign trade, unlike Canada, which depends on foreign trade for 40 percent of its income. Imports of manufactured goods from developing countries account for only 4 percent of overall U.S. consumption, with 30 percent of all clothing purchases coming from Third World countries. As a result of these imports, the price of shoes and clothing has fallen by over 20 percent (after discounting for inflation) during the past ten years.

On the other end of things, 42 percent of America's exports now go to developing countries—which is more than to Japan and Western Europe combined. These Third World exports are also growing at a rate of 12 percent per year versus 2 percent to other industrialized nations. Adding everything altogether, we find that the Third World countries increased their imports by 37 percent between 1990 and 1993, yet their exports grew by only 22 percent. Put simply, it has been trade with developing countries that has helped the United States pull out of the last recession. The United States has benefited more from the lowering of trade barriers than have less fortunate countries.

Over the next few decades, developing countries are expected to increase their rate of importation, especially of commercial services, branded consumer products, and capital equipment. The United States will be the net beneficiary.

The Benefits of Trade

Someone who does not understand economics is tempted to believe that trade is a zero-sum game—that is, the view that one country can benefit only if another country loses. This reasoning is the natural product of the linear logic or serial-time model that is incapable of understanding how simultaneous growth is possible through mutual exploitation. Organic systems grow by exchanging information or material (trading openly) with their external environment.

Between 1870 and 1913, when America was a developing nation, the U.S. economy grew at double the rate of Britain's, although the latter was a well-established economy. During that time period the U.S. economy surpassed the British economy in size, yet the rate at which the British economy grew throughout those years never declined. In fact, it was the growth of the American economy that allowed the British economy to continue to grow at its former pace. Had the American economy not grown so strongly, the British economy's growth rate would have slowed drastically. As it turned out, the First and Second World War, the Great Depression in the United States, and the rise of protectionism put an end to the growth of the British economy. Thus whatever reduces trade between countries—that is, fosters the closing of systems—hampers growth and prosperity.

What about investors diverting their money into foreign investments that pay higher rates of return? Back in 1913, Britain's investment in bonds that financed the development of infrastructures in the United States, Argentina, and Australia amounted to 180 percent of its GDP. Were it not for the First World War, these foreign investments would have spurred on Britain's economic growth even further. Why? Foreign investment always stimulates the economy of the receiving country so that it ends up importing even more goods and services to help it grow at a faster rate. Each country comes out ahead.

Who Loses?

Although Paul Krugman, author of *Peddling Prosperity*, asserts that American deindustrialization caused by foreign competition has lowered average U.S. wages by only 0.07 percent of the nation's total income, it has and will affect some workers much more than others. Economic evolution, according to economist David Ricardo, always tends to encourage countries to compete on the basis of comparative advantage.

Countries succeed by specializing in industries in which they have a natural advantage. Developing countries utilize their lower labor costs to focus on labor-intensive activities, such as clothing and shoe manufacturing. Developed countries must differentiate themselves by focusing on industries requiring high technology and high skills.

For instance, Germans are experts in high-quality engineering and chemicals, the British at publishing and pop music, the Japanese at electronics and miniaturization, and Americans at computers and film. Over time, developing countries begin to move up the evolutionary industrial ladder and to create industries requiring higher skills and technologies. For example, developing countries increased their share of the export of high-tech products from 12 percent in 1980 to 28 percent in 1993. Advanced industrial nations are then required to keep pushing on with new innovations at the higher end of things.

The further up the evolutionary ladder you climb, the higher the wages climb as well. Thus in developing countries, between 1985 and 1995, income per person climbed by 40 percent, with China's tripling. In the process the value of a country's currency begins to rise. When this happens, the price companies have to pay low-skilled workers in industrialized countries—compared to plentiful cheap labor and low currency rates in less-developed countries—makes it less expensive and more attractive for the developed countries to automate low-skilled functions as much as possible to keep these functions within the country. As James Baker, former executive vice-president of General Electric, observed, "The choice that confronts western industry is to automate, emigrate, or evaporate." The automation process is an undeniable one, for as the *Economist* notes, "No trade barrier will keep out the technological changes that are revolutionizing work in the rich world."

Put simply, developed countries cannot afford to have a surplus of low-skilled workers: their earnings dwindle over time, while everyone else's pay rises. By 1993, male college graduates earned 89 percent more than high school graduates, up from 49 percent more in 1979. Males with a doctorate now earn 40 percent more than four-year college degree graduates, while those with a professional degree earn twice as much.

Not surprisingly, employment has fallen fastest in industries with the largest percentage of unskilled workers, such as manufacturing, which employs 16 percent of the workforce. Imports from developing countries are estimated to have reduced low-skilled employment by 6 percent, and the competitive need to replace unskilled workers with more productive machinery or automation has displaced an additional 14 percent during the 1980s.

Obviously, the larger the growth in imports from developing countries, the faster the unemployment rate among low-skilled workers is bound to rise, and the wider the income disparity among workers. Over time, workers end up moving from these import-competing industries to the higher-technology exporting industries.

The attraction lies in export-related workers in America taking home 17 percent more in pay than the average worker. And they are growing in number as well. As already indicated, with increasing imports from developing countries, companies in developed countries create more jobs in high-technology or high-skill areas because the developing countries now have more money (from the sale of their exports) to import the more sophisticated products and services they are lacking.

So even though America as a whole is increasing its prosperity considerably by lowering trade barriers and importing and exporting more, those with lower skill levels suffer from the economic natural selection process. However, if the government tried to protect these workers by putting up trade barriers, the net result would be a reduction in the number of higher-paying jobs in the export market because the tariffs would increase the raw material or supply costs to the high-technology companies, making them less competitive.

Thus everyone ends up losing in the attempt to protect those who are less fortunate. Low-skilled workers are running out of time, and retraining is usually a time-consuming pursuit. The average hourly wages of various countries is a sobering wake-up call for low-skilled workers: Germany, $25; America, $16; South Korea, $5; Mexico, $2.40; Poland, $1.40; and India, China, and Indonesia, less than 50 cents. New technologies now find their way to almost every country in far less than two years. In some cases, it is less than three weeks. Each country is trying to scramble up the economic evolutionary ladder.

Developing countries are quickly improving their education levels. For example, there is a higher proportion of twenty- to twenty-four-year-olds in education in South Korea than there is in most European countries. Even though the average worker in China or Mexico has only five years of schooling, there is still a large number of highly trained workers in both countries. If only 1 percent of the population of India and China were highly educated, that would amount to twenty-five million highly skilled workers.

When you consider that for every 10,000 people, Japan graduates 535 engineers; Mexico and the Philippines, 200; the United States, 139; and Canada, 50, the repercussions for low-skilled workers can be staggering. Dataquest estimates that there are at least 350,000 Chinese information-technology engineers earning $105 per month, and Ph.D.'s less than $10,000 a year. So even high-skilled workers in the United States are not immune.

In 1994, electronic engineering experienced its highest level of unemployment ever because of the 150,000 information-technology engineers in Taiwan who now produce 60 percent of PC motherboards for the U.S. market for $25,000 per year (versus $60,000 to $100,000 in the United States for an equivalent circuit-board designer). Five years ago they were almost all made in-house in the United States.

India has the second largest number of scientifically trained, English-speaking workers in the world. As a result, Silicon Graphics, Inc., has a joint venture in Bangalore, India, where software designers are paid $300 a month to develop 3-D brain disorder diagnostic software.

When you consider that mathematics is the basis for all digital innovations and that India, China, and Russia have strongly stressed math, technical skills, and sciences in their education systems, you can begin to appreciate their latent competitive strength. American software designers, mechanical engineers, librarians, draftsmen, and bookkeepers will need to keep looking over their shoulders if they hope to compete in the future.

Normally as countries become more developed, their wages rise accordingly, thereby eliminating some of the competitive advantage that initially spurred their growth. However, Klaus Schwab, president of the World Economic Forum, claims that given the ability of capital and technology to move around the world so quickly, the normal link associating high productivity and high technology with high wages has been broken.

For instance, in Mexico, output per steel worker went from 21 percent to 37 percent of America's between 1989 and 1993, yet their salaries are one-sixth of those of U.S. steel workers. With Latin American productivity levels expected to reach the 80 percent mark soon, many U.S. steel workers could end up looking for work. The good news, however, is that wages do normally rise significantly in developing countries (they rose by an average of 8 percent per year over the last 20 years in South Korea). The end result is that even developing countries must keep climbing the economic ladder or value-added chain to stay ahead of the other lesser-developed countries hot on their heels (e.g., Taiwan is now second in the world in making notebook computers). Consequently, many of the Asian tiger countries find their labor costs too high, so they find themselves having to outsource production to lower-wage countries. And so it goes.

With the advent of modern communication technology, innovations spread around the world quickly. So it is becoming far easier to play the game of catching up, than it is to remain a world leader. This is the challenge facing all of the industrialized nations in the world. They must continue to innovate at a faster rate than lesser-developed countries can effectively enter these lucrative sophisticated industries. If you can stay far enough ahead, your competitors will never be able to catch up to you, or it will be too costly to try. (This same challenge applies to individuals.)

What kind of a lead do America and other industrialized countries have on the developing countries nipping at their heels? In some ways, quite a bit. To understand why, it first is worth elaborating on how you build a complex system or ecology.

Complex systems must be built one layer at a time, though each layer requires the synchronous development of all factors in that layer. In nature, evolutionary competitive forces put any new layer through a grueling set of destabilizing influences to test the integrity of the system. A strong foundation is needed, therefore. And each subsequent layer must prove itself as well. For this reason, the growth of complex systems takes time to evolve and often requires a lot of tending to in order to ensure that each new layer manages to take hold and weather the test of time. In a synchronous world of change, it is necessary to be continually building, maintaining, and altering more than one layer at a time even while adding new layers. For many countries, this is a challenge beyond their internal resources at various times in their history. This explains why Africa is not about to become a major competitor in the foreseeable future.

Many companies and individuals suffer significant setbacks for similar reasons.

What do the various layers consist of? First of all, you need enough social and political stability to allow for the creation of some system that can manage change without spinning out of control. Second, you need laws and business practices that encourage and facilitate the accumulation of wealth and knowledge. Third, an excellent infrastructure is needed so that all parts of the system can easily and effectively communicate with one another and with the rest of the world. Fourth, a complex system or organism requires a unifying purpose that is well suited to its environment and is clearly understood and shared by its constituent parts. Lastly, the system must be capable of evolving fast enough to take full advantage of new opportunities as they present themselves in a changing environment. In other words, all growth is a complex, interdependent, building process (so these principles or criteria can be applied to your own life as well).

Many of the economically emerging countries in the world are far more lopsided in developing the various layers needed to sustain continued growth. In a sense, most developing countries are not very integrated. The over one trillion dollars that are going to be spent by Asian Pacific Rim countries to create a modern infrastructure of power plants, dams, roads, airports, and ports stem from their obvious awareness of how important a country (system) must become integrated or else it slows the pace of economic growth (complexification) in newly industrializing countries (for example, poor countries have roughly 40 percent of their power-generating capacity out of action at any one time). Parts of their economy may be feudal or mercantile in nature.

Progress often consists of one step forward, two steps back. Russia, China, and India risk slipping back into their past as a result of various political backlashes in response to the destabilizing effects of rapid change. Look what happened in Iran when the former Shah tried to drag the country into the twentieth century. Even Mexico is not what you would call a well-organized or politically sound country. Not surprisingly, low wages are not necessarily the prime reason for where companies decide to locate their operations; nor are they likely the sole criteria on which you decide whether to accept employment or quit.

Ironically, even when countries do finally get their acts together, their growth rates begin to slow. As Paul Krugman notes, many of the competitive leaps forward made by Asian countries represent one-time accomplishments that cannot be repeated. You can build only so many roads or airports. So even the fast-growing Asian countries will likely find their growth rates leveling off as their economies begin to mature.

As competitors, they will find themselves slowing down as they begin to catch up with the rest of the developed countries, since they will need to consolidate whatever gains that have made and shore up any existing weaknesses before moving on. They too will likely have to go through many of the growing phases and cultural pains associated with countries that usually find that wealth tends to create culturally destabilizing levels of freedom (for example, spoiled teenagers and lawsuits galore).

For individuals, promotions can have the same effect as they climb the corporate ladder—there are only so many places at the top, and the higher you get, the more challenges await you.

Why the United States Will Benefit from Crumbling Borders

So which modern nation is best positioned to take advantage of the growth in free trade? The nation likely to reap the most benefits and come out ahead is the United States. Why? There are twelve main reasons:

1. The United States has already largely shifted to a service economy from a manufacturing one, unlike most of the other developed counties (such as Japan and Germany), which will need to go through this adjustment process. Lacking the United States' highly integrated service capabilities, Japan ranked tenth in the world in measured output per person in 1991. The United States and Canada were first and second in the world.
2. The low rate of unionization and the ability of wages to fluctuate according to demand in the United States (unlike Europe and Japan) will allow it to make a quicker transition to the high-skilled, high-technology industries that will increase the standard of living for Americans as a whole.
3. Much of the downsizing and reengineering necessary in the adjustment process has already occurred.
4. Americans have accepted the need for computers in their households, unlike Europeans or the Japanese.
5. The United States is a world leader in many high-tech or high-skill industries because of its postgraduate education programs, which are the best in the world.
6. Americans are culturally more willing to experiment and try new solutions than are most other cultures, so there are more opportunities to learn faster.
7. America's multicultural society will give it a wider range of perspectives, which will lead to more innovative solutions in capturing global markets.
8. America has more multinational corporations than any other country in the world, so its market reach and ability to learn in a global setting are unrivaled.
9. Americans believe in free trade and "teaming up" with other countries to facilitate trade, which is absolutely essential for survival in a global economy. NAFTA and

other trade agreements in process with Europe and the Pacific Rim will boost the American economy.

10. Over 60 percent of the aging boomer generation have private pension plans, compared to 6 percent in Germany. Once the American government realizes that it has no option but to allow pension plans to increase its foreign holdings, the American economy will benefit from a booming export market and the pension plans will not go broke.
11. The United States's diverse energy resources and expertise will become increasingly vital, since oil prices will double within ten years given the large growth in developing nations' economies and their overall increase in energy consumption as they achieve middle-class status (for example, there is only one car per one-thousand people in China at the moment, yet more people can now afford refrigerators that require electricity).
12. The United States will privatize more government functions before other developed countries do, so they will have more expertise in these areas that can be exported.

Getting to the Future First

During times of transition, we live in a "no pain, no gain" world. All change is painful, so avoiding pain is the same as avoiding change. America has been willing to accept the pain associated with transforming its economy, unlike most European nations. Even Japan must eliminate its bloated middle-management sinecures, which rose by 14 percent between 1984 and 1992. By being willing to make the necessary decisions before other countries, the United States has a significant learning curve advantage when scores of developing countries are getting better at playing the game of catch-up every single day. The global marathon is on.

Many of the other industrialized nations lack a high enough percentage of private pension plans and will experience problems in funding their pension plans. Most of the aging boomers are past their prime consumption years now that they have homes, fridges, TVs, etc. The first boomers, born in 1946, are likely empty-nesters whose kids have long since graduated from college. They are at their peak income earning power and are now the presidents and vice-presidents of most of America's corporations.

Bill Clinton symbolizes the conferring of the leadership role upon the boomer generation. In addition, they stand to inherit a significant amount of money from their parents who, having lived through the Great Depression, were great savers. Quite simply, they will be the richest generation in the history of the United States.

Most aging boomers are devoting an increasing portion of their incomes to retirement planning rather than to consumption. Now that emerging market funds are expected to outperform bond and equities in the developed countries by 6 percent for the rest of the decade, we will see a shift in stock portfolios to reflect this obvious opportunity. Governments will need to allow pension funds to invest a larger percentage in these emerging markets in order to stabilize the pension funds and to generate more export business.

The United States, unlike many other countries, is well positioned to take advantage of this opportunity, since Europe did not experience a baby boom following the Second World War and neither did Japan. Fortunately, the high savings rate among the Asian developing countries will limit the amount of foreign investment required by rapidly growing nations, so there will still be lots left over for American companies looking for investment funds.

America's willingness to become part of economic teams through trade agreements is essential for its success. The

European Common Market or Union is another attempt to exploit the advantages inherent in teams. Companies of every size are getting into the "team" mode through joint ventures, alliances, mergers, acquisitions, and stock swaps. To gain a helpful understanding of the dynamics behind this growing trend, let's look at what the biggest players in the world league are doing and examine why.

Multinationals

The existence of trade barriers was one of the original reasons for multinationals. Trade barriers, however, have been on a steady decline for the last fifty years, so the reasons for the existence of multinationals are having to change along with the ways in which they are run. With falling trade barriers and regulations, the need for multinationals would normally diminish since companies could just export their products directly to foreign markets without having to establish an operational presence in each country or simply license their product or service to foreign providers.

Although many of the structural restrictions that encouraged the existence of multinationals are disappearing (for example, transportation costs, import taxes, subsidies, investment restrictions, poor investment opportunities, and financial funding considerations), significant market imperfections continue to support their reason for being.

The *Economist* offers several examples:

> ... the uncertainty that a suppler will deliver on his promise; the volatility of exchange rates; the difficulty customers face in evaluating unfamiliar products; the cost of negotiating deals; economies of scale ...; uncertainty about competitors' actions; the opportunity to spread risk through diversification.

When trade barriers were more significant, multinationals tended to create branch plants, which completely manufactured enough items for the local market. With the barriers falling, some multinationals manufacture everything in one appropriately situated country and ship to the neighboring countries (or those covered by a free trade agreement). However, more are finding that it usually makes better sense to rationalize and integrate various aspects of the production process across the whole region rather than reinvent the wheel in each country. So teaming up or networking factories is proving more effective and efficient than cloning individual factories.

Once the region surrounding the home market is mastered, multinationals move on to other promising regions around the world that are as similar to the home region as possible. The attempt to minimize the number of diversity challenges multinationals wish to take on stems from the increasing complexification of products, technologies, marketing strategies, and management processes. In the cost-benefit trade-off, it usually makes more sense for a multinational to remain regional rather than global, at least until each region's opportunities are thoroughly exploited.

This same logic applies to individual countries or companies as well. Conglomerates failed miserably because—although each company in the conglomerate may have individually made sense as an acquisition for a diversified portfolio—there was no natural relationship among the various companies that contributed to the creation of some larger synergistic whole.

Instead, what happened was that centralized head offices tried to run companies with a diversity of cultures, structures, markets, industry dynamics, technologies, problems, and levels of complexity. In no time at all, they simply became nightmares. Never make your life more complicated than you can handle. But since complexity is unavoidable in today's world, build each layer of complexity on a strong underlying foundation.

Although most of us in a synchronous world must be building more than one layer at once, we must try to integrate the various layers. The layers can be in a state of continual change; however, the trick is to manage the changes in an integrated fashion. This is precisely what multinationals, countries, and companies find they have to do in order to succeed. Just as every trade agreement, joint venture, alliance, merger, or acquisition should make some sort of overall sense, so should the various relationships and goals in our lives (e.g. lateral career moves).

Many multinationals use alliances to extend their reach, speed up product development (sharing or dividing R & D), and reduce risk. Alliances make up for a country, company, or individual's limitations.

By teaming up with other partners, complementary talents can be exploited and strategies combined. In a world where it is essential to meet global standards of quality, few companies can be good at all aspects of the product development or delivery process. By each partner's bringing a high level of quality to their part of the alliance, any weaknesses or limitations are adequately compensated for.

It is preferable to outsourcing a function to another company or individual because of the comprehensiveness or scope of the arrangement and the obvious mutual benefit associated with coordinating activities closely. As the world and the nature of products and services become more complicated, partnerships tend to take the place of merely outsourcing because of the ongoing education and learning process associated with any flexible coordination of complex activities.

Since speed of innovation or product development is increasing in importance at the same time the products are growing in sophistication, it is essential to have a close working relationship with the partners so that a seamless, well-integrated wholeness is the end result.

By combining, smaller companies are able to take on the characteristics of larger firms either to prevent smaller companies from entering the market or to allow them to leapfrog over their limitations (for example, technological, geographical, core competence, R & D funding). So teaming may be necessary even to become a competitor in the first place.

The big challenge for multinationals is managing in a world where Harvard's Theodore Levitt's slogan, "Think globally, act locally," has become a pressing reality. In an era of customization, local realities need to be fully addressed. Products and services need to be adapted much more than ever before to meet a wider range of preferences.

In a world where "lean and mean" governs the size of organizations, many multinationals have gone on a diet and restructured their operations. Centralized control has given way to decentralization and complex integration of various activities. At the beginning of 1995, Ford got rid of its branch plant operations approach. Unilever is following suit, and IBM has diminished the influence of each country's top executive and redirected power to fourteen broad-based global teams.

Even Toshiba is reducing its home office staff by 30 percent by 1997. Fujitsu has already let go 20 percent since 1992, and Nissan downsized its local staff by five thousand by the end of 1995. Headquarters for products are now leaving the home country and moving to countries that possess a competitive advantage in individual product areas. R & D is moving in the same direction as well.

The traditional practice of sending home-country executives to manage foreign operations is changing. Procter & Gamble suffered a number of serious product failures until they changed their traditional ways. Mergers and acquisitions, especially prevalent in banking and chemicals, demands that managers become much more multicultural. Local managers now run their own offices since the increasing complexity of business practices everywhere requires an intimate knowledge of all of the subtleties likely to be experienced in each country. At the same time, these managers report to global product managers to take advantage of worldwide coordination possibilities, any global economies of scale possible, and what has been learned elsewhere.

By coordinating knowledge and practices globally, multinationals are transforming themselves into learning organizations. Canon is trying to promote a global mind-set, while Nissan is stressing a global team spirit.

Running the New Multinational or Transnational

Formal controls are being replaced by more organic or informal methods that flourish when communication among the various parts is good. The matrix structure of management, which has everyone reporting to local and global teams, requires excellent communication and negotiation skills in a multicultural setting.

The challenge for organizations is to maintain a strong corporate culture within globally diverse settings. To do so, corporations are emphasizing the instilling of company values. Local managers are now typically sent to the home country for up to two years of training (for example, Gillette and AT&T), using simultaneous translation.

To further encourage communication globally, Lotus Notes, videoconferencing, and electronic whiteboards are now used extensively. Coopers & Lybrand recently purchased 28,000 copies of Lotus Notes so that each staff member could act as a resource for each other. The U.S.-based Daimler-Benz managers teleconference for two hours daily with the German head office.

In order to promote the kinds of personal ties necessary for the development of widespread cultural familiarity and trust, managers are being flown around the globe even more than in the past to supplement the other technological communication strategies. Rotating postings helps to break down barriers as well. Thus the greater the diversity and teamlike nature of organizations, the greater the need for excellent communication abilities and systems. Alliances require more trust than a strong sense of contractual obligation, so they too up the communication quotient.

You might wonder if all the headaches associated with trying to communicate and coordinate activities across cultural boundaries make it worth while even to strive to become a multinational company when some of the economies of scale have been lost to flexible manufacturing, which is limited to smaller production runs to accommodate the customized needs in each market. Can't local competitors achieve the same economies of scale?

Global teams, as it turns out, are capable of making quite a difference. Such teams are capable of working on projects twenty-four hours a day from various parts of the world, and are a good way to coordinate knowledge gathering and dissemination around the world. Economies of scale exist in global learning. Global talent pools are capable of producing a more powerful team, as everyone in the sports world knows. Chief knowledge officers have been created to coordinate the activities of the best individuals or teams of specialized talent each country has to offer.

Ikea uses store start-up teams who spend a year getting a store on its feet before handing it over to local staff. The team ends up learning how to improve the start-up process each time. Learning can also take place through internal benchmarking and the sharing of best practices. With all the information internally available and sharing encouraged, corporate learning can take place on a much larger scale. The end result is more flexibility and adaptability in the face of changing customer demands.

So economies of scale still exist, but it is teams that make it possible to take advantage of them. R & D costs for sophisticated technologies can be so expensive that a significant share of the world market may be needed to recover initial investments. Many companies band together to fund such projects given the hugeness of the scope. The telecommunication wars we are witnessing have led to the combining of many extremely large multinationals together in an attempt to establish worldwide multimedia delivery services. Such a convergence of various media represents a cultural communication challenge in itself.

The Personal Perspective

Applying this same logic to individuals, it makes more sense to build on your obvious strengths, to make career changes or lateral moves that are natural extensions of your employment background, to master a core set of competencies that can integrate well with other skills similar in nature, to explore finding employment in areas where you know the turf and corporate culture fairly well, and to aim for the high-skill or complex areas of employment. As Barbara Moses suggests in *Career Intelligence,*

> Always try to attach yourself to the project that is the most leading edge, uses the newest technology, and adds the most to your abilities, in particular, skills and knowledge that are the most transferable to other work settings.

Does your resume build strategically, or are you like a conglomerate or a one-trick pony? In addition, it makes more sense to have a variety or friends who are slightly different from one another but integrate well in some sense than to merely have a lot of friends just like yourself. Are you actively involved with career-related associations? If not, why not? If so, what connections exist between your association and other closely related associations? If none, could connections be meaningfully established?

From a personal perspective, it should be clear that each of us needs to become part of many larger strategic wholes in order to reap the benefits that accrue to a higher level of competitiveness. The kind of war movies where Sylvester Stallone takes on the rest of the world and wins through sheer determination and guts is becoming more limited in scope and opportunity nowadays. Small may be beautiful, but as the Beatles song says, "I get by with a little help from my friends."

More and more, however, your potential friends or team members will come from diverse backgrounds and cultures. To complicate matters further, they all have unique psychological predispositions, needs, values, perceptions, and life circumstances. In a complex world highly dependent on high quality, overcoming the potential "tower of Babel" problem may be the toughest career challenge of all. As many newly minted MBAs find out, their biggest challenges are not on the business theory side, but in the realm of human communication. Unlike Jean Luc Picard, who on Star Trek merely had to authoritatively demand the others to "make it so," we now require considerable "emotional intelligence" in order to make things happen and to create a psychologically comfortable environment. Powerful visions, relationships, cultures, values, and beliefs have become the preconditions for success; yet creativity, innovation, and growth require constructive conflict in order to flourish. Such a potent combination presents us all with a challenge of Herculean proportions if we hope to succeed and maintain our peace of mind. Mastering the communication challenge is essential for stress reduction. And few of us perform well or are very creative if we are overly stressed.

The next chapter will help you prepare for a world where careers may consist of progressing from one project to the next, and where your ability to get up to speed as fast as possible with your coworkers or organization will play a major role in each project's success.

PART III

Reengineering Yourself

CHAPTER 7

Dealing with Diversity

Everyone you come in contact with is now considered a customer. Even more intimidating is the fact that everyone you have dealings with—both inside and outside your organization—is evaluating your performance. At best, this presents you with an ego-bracing challenge.

We all know that there are certain people we have trouble getting along with—often the customer purchasing the good or service. How do we make dealing with other people less painful while still acknowledging that human beings are naturally different from one another? In an age where leaders are expected to be able to manage upward, sideways, outward, and downward, it is essential to have a broad repertoire of tools to help in minimizing and resolving conflict and in negotiating optimal decisions. This chapter looks at some perspectives likely to help you deal with others. Feel free to skip over sections you are already familiar with, or proceed to the next chapter and return to this chapter at another time.

Personality

One system of looking at preferences that has rapidly grown in popularity in the business world is I-SPEAK Your Language, a study of personal communication styles. Drawn from psychological theories developed by Carl Jung, I-SPEAK®

is based on four major personality styles that people adopt in their characteristic approach to work and life. The assumption is that all people have easily recognizable and consistent communication styles. Understanding and reacting to these styles will enable you to get a better sense of which style describes you, people you know, and many of the companies you may be familiar with. Once mastered, this is an extremely easy tool to use in helping you get what you want and making you understand why there are limits to what may be possible with certain companies and people in specific situations.

The I-Speak Questionnaire

Before trying to understand these types, try the following simple exercise. To create a snapshot of your dominant communication style, answer the questions that follow.

Instructions: For each self-descriptive statement below there are four different endings. Rank in order each ending, using the following scale:

4 for the statement most like you
3 for the statement much like you
2 for the statement a little like you
1 for the statement least like you.

1. I am likely to impress others as
   a) practical and direct.
   b) emotional and somewhat stimulating.
   c) astute and logical.
   d) intellectually oriented and difficult to understand.

2. When I work on projects, I
   a) want the project to be stimulating and involve lively interaction with others.

   b) concentrate to make sure the project is systematically or logically developed.
   c) want to be sure the project has a tangible benefit that will justify my spending time and energy on it.
   d) am most concerned about whether the project is innovative or advances knowledge.

3. When I think about a job problem, I usually

   a) think about concepts and relationships between events.
   b) analyze what preceded it and what I plan next.
   c) remain open and responsive to my feelings on the matter.
   d) concentrate on reality—on things as they are right now.

4. When confronted by others with a different point of view, I can usually make progress by

   a) getting at least one or two specific commitments on which we can build later.
   b) trying to put myself in someone else's place.
   c) keeping my composure and helping others to see things simply and logically.
   d) relying on my basic ability to conceptualize and pull ideas together.

5. In communications with others, I may

   a) appear to lose interest with talk that is too detailed.
   b) convey impatience with those who express ideas that are obviously incomplete.
   c) show little interest in thoughts and ideas that show little or no originality.
   d) usually ignore those who talk about the future, and direct my attention to what needs to be done right now.

Scoring: To obtain an approximate indication of your primary communication style, enter below the number (1, 2, 3, or 4) you wrote next to each ending.

	Intuitor	Thinker	Feeler	Sensor
#1	d	c	b	a
#2	d	b	a	c
#3	a	b	c	d
#4	d	c	b	a
#5	c	b	a	d

Totals: Total each column. The column that has the highest total indicates your favored communication style; the column with the lowest total is your least-used style.

Understanding the Scales

Sensors versus Intuitors (S versus N)—People who are sensors stress their physical senses as the means of receiving and interpreting information. They are therefore very focused on the current, tangible, highly detailed reality in front of them. Missouri's "Show me" slogan would nicely capture how they evaluate any new idea. The phrases "hands-on" and "practical" convey their down-to-earth quality. Sensing types often view intuitive types as being lost in the clouds, out of touch with what is practically possible, great oversimplifiers, and sloppy with details.

Intuitive individuals look at and interpret reality through the lens of concepts and ideas. Their concepts are like dreams or abstractions that extend beyond the moment into future possibilities. The present is only a stepping-stone along the way to a much better, more exciting future. Ideas excite them, whereas current reality is too confining and boring. As John Scully, Apple's former CEO, said, "The best way to be ready for the future is to invent it." Intuitive types may consider sensing individuals to be limited in imagination, too caught up in what works at the moment, intolerant of change, and overly preoccupied with mundane details.

Sensing organizations believe in the here and now. They demonstrate a sense of immediacy and are ready to address problems with expedient solutions. The way in which Johnson & Johnson crisis-managed their Tylenol tampering scare (here's the problem; here's the way to fix it) exemplifies the behavior of the sensor organization: smart, sensible, and customer sensitive.

Intuitive organizations are more vision- or belief-driven. Inventing the future means transforming the present. They are out to change their industry, just as Apple wanted to revolutionize computing. Overall concepts are more important than individual details. Present concerns don't count in the new and improved future that will arrive shortly. Creativity, trust in ideas, and belief in a common vision are essential to working in one of these organizations. Both Motorola and GE are heading in this direction.

Thinkers versus Feelers (T versus F)—Thinkers use rational analysis to arrive at a decision or conclusion. The facts are clearly examined, and the merits of the pros and cons are tallied. When you add up the results, you have your decision largely made for you. Feelings are considered as only one element in the equation. Arguments and differences of opinion are settled by resorting to a full, frank, and fair objective critical analysis of the issues debated. The end frequently justifies the means. Thinkers often view feelers as wishy-washy, incapable of making difficult decisions, not focused on getting the job done, and bleeding hearts for people who should not be defended.

Those who use feelings as a basis for making decisions go with their gut reactions and usually are very sympathetic to the personal circumstances that surround the results of any decision. Consensus and social harmony are the ideal outcomes of any decision. Conflict is avoided if at all possible, though human feelings are always defended. With the emphasis on human process, the means is as important as the end. Feeling types tend to consider thinkers to be cold, hard-hearted, ruthless, and lacking in ordinary human compassion.

Thinking organizations stress responsibility because they are bottom-line-oriented. Principles are used to arbitrate among options, to set priorities, to plan, and to measure the results against. The key principle in such organizations is usually efficiency. By logically working out what productivity-enhancing rules need to be followed, participants assume that desired results will logically follow. All problems are assumed to be solvable in some intelligent fashion. Emotions are usually shunned because they are assumed only to cloud issues, such as special pleading or the excessive stressing of the exceptional nature of every person likely to be adversely affected by any decision. Generalized solutions that apply equally to everyone tend to be sought. Tasks take priority over relationships. Relationships and reporting lines tend to be formal and clearly defined. Large firms such as Hewlett-Packard and manufacturing and financial firms typically fall into this category.

Feeling companies prefer values to efficiency and are often more customer-service-oriented. The primary focus is on people, taking into account all of their needs, values, dreams, personal differences and circumstances, backgrounds, and feelings. Formal organizational structures are less important than relationships. By encompassing all aspects of humanity in their relationships, employee relations end up playing a large role in the company. Teams and trust go together well in feeling organizations. Everyone is in the same boat, so working well together makes the most sense, and fostering a culture of participation will pave the way. United Airlines with its "friendly skies"; Levi Strauss, which tries to get employees to balance work and family or community life; and Ben and Jerry's, with its emphasis on peaceful causes, capture the flavor of the feeling-type of organization.

Other Personality Dichotomies

There are four other common ways of differentiating people's personalities—and the personalities of corporations. William Bridges related personality type to organizations in his book, *The Character of Organizations*, an interesting application of Myers-Briggs theory to organizational development.

Introverts versus Extroverts (I versus E)—Extroverts get their energy and inspiration by being around people and talking through issues. They tend to act or speak and think later. They may see introverts as being too caught up in themselves, unfriendly, secretive, socially inept, and out of touch with most other people and the world around them.

Introverts welcome time alone to reflect and recharge their batteries. They also tend to limit the number of external relationships they engage in, though these relationships can be quite close in nature. Unless you know them well, introverts prefer to keep conversations short and to the point, since they have probably planned in advance what they are going to say. Extroverts are often considered to be mindless talkers, insensitive to subtleties, unappreciative of expertise, and time-wasters preoccupied with social platitudes.

Introverted organizers emphasize written (that is, precise or thought through) communication, expertise or compartmentalization, internal solutions (for example, GM focuses on cutting costs and upping quality), promoting from within, limiting participation in meetings or decision making, and examining options in detail. Extroverted organizations look for answers in the external environment, such as through benchmarking the progress of other companies (for example, Ford comparing itself to Mazda). Oral communication predominates, so there are typically many meetings, both formal and informal. Collaboration and teamwork appeal to these companies (Ford's Taurus was designed using teamwork).

Judgers versus Perceivers (J versus P)—Individuals who are judging in nature place a strong belief in the importance of order, schedule, time management, planning, neatness, punctuality, and control. Disorganization is condemned, and surprises are not appreciated. Judgers have their social calendar planned well in advance and manage to accomplish a lot in the way of sightseeing when on vacation. Closure is important. Checking off "to do" lists once tasks are out of the way brings great satisfaction. Personal accomplishments of various kinds are considered the mark of success. Judging types often view perceiving types as irresponsible, lazy, disorganized, and procrastinating.

Perceivers are people who like to keep their options open. Rather than plan, they would rather see what opportunities arise naturally over time and probably go with the flow of the moment. Spontaneity, informality, and creativity are valued; structure is usually seen as too confining or limiting. Chaos is interesting rather than frightening. Judging types are often considered to be uptight, stubborn, and square-headed. (To analyze your Myers-Brigg type, try the on-line free tests at http://sunsite.unc.edu/mb.pl and http://www.career-pro.com/profile.com).

Judging organizations like to make decisions as soon as possible so that they can get busy accomplishing the goals and objectives set out. Rather than gather a lot of information, they would prefer to go quickly with what information is available or spend only a minimal amount of time on research before getting down to business. Order and control demand that policies and procedures be clearly defined so that things get done with the least waste of time and effort. Since there is a lot of work to be done, it is best to get on the task as soon as possible in the most organized possible way. Line personnel often perceive their role from this perspective. UPS, which organizes every aspect of its delivery process in a clock-like manner, exemplifies this approach.

Perceiving organizations are more into the kind of creative chaos Tom Peters likes to celebrate. The excitement of trying different things and constant brainstorming about possibilities makes for a lot of innovative exploration. Much experimentation and grandiose planning continually stir the corporate culture. To some extent, anything seems to go as long as it sounds good. Perceiving companies are always trying to find a more novel way of tackling a problem as a way of staying ahead of competitors. Research and staff functions often require this kind of thinking in order to come up with new approaches to exceptional problems or new interpretations of information for specific purposes. Innovative companies like PC Connection are always trying to figure out better ways of serving their customers.

The Sixteen Basic Personality Types

Companies and individuals are a composite of the four dichotomies, which create a total of sixteen possible types. In some cases, an organization or individual may fall somewhere in the middle in one or two categories (which is desirable, given the potential ability to adapt either way), but in others a clearer preference usually prevails.

The room for conflict among the various individual and corporate types should be rather obvious. An approach likely to work with one type may not find any success with another at all. This is precisely why most management fads tend to fail and why many people have bosses or coworkers they can't get along with. Every person and every organization is unique, even if they share the same type, because the tendencies can vary in degree and according to situations. Someone who is judging in most instances may be perceiving in certain other realms, which one could not predict from a knowledge of their type. It is the idiosyncratic nature of all companies that led Eileen Shapiro in her book *Fad Surfing in the Boardroom* to stress the importance of understanding a company's corporate culture before initiating any changes.

As you might imagine, all types play a very useful role in organizations, families, and society. Any firm with only one type of person has a very limited perspective on the world and is likely to run into serious trouble sooner or later since change is inevitable in every organization and departments need to be able to communicate openly with one another in team settings.

The key then is to learn how to take advantage of the valuable perspectives each type brings to the table and to recognize which type is better suited to lead at any given moment. In addition, it is equally vital that each type come to appreciate its shortcomings and try to counterbalance them with increased receptivity to the worthwhile concerns of their opposite types.

Knowledge of an organization's or individual's type can help resolve potential conflicts in partnerships or teams. Points of likely conflict can be easily anticipated and appropriate strategies (for example, "polarity management") adopted to help reconcile approaches to a common goal. For instance, if you walked into an associate's office and noticed family pictures in abundance on his desk, you would know that you must address the human side of the equation in persuading in favor of any organizational change. If Sue down the hall is a by-the-numbers "quants" stickler, you better have your facts and figures in place including an analysis of possible variances and their effects on the bottom line.

Although many individual differences are bound to exist among people, it is important to take into account the overall context of the situation and the individual context of each person in this setting. Let's briefly examine some organizational contexts that may typically frame the way problems are viewed.

Using Your Knowledge of Personality Types

The Myers-Briggs Type Indicator combines these personality dichotomies into four-letter abbreviations to provide a sort of shorthand label for each personality combination. The four dichotomies go in the order Introvert-Extrovert; Sensor-Intuitor; Thinker-Feeler; Judger-Perceiver. Thus INFJ is an introvert/intuitor/feeler/judger. Intuitor is abbreviated N to avoid confusion with introvert.

Certain personality factors contribute to organizational design. With respect to age and size, formalized behavior is typical in older and larger organizations (-STJ). The structure typically reflects the historical origins of the industry as a whole with larger companies having more elaborate structures (--TJ).

With respect to technical systems, those that are more controlling of workers are more formal and bureaucratic in nature (-STJ). The more complex technical systems become, the greater the need for professional support staff (-N-P). When the operating core is largely automated, however, bureaucratic structures are transformed into organic ones since control is now built into the technology itself (-NFP).

Power concerns can also lead to structural definition. For instance, companies controlled by an external parent are likely to have more formal and centralized structures to keep them within allowed boundaries (-STJ). A politically divided external environment tends to foster internal division, just as political unity is also reflected internally. Management fad or fashion also can play a significant role in organizational design, regardless of its appropriateness.

Table 7.1 Personality Dynamics

Type	*Orientations*
Intuitive	Highly conceptual—inspired by ideas and future possibilities. Dreams and abstractions lead to exciting new developments—averse to details. Vision-driven to transform the present and create the ideal future. May be considered by sensors as out of touch and impractical.
Sensing	Reality-based with practical here-and-now orientation. Methodical, sensible, good with detail and immediacy of day-to-day business. Often are expedient problem solvers and troubleshooters. May be considered by intuitives as narrow or shortsighted.
Thinkers	Rational perspective based in analytical, objective orientation. "Just the facts please"—comfortable with argument and debate. Critical issues get full, frank, and fair analysis, with less interest in emotions. May be considered by feelers as cold, ruthless, or hard-hearted.
Feelers	Consensus and social harmony are important aspects of decision making. Conflict is avoided if possible, and the human side of issues is very important. Compassion and empathy are natural orientations that promote goodwill. May be seen by thinkers as wishy-washy or bleeding hearts.
Extroverts	Derive energy and ideas from being with others—natural focus is on external world; stimulated by group activity, like variety and action. Develop ideas by verbalization with others. Often enjoy numerous acquaintances and multiple relationships. May be considered by introverts as too talkative, superficial, or gregarious.

Introverts	Derive their energy from time alone to reflect and recharge their batteries. Natural focus is on the internal world; energized by time alone. May prefer to think through things before verbalizing responses; develop ideas through quiet reflection. Often enjoy a small number of close friendships. May be considered by extroverts as unfriendly, unresponsive, or secretive.
Judgers	Believe in the importance of order, scheduling, time management, planning, neatness, punctuality, completion, and control. Disorganization is condemned, and last-minute surprises not appreciated. Enjoy systematic, methodical processes. May be considered by perceivers as uptight, stubborn, or square-headed.
Perceivers	Like to keep their options open and see what opportunities arise naturally over time. Spontaneity, informality, and creativity are values; structure is usually seen as too confining or limiting. Chaos is interesting rather than frightening. Enjoy flexible, casual processes. May be considered by judgers as irresponsible, lazy, disorganized, and procrastinating.

Mintzberg's Organizational Types

Henry Mintzberg in *Mintzberg on Management* describes seven types of organizational configurations: entrepreneurial, machine, professional, diversified, innovative, missionary, and political. Each configuration is derived from the organization's evolutionary forces in its external environment. The resulting shapes are a product of a suitable fit with the external environment and a synergistic internal consistency based on a unifying theme that acts as an organizing principle. If you know yourself and understand the company, you will get a feel for whether that is an environment that will suit you.

In entrepreneurially structured companies, the personality, vision, attitudes, and habits of the chief executive tend to govern its success. Although the corporate structure is simple and relationships flexible and informal, the chief executive tends to centralize control and is therefore usually the key to the company's success or failure. Conflicts can arise over whether strategy or operation should act as the primary focus. As a result, there can be a lot of trial and error in attempting to sort out structure and function issues.

Those best suited to such an environment are often -NFP and -NTP in nature particularly if the environment is rapidly changing, yet -SFJs are useful in maintaining some sense of internal consistency.

Machine-structured organizations are usually consistent, reliable, efficient, and precise. Because the structure is common to large, centralized, mature bureaucracies, -STJ types predominate. Unfortunately, this structure is useful only so long as the operational context remains simple and stable. Given the preoccupation with control, any significant environmental changes are likely to set off considerable internal conflicts, which probably cannot be resolved without a corresponding restructuring of the organization—something bureaucracies resist with a passion.

This is why there was much amused puzzlement regarding the tentative alliance formed between IBM and Apple (INTP and an innovative organization). Some people described it as a banker dating a surfer girl. Or as one wag put it: "What do you get when you put IBM and Apple together?" Answer: "IBM." Getting IBM or GM to change or adapt quickly is the equivalent of getting an elephant to dance.

The diversified organization or conglomerate consists of a number of divisions loosely cobbled together much the way most large institutions are and the way many multinationals used to be. Centralized administration's (ISTJ) closed-system attempts to manage diverse markets (which favor ENFP managers), so conflicts, misunderstandings, and inefficiencies are usually created. Communist countries and all centralized government bureaucracies are the stellar examples of this structure, where often one hand has no idea what the other is doing despite centralized attempts to coordinate activities.

Professional organizations tend to be bureaucratic though decentralized. Many professionals (-N-J) work autonomously within a bureaucratic pigeonhole of sorts (for example, doctors in a hospital).

Collegial peer pressure (E-F-) and professional standards (INTJ) are the control measures that moderate the activities of autonomous professionals and are therefore a source of conflict. The relationship of autonomous professionals to the large supporting staff (-S-J) and the bureaucratic structure (-STJ) also provide potential friction points. Moreover, areas of coordination among professionals can give rise to conflict where professional standards differ and expertise is not overlapping.

Innovative organizations are the complete opposite of machine bureaucracies. These firms are fluid, organic, decentralized, and multifunctionally team-based. Whereas entrepreneurial organizations are capable of innovating on a rather simple level (that a single manager can organize), innovative organizations can tackle complex and sophisticated projects. Information flows freely, and decision processes tend to be informal (-N-P). Supervisors or control are secondary to getting the job done, or as one person at Apple computers joked, "If my boss calls, get his name for me." Strategy and structure are always in the process of emerging (-N-P), though there tend to be alternating styles of convergence (-N-J) and divergence (-N-P), which can occasion disputes as to which is the appropriate direction or approach. These learning, grass roots organizations are ad hoc in nature because they combine democracy with a lack of bureaucracy. The direction or focus can change as rapidly as people can collectively decide to make adjustments. Since machinelike efficiency is often sacrificed for the sake of innovative effectiveness, conflicts can occur over this trade-off.

Missionary organizations are governed by a compelling vision or set of values that takes precedence over structure and control in many cases (ENFP). Such organizations ideally are centralized and more informal in structure and strategy. To maintain coherence or unity, they most have an inspiring, clear, focused, and distinctive mission.

Everyone in missionary organizations is expected to share the zeal, so careful personnel selection, indoctrination, appeals to proud historical traditions, and informal socialization are used to sustain the missionary focus. Organizational units tend to remain small so as to encourage continuous informal personal contact and a strong sense of loyalty. Although the missionary or ideological focus can act as an overlay on some of the other organizational types, it works best in entrepreneurial and innovative organizations and in professional organizations. Machine organization examples like McDonald's are rather rare. The smaller the organization (or even institution, such as a college), the easier it is to maintain such a focused identity, so new units are frequently established once membership or personnel growth reaches a certain level. Conflicts tend to arise not over the ideology but over how the mission can best be accomplished (-S-T) and the various spun-off chapters or business unit activities coordinated.

The political organization is like an ideological organization insofar as politics can dominate its processes. To ignore politics as a source of conflict or as a powerful organizational force would be naive. Politics even extends into our relationships with family and friends. Politics is about playing games and making deals—relationships are meant to be exploited, and the art of the deal triumphs. Once organizations become highly politicized, they are highly unstable since there is no social "glue" that is capable of withstanding change.

Politics tends to be inherently divisive, so alienation is rife, and people end up working at cross-purposes. Although informal in nature, politics does not lend itself to increased communication so much as to the hoarding and manipulating of information for strategic purposes. Organizations in the midst of restructuring or reengineering often run into these problems, especially in connection with those who are likely to be adversely affected by any change. Sometimes intercompany alliances fall prey to one side trying to take advantage of the other.

In cases where the politics has gone beyond a simple defensive reaction to a perceived threat or when it is no longer possible to strike an acceptable deal to balance what may be naturally irreconcilable forces within an organization or between partners, the only solution is to dissolve the relationship or leave the company. Unless politics is used as a means of correcting something that has become dysfunctional, it is the equivalent of a virus—it makes you aware of what you want to avoid getting. Remember, the tragedy of NASA's *Challenger* mission was largely the result of intercompany politics.

Table 7.2 Mintzberg's Organizational Types

Type	*Orientations*
Entrepreneurial	Personality, vision, attitudes, and habits of the CEO exert a strong influence. Structure is usually simple, and relationships flexible and informal. Usually marked by centralized control and strong leadership. Conflicts may arise over whether primary focus is strategy or operations. Characterized by action learning, trial and error. Best suited to this environment: NFP or NTP for strategy, SFJ for operations.
Machine	Consistent, reliable, efficient, and precise. Structure is represented by large, centralized, mature bureaucracies. Strong

	controls and stable systems predominate. Challenges arise from difficulties in adapting to environmental changes, which often precipitate restructuring efforts and resulting upheavals. STJs predominate.
Diversified (Conglomerate)	Highly centralized administration and a closed-system attempt to manage diverse markets, often loosely connected. Communist countries and all centralized bureaucracies exemplify this organizational configuration. Inefficiencies often abound. Central administration (ISTJ) and diverse markets (ENFP) engender potential conflict and misunderstanding.
Innovative	Fluid, organic, decentralized, and multi-functionally team-based. Free flow of information and informal decision-making processes enable complex and sophisticated project management. Strategy and structure are continually emerging (NP), and give rise to alternating styles of convergence (NJ) and divergence (NP). Grass roots, ad hoc, democratic. Conflicts may occur over the trade-off of machine-like efficiency (SJ) for innovative effectiveness (NP).
Missionary	Compelling vision and set of values (NFP) take precedence over structure and control (STJ). Centralized focus and coherence maintained by inspiring, clear, and distinctive mission (NFP) with informal structure and strategy. Organizational units tend to remain small to encourage necessary continuous informal personal contact and loyalty. Ideology is not usually an issue, but conflict may arise over how mission can best be accomplished and coordinated (ST).
Political	Similar to an ideological organization in that politics dominate processes. Game playing and deal making predominate, causing divisiveness and alienation.

	Can advance to dysfunctional counter-productivity and instability since there is no social "glue" to bond people, a necessary element to weather organizational change and competitive challenge.
Hybrids	Combine diverse aspects of each structure, often in response to challenges from external forces (e.g., technology), evolutionary growth (often requiring a balancing of structure and innovation), and changes in the environment (competitive threats).

The Effect of External Forces

An organization's shape is essentially its response to external forces. The stronger the force, the more defined the organizational form that emerges to deal with it.

Because organizations are subject to many forces, which can differ from company to company and industry to industry, evolving hybrid organizational designs are common, although there tends to be variations of the designs discussed, which are the species-like evolutionary survivors so far. During periods of change, hybrids that amalgamate the best aspects of flexible and adaptable organizational design tend to flourish (for example, entrepreneurial, professional, innovative, and missionary).

Combining diverse aspects of each structure engenders conflict among those members who would normally be comfortable with any one of the purer designs forms. Change requires that roles evolve, so roles constantly need to be renegotiated and new structures adopted. The implicit challenge this represents is the source of many conflicts among diverse types of individuals. The need to get beyond political solutions should be obvious, since relationships and not deals form the basis of long-lasting conflict resolution.

Relationships lead to mutual understanding, trust, and benefit over the long term; deals and the structures that arise from them are only as good as the fragile conditions surrounding the arrangement.

During periods of change, who benefits the most can alternate, so deals often end up getting called off. No structure can weather that kind of instability. Structures, which are marriages of sorts, require internal consistency to remain harmonious.

Structure is the compromise that organizations make as an attempt to capture efficiency. Innovation, which is a restructuring force, is often sacrificed to some extent for the sake of efficiency, order, and sanity. While innovations lead to more effective organizations, they nonetheless compromise efficiency until they are fully incorporated into a new company configuration. Thus organizations are always making compromises between keeping an efficient system going despite its growing irrelevance and innovating to the point of chaos and confusion.

Imagine trying to keep up with every computer advance and turning your equipment in as soon as something new and improved came along—it would drive you crazy after a while just trying to keep up and master each new technology. Similarly, if professionals were allowed complete autonomy, chaos and anarchy would ensue. Thus structure is the price paid for some containment of opposing forces. Conflicts in many organizations surround these inherent contradictory trade-offs that present ongoing decision dilemmas.

On the other hand, each organizational design carries within it the seed of its own destruction. Automation or technological control eventually supplants the machine configuration, and entrepreneurs need to be replaced by managers once a company begins to grow in size. Each structure defines and reinforces the culture of an organization: machine organizations are control-oriented, and innovative ones are free-spirited in nature.

As each organization evolves to another configuration because of changes in both the internal and external environments, conflicts naturally arise as the structure and culture must change. John Sculley was forced to fire Steve Jobs from Apple even thought it was Steve who tried hard to get Sculley to leave Pepsico to join Apple. Jobs, an entrepreneurial type, began to get in the way of Apple's growth beyond its grass roots origins.

The Role of Ideology

It would seem from the foregoing that conflicts are both inevitable and that one force, structure, or person is likely to win at the expense of another at any given moment, but that is not necessarily the case. The way out of the conflicting situations that can lead to divisive and bitter political wrangling is ideology.

As Mintzberg notes,

> Ideology encourages people to look inward—to take their lead from the imperatives of the organization's own vision. People in the organization can more easily reconcile opposing forces when it is the organization itself they believe in rather than any one of its particular parts. If you believe in IBM instead of productive efficiency or marketing finesse per se, then when things really matter, you will suspend your departmental rivalries to enable IBM to adapt. Great organizations simply pull together when they have to, because they are rooted in a great system of beliefs.

When workers feel part of a compelling vision, even contradictory things become possible. Toyota manages to produce world-class cars at reasonable prices—something normally not feasible. But everyone in the organization has respect for everyone else's work, and no job is considered too menial. Company managers will often sweep up the floor to teach new hires that even the administrative staff believe that employees should do whatever it takes to make the company a success and gives them the decision-making power to follow through, including stopping the production line when they deem it necessary.

Is ideology or vision then the holy grail that needs only to be appealed to in order to solve all problems? Unfortunately, there is no panacea. The solution requires a balancing act. Ideology and vision are desirable when authentic; however, their gospel-like quality can get in the way of challenging the vision or ideology itself. A certain amount of politics is both inevitable and even desirable so long as it allows an organization to redefine its mission when the need arises. The key is that the good of the organization must remain the overriding consideration. And what is good for a company's customers is the ultimate arbiter of what is good for the organization—rather than the old claim that what is good for GM is good for America.

Needs

In many ways, structures can influence needs. Hierarchical designs tend to foster parent-child relationships within such organizations. As a result unresolved childhood problems tend to resurface, and unhealthy need-based relationships get established and reinforced. Eventually these untenable situations give rise to resentments, unresolvable conflicts, and dysfunctional relationships that don't serve anyone's real needs.

Before we try to tackle such thorny issues, perhaps we should clarify what exactly needs are. Needs are internal states of tension surrounding goals that are not being met.

Their power is such that they are capable of strongly influencing our thoughts, perceptions, emotions, decisions, actions, plans, and goals.

Psychologist Abraham Maslow developed a hierarchy of needs beginning with the lowest level being physiological needs (for instance, hunger, sleep, water, warmth). The second level of needs concerned safety from external dangers. The third level was devoted to the relationship needs of loving and belonging. The fourth level comprised self-esteem needs in one's own mind (strength, confidence, independence, achievement) and in the eyes of others (prestige, reputation, recognition, importance). The final or highest level of need was to fulfill some sense of personal destiny by becoming more fully oneself and by using one's talents or potential to the utmost.

In the past, many organizations barely managed to satisfy some of the third-level needs at best. As a result, many workers were bored with their work and resentful of not being allowed to contribute to the organization in ways which would have met their higher order needs. Most likely, unions were the natural outgrowth of such conditions. Now that workers are being asked to work in teams and make better use of their entire personality, higher order needs are beginning to be met and unions are losing much of their former clout.

As distinctions connected with title, function, and task continue to disappear, internal linkages within organizations tend to become psychological rather than functional in nature. Dealing with other employees face-to-face has replaced the idea of pulling rank or passing the buck to some higher arbitrating authority, as one would in a bureaucratic organization.

At Apex, a division of a large company, a group was formed to deal with a conflict between two senior managers. The group consisted of the two managers plus everyone likely to be affected by the outcome of the conflict. Everyone was expected to work together to achieve some sort of consensus, rather than just arbitrate as was more common in the past—which probably would not satisfy either side and likely leave a residue of bitterness. As it turned out, the group was able to arrive at a solution that was better at meeting everyone's needs than the proposals conceived by the two disagreeing managers. Obviously neither manager had a good grasp of the needs of everyone involved, nor did they possess the required conflict resolution skills to solve the problem.

In going one-on-one with someone, an individual must understand the needs, values, and larger contexts of the other person. The needs identified by Maslow and psychologist Henry Murray can be briefly described so that at least it is possible to know what to look for.

The Need for Achievement

A well-recognized need that has been studied at length by David McClelland is the need for achievement. More than 80 percent of all successful executives score high in this category. In the age of teamwork, managers need to be able to satisfy this need not through individual effort in isolation, but through group success.

The desire for dominance over one's environment reflects a need for power and security. In the past coercive or authoritative power were used liberally to influence people; today, however, power can consist of expertise (having specialized knowledge), referent power (charisma or role model identification), information power (access to vital sources of information), affiliative power (association with someone else who is powerful), and group power (many agree with you).

The need for affiliation (-F-) describes the desire to work with other people rather than alone. Relationship takes precedence over task for those high in this particular need.

Deference is a need to respect those who appear to be more knowledgeable or talented than oneself. It is akin to the acknowledgment of natural authority or ability.

The need for autonomy, on the other hand, reflects the desire to make decisions independently and suggests a high level of self-confidence and self-knowledge. Nurturance is the need to support others and offer them care, affection, or empathy (E-F-). Succorance, however, is the need for support, care, affection, and empathy. Abasement represents the willingness to accept the blame for whatever has gone wrong. Carried to an extreme, it leads to a kind of masochism.

Robert Benafari, in his book *Changing Your Management Style,* uses these and other terms to provide a useful framework for dealing with a broad diversity of individuals. Applying the preceding needs to the Japanese, he notes:

> In Japan... the modal pattern of managers are high achievement, moderate dominance, and high affiliation. In terms of Bosses/Peers/Subordinates/Relations/Needs, autonomy needs to be low, deference high, nurturance high, succorance moderate, and abasement high.
>
> The Japanese succeed because they can readily sacrifice their individual egos for the team effort. They do not demand excessive autonomy or dominance. They readily defer to others' opinions and give positive strokes to one another. The cementing factor is that they are hyper-responsible (they have a high need for abasement) and do not want to lose face with their colleagues by failing.

Benafari also cites the following task factor needs: change (variety, experimentation, movement, or perceiving type qualities), order (detail, precision, schedules, or judging-type qualities), endurance (stay on job until finished), and intensity (bouts of concentrated effort). Three other needs (introspection, aggression, and exhibition) act as interpersonal modifiers since they determine the nature of how the other needs manifest themselves.

For instance, a manager who is achievement-oriented could be either high in introspection and low in aggression or low in introspection and high in aggression. The former might be considered "cautious, thorough, and sensitive" while the latter might be deemed "domineering, impatient, and insensitive." The key is to look at the combination of needs before deciding on a conflict resolution or negotiation strategy.

Table 7.3 Needs Theory

Maslow's Hierarchy of Needs		
1. Physiological	Lower order	Hunger, thirst, shelter, sex, and other bodily needs.
2. Safety	Lower order	Security and protection from physical and emotional danger.
3. Social	Higher order	Relationship needs of affection, belongingness, acceptance.
4. Esteem	Higher order	Internal factors such as self-respect, confidence, independence. External factors such as status, recognition, and reputation.
5. Self-actualization	Higher order	The drive to become all that one can be, to fulfill personal destiny, to realize one's potential, fully using talents and abilities.

McClelland	
Achievement (nAch)	The drive to excel, to reach standards and goals, to succeed. High achievers perform best when they perceive moderate risk and have performance feedback and personal responsibility for outcomes. Achievement today is often a function not so much of individual effort in isolation, but of a team effort.
Power (nPow)	The drive to have impact and be influential, the need to be in charge or have influence over others. Power can consist of expertise in—or access to—a field of specialized knowledge (information power), charisma or role model identification (referent power), connection with vital individuals (affiliative power), or persuasive ability to sway the opinions of others (group power).
Affiliation (nAFF)	The desire for close relationships and friendships. Prefer cooperative situations rather than competitive ones and desire relationships with mutual understanding and reciprocity.

Other Influences/Needs	
Autonomy	The need for independence.
Nurturance	The need to support others and offer them care, affection, and sympathy.
Succorance	The need to receive support and empathy from others.
Deference	The need to acquiesce, comply, and conform to the requirements of a situation.
Abasement	Defined here as the abilty to sacrifice individual ego.

Learning Styles

Learning styles are also needs in that they strongly affect how people prefer to behave in situations. When denied their preferred style, people often tune out and become bored. It is the difference in learning styles that accounts for the fact that people hate the teaching style of certain teachers. In an organizational, team, or sales meeting, these preferences can make the difference between bringing people on board, losing their interest, or making the sale.

The learning styles consist of opposite polarities, such as concrete versus abstract and active versus passive. The concrete types resemble the Myers-Briggs -SF- types; the abstract types, the -NT- types; the active types, the ES— types; and the passive, the IN-- types. When the two polarities are placed on vertical and horizontal axes (see Table 7.4 "Learning Styles"), four distinct combined types emerge: accommodators (active and concrete), divergers (concrete and passive), assimilators (passive and abstract), and convergers (abstract and active). People will differ to the extent that each quadrant applies to them. Those with strong learning preferences frequently have difficulties adapting to styles that are opposite (accommodators vs. assimilators, or convergers vs. divergers) in nature.

Accommodators (ESFP) are active experimenters. They enjoy flexibility, variety, risk taking, action, carrying out plans, change, and tangible results. They are attracted to marketing, sales, and action-oriented managerial jobs. As learners or team members, they hate lectures, fixed seating arrangements, standard or rigid routines, vague theories, attention to detail, quiet classrooms, lack of visual and hands-on applications, and knowledge for its own sake.

Divergers (INFP) look for personal meaning in everything as a unifying factor in their broad interests. They enjoy listening; sharing ideas; people of various cultures; multiple perspectives; and people they can look up to, admire, and model themselves after. Careers that interest them include organizational development, personnel, counseling, and the humanities. As learners or team members, they hate time limits, lack of interaction, debates ("feelings can be hurt"), insensitive comments, dogmatic opinions, austere environments, superficial discussions, "just do it" approaches, repetition, impersonal attitudes, and conflict situations.

Assimilators (INTJ) try to integrate everything into a concept that is capable of explaining all questions you might have. Ideas and concepts are more interesting than people, other than what people think, particularly the experts. Traditional classroom approaches are preferred since straightforward explanations from experts are valued rather than aimless classroom or group discussions. Careerwise, many assimilators end up in the sciences, math, and planning and research. As learners they have a distaste for role playing, criticism, subjective evaluations or opinions, ambiguity or wandering conversations, poor planning, noise, open classrooms or work areas, and group evaluation.

Convergers (ISTJ) like to apply thinking to practical object-related problems (for example, when all else fails, they will read the instruction manual on how to put something together or get it up and running). They are fascinated by how things work, enjoy solving tangible problems, love hands-on experience, and need to know the commonsensical relevance of anything before treating it seriously. Convergers are attracted to careers in the physical sciences, engineering, nursing, and technological areas. As learners or team members, they hate lectures; reading assignments; group work; discussions regarding feeling, philosophy, or grand ideas; poor workmanship; tools that are broken or inadequate; sitting in one place; and a dearth of field work or lab experiments.

Each type has a place in the problem-solving process since all of us actually go through all types or phases as a natural part of learning in our lives. For instance, learning often begins with an experience of sorts, let's say a first date. During the first date, people usually listen carefully to each other and explain their personal preferences on a wide range of topics. At the conclusion of the date, each party goes home and begins to reflect on the events that transpired and comes up with a theory or explanation for how he ended up feeling by the end of the date. After additional reflection a decision is made whether to pursue the relationship further. If the decision is mutually favorable, another date is arranged, which acts as another lab experiment to see how things are likely to work out in a different setting. After each successive date, the people involved are likely to become less restrained and more spontaneous in their social interactions, but the reflective theorizing continues ("Is this the right person for me in some sense?"). Eventually practical problems begin to play a larger role than they did at first blush, especially if a decision is made to move in with one another. Living together and perhaps eventually raising children set the wheel of experience in motion, each time generating new experiences, theories about the others involved, practical solutions to concrete problems, and discovering new ways to continue to have fun to make it all worth while.

Teams, groups, and organizations go through cyclical experiences as well, which need to take advantage of the strengths of each type and minimize the weaknesses and alienation latent in the process if attention is not paid to managing significant differences.

In the problem-solving process, accommodators are extremely helpful in initiating the process, exploring opportunities, getting people involved, committing to goals, trying things out, and implementing plans. Divergers are useful for creative thinking, which can help in identifying problems and opportunities and generating new ideas and alternatives. They are also good at collecting relevant information and in sharing feelings and the importance of the task with others. Assimilators can help define the problems involved. Using quantitative analysis, they are likely to come up with theories or models that explain what is going on. In addition, they are helpful in drawing up implementation plans and evaluation criteria so that a sensible solution can be tried out. Convergers can contribute to setting priorities based on practical considerations, designing appropriate experiments or pilot study situations, measuring and evaluating the success of initiatives undertaken, interpreting the raw data in a commonsensical fashion, and in offering input into the decision-making process regarding whether something is likely to fly. From a trend perspective, the accommodators and the divergers are the ones who are gaining in importance in the new economy, given their multiple perspective and relationship-orientation advantage.

Behavioral Styles

In addition to taking advantage of multiple learning perspectives necessary to solving new problems in a rapidly changing environment, it is also important to be able to understand the behavioral styles likely to be encountered in teams and in individual situations for the purposes of conflict resolution and avoidance and negotiation. It is possible to take the Sensing, Intuition, Thinking, and Feeling scales of the Myers-Briggs assessment and turn them into four commonly recognizable behavioral styles. This can be accomplished by creating two polar scales (low assertiveness vs. high assertiveness and low responsiveness vs. high responsiveness) and putting them on horizontal and vertical axes.

Table 7.4 Learning Styles

CONCRETE EXPERIENCE (SF TYPES)
FEELING

ACTIVE (ES TYPES) DOING	PASSIVE (IN TYPES) OBSERVING
Accommodators (ESFP) *Active Doers* Enjoy flexibility, variety, risk taking, action, tangible results, hands-on practical processes. Dislike rigid routines, vague theories and knowledge for its own sake. **Preference: Initiating action.** **Strength: Getting things done, implementing plans, accomplishing tasks.** **Focus: Let's do it.**	*Divergers INFP* *Reflective Watchers* Enjoy listening, generating and sharing ideas, multiple perspectives, sensing values and feelings. Dislike "just-do-it" approaches, insensitivity, time limits. **Preference: Identifying opportunities** **Strength: Imaginative ability, collecting information, seeking advice.** **Focus: What do we have here?**
Convergers (ISTJ) *Active Experimenters* Enjoy applying thinking to practical problems, deductive reasoning, defining problems, and conceptualizing solutions. Dislike lack of focus, lack of experimentation with ideas. **Preference: Interpreting data, making decisions.** **Strengths: Evaluating consequences of various solutions and setting priorities, goals.** **Focus: Will it work?**	*Assimilators (INTJ)* *Abstract Thinkers* Enjoy ideas and concepts, formulating theories, creating models, integrating different observations into a unified conceptual framework. Dislike ambiguity, subjectivity, poor planning. **Preference: Defining problems, planning.** **Strengths: Quantitative analysis, using theory and models, planning implementation, establishing evaluation criteria.** **Focus: How does it come together?**

ABSTRACT (NT TYPES)
THINKING

People who are low in assertiveness are often described as being quiet, shy, easygoing, reserved, supportive and pleasant. They are also thought of as being slow to act, good listeners, risk avoiders, thoughtful decision makers, and weak opinion holders. High assertiveness people are commonly referred to as being verbose, active, impatient, confident, confronting, and powerful. Moreover, they are quick to act, good talkers, risk assumers, fast decision makers, and strong opinion holders.

Those who are low in responsiveness are considered to be aloof, proper, formal, guarded, controlled, and disciplined. They are also thinking, fact- and task-oriented, and not given to divulging their personal feelings. Highly responsive individuals tend to be personable, relaxed, warm, open, dramatic, and flexible. In addition, they are often more oriented toward feelings, opinions, and relationships and are more willing to share their personal feelings.

If we combine the style categories, we end up with amiables (low assertiveness and high responsiveness), expressives (high assertivenss and high responsiveness), driving types (high assertiveness and low responsiveness), and analytical types (low assertiveness and low responsiveness).

Amiables (I-FP) are supportive, pleasant, and reliable; however, they also can be overly soft-hearted, retiring, and too willing to go along with what may be the wrong decision. They have a high need for belonging and security, which makes them favor close, personal relationships; but they are fearful of setting direction and goals on their own. Security needs cause them to avoid conflict and wait for a consensus to emerge before acting. They enjoy counseling others as a means of reaching a common understanding.

Expressives (ENFP) are optimistic, animated, and invigorating; however, these same qualities can lead to their becoming impatient, excitable, and manipulative. Their excitement shows itself in spontaneous actions and decisions, high involvement, and a tendency to exaggerate, overgeneralize, and jump from one activity or dream to the next. Their need for belongingness and esteem causes them to dislike working alone and use their persuasive skills and energy to gain acceptance.

Drivers (-STJ) are usually very comprehensive, productive, and firm in their activities; but their corresponding downside can make them overbearing, pressuring, and uncompromising. Their bias toward action and commitment to decisions makes them somewhat intolerant of the attitudes, feelings, and opinions of others inasmuch as relationship and interpersonal process get in the way of getting things done. Thus they prefer to work alone and have the authority to manage themselves and those whom they must depend on for getting tasks accomplished. Their esteem and self-actualization needs are met through their achievements, which are meant to speak for themselves.

Analyticals (-NT-) are characteristically persevering, systematic, and diligent; but they can also be rigid, righteous, and overly picky. They are biased toward organization, structure, tasks, and excessive amounts of information. Their desire to work alone manifests itself in a preference for objective problems requiring intellectual expertise. They are slow to decide and act because they are afraid of being wrong and tarnishing their image as experts. This insecurity leads to continuous, precise information gathering and highly qualified opinions.

Table 7.5 Behavioral Styles

Categories	*Characteristics*
Amiables *Low assertiveness* *High responsiveness* I-FP	Supportive, pleasant, and reliable, but may be overly softhearted, retiring, and complacent. They have a high need for belonging and security, and favor close personal relationships. Prefer to avoid

	conflict and risk, sharing personal feelings and emotions. Good listeners. Motivated by needs for belonging, acceptance, and security.
Expressives *High assertiveness* *High responsiveness* ENFP	Optimistic, animated, and invigorating, but may also become impatient, excitable, and manipulative. Enjoy spontaneous actions and decisions, a quick pace, and high involvement. Possible tendency to exaggerate and overgeneralize. Prefer to work with others, using persuasive skills and energy to gain acceptance. Motivated by need for belonging and self-esteem.
Drivers *High assertiveness* *Low responsiveness* STJ	Usually very comprehensive, productive, and firm, but may also be overbearing, pressuring, and uncompromising. Seek control, action, and commitment to decisions. Possible tendency toward intolerance of attitudes and feelings of others. Prefer to work alone with management authority to accomplish tasks. Motivated by power orientation and needs for self-esteem and self-actualization.
Analyticals *Low assertiveness* *Low responsiveness* NT	Tend to be persevering, systematic, and diligent, but may also be rigid, righteous, and overly picky. Biased toward organization, structure, task, and quantities of information. Prefer to work alone and use intellectual expertise to tackle objective problems. May fear being wrong and tarnishing the "expert" image. Motivated by achievement orientation and self-esteem needs.

Your Personality Type

Although most of us are a combination of types, it is likely that we nonetheless have a dominant personality style. The area where we clearly reveal our biases is in the values we hold dearest. Since people tend to have coherent identities, it should come as no surprise that values overlap with needs, personality preferences, and learning styles.

Michael Maccoby, in *Why Work,* used extensive research to come up with five types of individuals whose values were their prime motivators on the job. The eight value drivers he found to be of key importance in the workplace are survival, relatedness, pleasure, information, mastery, play, dignity, and meaning. Although different situations are likely to provoke different value drivers, each of the five types possesses a dominant value drive. His five character types he has called experts, innovators, helpers, defenders, and self-developers.

The experts are much like the analytical types (-NTJ) just discussed. Their dominant value is mastery and information, and the secondary value is the means by which this goal is realized. Professional organizations and research/technical service departments attract this type of individual, who relishes complete control over his or her area of expertise and resents anyone's criticism. University departments are filled with these types who jealously guard their knowledge and are somewhat paranoid of administrators looking into their bailiwick. Meeting and ideally exceeding a widely recognized standard of achievement is more important to them than customer service. For them, the ideal boss must clearly establish goals and high standards that she must equally clearly recognize when they are met. The boss's role is to act as a sounding board, an advice-giver when asked, and a delegator of responsibility to the professionals. As a sign of respect, the boss is expected to give the experts free reign in carrying out their functions.

One has only to think of most computer experts, doctors, lawyers, and teachers to get a sense of this kind of person. The key missing ingredient in this equation is the ability to work together for a common goal—that is, serving the customer or having the organization function in an innovative and congruent manner by sharing information more freely and working more closely as a group. Many people often complain about doctors, lawyers, technical experts, and professors because they feel that these professionals care more about their profession and their standing in it than in delivering caring customer service.

At some universities in the United States, being a good, dedicated teacher is considered reasonable grounds for dismissal—after all, it is research that brings in the awards, prestige, and money. Only recently Stanford became the first university to appoint professors separately according to teaching or research functions.

Whereas experts are driven to perform according to some standard, innovators (ENTP) are leaders who like to motivate people into trying new approaches. Wal-Mart's Sam Walton and GE's Jack Welch fall into this category. They spend their time instigating, organizing, and strategizing how to create innovation throughout a company. Their high tolerance for ambiguity allows them to take to heart Tom Peters' suggestion regarding thriving on chaos. Essentially they see their mission as challenging bureaucracy.

People at the bottom of the organization who are like this steadfastly refuse to become part of the bureaucracy and will leave unless given entrepreneurial opportunities. Hewlett-Packard, Cummins Engine, Westinghouse Furniture Systems, Scandinavian Airlines, and the Dana Corporation fit into this mold. Their weaknesses include grandiose or utopian visions, intolerance and impatience, and manipulative means to achieving their goals.

Helpers (E-F-), on the other hand, care about a client as a whole person. Unlike the experts, if someone has a medical or legal problem, solving the particular problem is only part of the solution in the eyes of the helpers. Caring police officers are more concerned with preventing crime than just maximizing the number of arrests. Because of their holistic focus, helpers are rarely promoted since they refuse to concentrate mainly on number-related goals.

Their strengths lie in developing one-to-one relationships, understanding the strengths and weaknesses of individuals, and thinking in terms of relationships and community rather than autonomy. Weaknesses include their avoidance of necessary conflict and hard decisions, and overestimation of their ability to help. By avoiding conflict, they often fail to defend their views; and by misjudging their ability to help, they sometimes create unhealthy dependencies.

By focusing on people issues, they also sometimes fail to see organizational structural remedies that might help them achieve their goals. One-fifth of the service sector consists of helpers, but the helping professions naturally attract this type of individual.

Defenders (-NTJ or -STJ) act as advocates for clients, customers, peers, and subordinates by defending and protecting them. From an organizational perspective, they may try to protect large institutions from unfair criticism, cheats, and people who attempt to undermine its proper functioning. They are usually impatient with helpers who won't stand up for a cause, and are highly critical of experts and bureaucrats who avoid involvement in messy issues. For them, laws and institutions can take priority over individuals since their efforts are often in the service of large societal goals.

Unfortunately, they can politicize an organization into a "we-they" mentality that is not always productive, and they can end up harboring paranoid fears surrounding recrimination for their valiant whistle-blowing efforts. Machine bureaucracies, like the police force or the IRS, tend to attract this type of individual.

Self-Developers (I-TJ), according to Maccoby,

> focus on self-development to maintain a sense of authority, self-esteem, and security by upgrading marketable skills, integrating usable information, facilitating effective teams, and understanding customer needs ... Their weakness is the reverse of their strengths: detachment, reluctance to commit themselves and to take parental-type leadership roles.

While self-developers dislike bureaucracy for circumscribing learning opportunities, they dislike intimacy in work relationships. Although they appreciate helpful and friendly relationships and believe in facilitating teams, they keep their personal life separate. Many Generation X types are reluctant to invest in an organization or society that doesn't seem to care about them. They admire people who help them or act as collegial role models; however, they put no one on a pedestal and therefore have a rather instrumental view even of their ideal boss. They demand to be treated as adults and equals free to express their views, and they expect superiors to fulfill their duties by clearly outlining expectations and by demonstrating competence and adequate coaching ability.

Feedback from managers and coworkers is important for self-developers because they want to gauge themselves in a benchmarking manner. They are intensely competitive but believe in a level playing field for everyone. Lacking intimate relationships, they measure their self-worth by standards of achievement. Their inability to commit to anything other than their self-development undermines the kind of trust and understanding necessary to become motivating managers of leaders—though their technical abilities are generally superior.

A "new and improved" version of the self-developers would be what I call the "professionals." These individuals bear all of the earmarks of the self-developer except they care deeply about both their own careers and the organizations that can help them to continue to learn and grow. They believe in openness, full involvement, and time-limited commitment.

They will need to move on once they have done all they can for companies. Staying on would be bad both for themselves and for the companies for which they work. Thus they do not allow themselves to be trapped by security needs; instead, they realize that change is the essence and spice of life. Because they have interests and affiliations outside the companies they end up working for, they bring a wealth of industry and competitive information, contacts, new perspectives, and an eagerness to see companies prosper within a changing and challenging market place.

Like all good leaders, they know when it is time to let someone else take their place who is better suited to lead the companies through some new phase of development. Unlike the self-developers, the professionals feel passionate about their goals, commitments, obligations, and learning needs. Where feasible and appropriate, reaching consensus with everyone is the challenge they value most.

Taking a person's values into account is critical because most decisions in life are made on the basis of values; however, living in an age where information is now plentiful and is now playing a larger role in decision-making processes, it is essential to understand how people use information to make decisions if conflicts are to be resolved and roles negotiated by referring to the information available.

Table 7.6 Value Drivers and Personality Types

*Value Drivers**	*Character Types*	*Brief Description of Role in the Technoservice Organization*
Mastery Recognized achievement	**Experts (NTJ)**	Relish complete control over their area of expertise and resist delegation, flexibility, and relationships. Driven to perform; not predisposed toward collaboration or customer service orientations. Ideal position allows for personal control and the exercise of independent judgment. Possible growing edge: ability to work independently.
Play Exploration, adventure, creativity, competition	**Innovators (ENTP)**	Organizers, instigators, and strategists. Their vision involves motivating people, developing human potential. Organizational structure is seen as a tool to be shaped to provide high-level, cost-effective service. Bureaucracy busters. Possible growing edge: Overcoming grandiose or utopian vision, intolerance, or impatience.
Relatedness Care, protection, sociability, community	**Helpers**	Holistic focus, care about people, especially those in need. Responsive, collaborative, relational. Tend to dislike experts and their world of hierarchy, status, and measurable performance. Possible growing edge: rounding out the holistic focus to include number-related organizational goals.

*Value Drivers**	*Character Types*	*Brief Description of Role in the Technosevice Organization*
Survival Self-defense and defense of one's group, sustenance, livable environment avoidance of danger	**Defenders**	Act as advocates for clients, customers, peers and subordinates by defending and protecting them. Laws and institutions take priority over individuals; one-fifth of the public sector consists of helpers. Possible growing edge: Overcoming a we-they mentality, which may include paranoia and be counterproductive.
Information Sensory stimulation, directions, cues, signals, knowledge, understanding	**Self-Developers**	Dislike bureaucracy and like to keep their personal lives separate. Put no one on a pedestal and therefore have a rather instrumental view even of their ideal boss. Demand to be treated as adults and equals, free to express views. Expect competence and coaching from superiors. Possible growing edge: strong self-interest may limit trust and understanding necessary to become motivating managers of leaders.

Derived from information in Michael Maccoby, *Why Work*.
*These are representative value drivers but not mutually exclusive. Other value drivers are pleasure, dignity, and meaning, which are shared by most everyone.

Personality and Decision Style

In *The Art of Managing People,* Phillip Hunsaker and Anthony Alessandra show how our basic decision styles can be derived by combining dimensions of information complexity and focus on two separate axes. Complexity is polarized according to the amount of information used (minimum or maximum), and focus is polarized according to the number of conclusions drawn (few or many).

The four decision styles that result from this are the decisive style (minimum information and single conclusion), the flexible style (minimum information and multiple conclusions), the hierarchic style (maximum information and single conclusion), and the integrative style (maximum information and multiple conclusions).

Decisives (-STJ) are biased in favor of consistency, speed, and efficiency. Action and results figure prominently, as they do with the driver types. Organizational objectives carried out in hierarchical structures with well-defined rules and spans of control are the natural context for this approach. Results and recommended actions are all that are required for decision-making purposes. Lengthy reports are ignored because they obscure the key issue. Decisions are typically unilateral and beyond question. There is only one right answer in every instance. Although decisions tend to be consistent, fast, and reliable, they are more than likely also to be simplistic, shallow, and rigid. Not surprisingly, President Dwight Eisenhower is reported to have run the White House in this kind of military manner. Loyalty to decisions made had to be unequivocal. Ironically, it was this same approach that led to Saddam Hussein's losing the Persian Gulf War once communication in the chain of command was fractured.

Flexibles (-SFP) are mainly interested in adaptability, speed, variety, and action. They are willing to change focus as needed rather than plan well in advance. Typically they pursue many goals simultaneously but will change their decision to match the needs and goals of each person they encounter. Choice is desired even if the amount of information required for short term decisions is only minimal. As opportunists, they prefer loose organizational structures and cultures that permit considerable participation and spontaneous decision making. Personal charm is often used to win over people to the desired solution. Surface appearance matters more than quality.

Although intuitive, adaptable and congenial, flexibles tend to be fickle, indecisive, and shallow as well. William Durant is supposed to have run GM in this fashion. He opposed planning, inventory controls, and the application of accounting to production, which may have accounted for the production of a large number of low-quality cars being made. Some people are of the opinion that President Bill Clinton falls into this camp with his changing policy positions that depend on which way the political winds blow.

Hierarchics (-NTJ) prefer one solution that is the result of extensive information gathering and analysis. The thoroughness, precision, and perfectionism that are expected as part of the process require considerable control over all aspects of the organization to ensure both the acquisition of the appropriate information and the clear implementation of the long-range plan that is forthcoming. The strategies for achieving the desired goal tend to be elaborately worked out through extensive policies and procedures. Communication tends to be formal, and instructions detailed. Leadership is based on information, logic, and analysis. Although decisions are unilateral, considerable input from subordinates is sought in order to make a better decision.

Unfortunately the downside to being rigorous, thorough, and precise is the tendency to also end up being nit-picking, overcontrolling, and dogmatic. President Richard Nixon was given to this style of decision making. He decided to be a lawyer at the age of twelve and planned his presidential campaign in 1952. Needless to say, the information-gathering tactics required of subordinates became his downfall.

Integratives (-NFJ) gather large volumes of information and generate a large number of conclusions. They like to juggle many personal and organizational goals at once, so looser, more fluid structures are preferred. Long-range plans consisting of detailed analysis are constantly being updated to take into account the feelings and opinions of all involved and the facts under consideration. The inclusive nature of the process tends to engender understanding, empathy, and ownership on the part of participants. The cooperative, inventive, and empathetic aspects of this approach are liable to the dangers of overcomplication, indecisiveness, and political agendas.

Benjamin Franklin and President Jimmy Carter were both voracious information gatherers and highly valued the opinions and feelings of others. By trying to micromanage everything, President Carter lost sight of the big picture economically and paid the political price for doing so. Typically the Democratic party is characterized by this style. Most people use more than one style depending on the situation. Although we all likely have a dominant style, we also have backup ones when information is either unavailable or overabundant and decisions need to be made quickly. When constrained by time, we might fall back on either the Decisive or Flexible style if information is minimal or on the Hierarchic style if there is an oversupply. Of course, mixed styles are also possible.

Table 7.7 Personality and Decision Styles

Styles	*Characteristics*
Decisive (STJ) *Minimum information and single conclusion*	Favor consistency, speed, and efficiency. Action is carried out via hierarchical structures, well-defined rules, and spans of control. Decisions tend to be unilateral and beyond question. The key issue is the single right answer; all else is ignored. Decisions tend to be consistent, fast, and reliable, but downside may also be simplistic, shallow, and rigid. Power is often used to bring people on board with decisions.
Flexible (SFP) *Minimun information and multiple conclusions*	Interested in adaptability, speed, variety, and action. Prefer to change focus as needed, rather than plan in advance. Pursue many goals simultaneously; choice is desired even if information is minimal. Prefer loose organizational structures and cultures that allow participation and spontaneity. Decisions tend to be intuitive, adaptable, and congenial, but downside may be fickle, indecisive, and shallow. Personal charm is often used to win over people to the desired solution.
Hierarchic (NTJ) *Maximum information and single conclusion*	Prefer one solution arrived at through extensive information gathering and analysis. Thoroughness, precision, and perfectionism are valued. Strategy-driven through extensive policies, procedures, and controls. Communication is formal, and instructions detailed. Decisions tend to be rigorous, thorough, and precise, but downside may be nit-picking, over-controling, and dogmatic. Information, logic, and analysis are often used to support the unilateral decision made.

Integrative (NFJ) *Maximum information and multiple conclusions*	Gather large volumes of information and generate many conclusions. Like to juggle personal and organizational goals so that looser, more fluid structures are preferred. Long-range plans and detailed analyses are constantly updated to maintain inclusivity for participants. Cooperative, inventive, and empathetic, but downside may be overcomplexification, indecisiveness, and political agendas. Involvement and ownership are often used to gain commitment to decisions.

Note: Derived from information in Philip Hunsaker and Anthony Alessandra, *The Art of Managing People.*

Personality and Conflict

Resolving and minimizing conflicts and negotiating roles require that a lot of factors be taken into consideration, as should be evident from the foregoing models. In many instances it will be neither desirable nor feasible to exhaustively explore all of the variables discussed since the permutations and combinations are obviously staggering. What is needed is a way of prioritizing the importance of decisions so that the amount of time and energy expended on any situation is directly proportional to the value of fully or partially achieving particular goals and the probability of actually accomplishing each goal.

There is no point trying to win an argument when your coworker will not even acknowledge or recognize the validity of what you are saying. If someone is acting completely unreasonably and all of your clever dealing-with-difficult-people tactics are failing, you might as well not bother arguing—concentrate on damage control instead. Similarly, it makes no sense to devote a lot of effort to reach complete consensus when the issue is of minor importance. For instance, it is not crucial that everyone in a household come to complete agreement about a shopping list. You can always make another trip if necessary. On the other hand, it would be foolish to get your way on some insignificant issue only to risk ruining an important relationship in the process.

Having said that, it nonetheless makes sense to risk ruining an insignificant relationship if the goal is of utmost importance. If satisfying an unreasonable customer is going to bankrupt you, it is obviously better to lose the customer. Identifying what is most important in each situation is paramount, after which it is necessary to evaluate the trade-offs in connection with the risks involved in each situation. But what are the common trade-offs?

Most goals can be divided into task and relationship goals, even though the two overlap increasingly in the customer-service revolution.

Conflict Style Questionnaire

The following questionnaire will tell a lot about your preferred style for resolving conflicts.

After each statement below, indicate how often you resort to the strategy indicated or find yourself with the statement, using the following:

Never 1 2 3 4 5 Very Often

1. Showing warmth in discussions can often win over stubborn people._____
2. Appealing to common sense works most of the time._____
3. Whoever sticks to their guns more often than not gets their way._____

4. It is important that both parties try to ensure everyone comes out ahead._____
5. Avoiding conflicts is preferable, whenever possible._____
6. It is best to speak calmly when someone else is hurling abuse or getting upset._____
7. Qualitative concerns are more important than quantitative issues in most cases._____
8. If you cannot persuade people to agree with your thinking, it is still possible to make them carry out the actions you want them to._____
9. A compromise is better than no agreement at all._____
10. It is best to avoid people who might like to get into an argument with you._____
11. Trying to soothe someone's anger with gentle words often works well._____
12. If you just argue long enough, most issues can eventually be sorted out._____
13. It is often better to walk away from an argument than to get into one you probably will not win._____
14. Arguments should be resolved in mutually beneficial ways._____
15. No argument is worth it if the end result is bitter feelings on both sides._____
16. Appealing to the kinder, gentler nature of the other person usually works._____
17. Persistence is often the key to winning an argument._____
18. Power and intimidation are often more effective than appeals to what is right._____
19. It is only fair to use other people's tactics against them._____

20. Whenever possible, simply avoid argumentative people since they will only end up frustrating you.____

Scoring: Write your numbered response (1-5) for each of the preceding statements beside the statement number in Table 7.8 and total each column.

Table 7.8 Conflict Style Questionnaire Scorer

Avoiders	*Forcers*	*Accommodators*	*Compromisers*	*Collaborators*	
5. ____	3. ____	1. ____	4. ____	2. ____	
10. ____	8. ____	6. ____	9. ____	7. ____	
15. ____	13. ____	11. ____	14. ____	12. ____	
20. ____	18. ____	16. ____	19. ____	17. ____	
____	____	____	____	____	TOTAL

The highest column total reflects your primary style of conflict resolution. You are likely to find that you fall into a number of categories, which is a sign of versatility (see Figure 7.1).

Figure 7.1

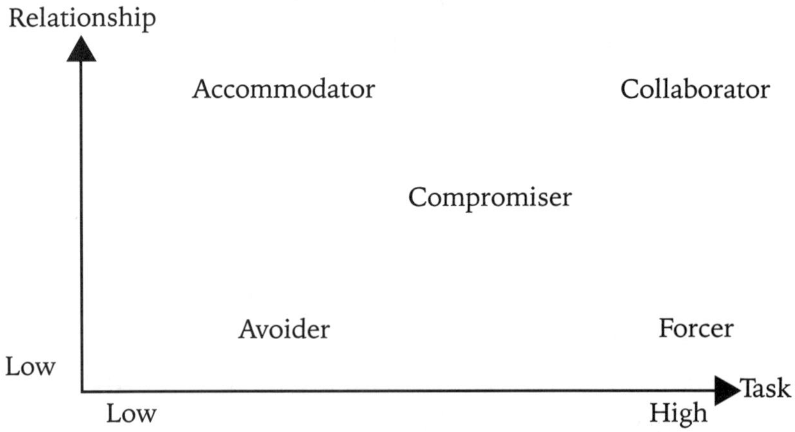

Conflict resolution matrix

If your score strongly favors one particular type, it suggests that you definitely prefer that style of conflict resolution in most situations, regardless of the context of issues involved. The ideal of conflict resolution is to match approximately the type of situation in each use.

Forcers: For these people, goals are usually more important than relationships. The needs of the other person are not given much consideration since it is often assumed that arguing is a zero-sum game—that is, there must be one winner and one loser.

Losing may suggest inadequacy, weakness, or failure, so there is a tendency to overcompensate to ensure victory by overwhelming, overpowering, or intimidating the opponent. This tactic is useful when fast action is necessary and is likely to work (for example, you don't have time to argue—your plane is about to take off), and when encountering a ruthless or untrustworthy opponent against whom entrenched positions or threats and posturing are effective.

Hardball negotiation when making a major purchase (for example, buying a house) or working through an unpopular but vital decision is quite understandable. This approach has the following disadvantages: a) it precludes investigation of other possible solutions; b)any agreement conceded will be devoid of commitment; c) the solution is usually temporary at best since the other side will likely regroup, given time; and d) it alienates someone perhaps unnecessarily—you never know when this person might be able to help you in the future. Defenders, decisives, and experts sometimes fall prey to these shortcomings.

Avoiders: Giving up both the goal and the relationship is preferable to engaging in conflict for these people. Confrontations are seen as so negative that it is worth sacrificing everything for the sake of retaining whatever peace of mind one can muster in such situations.

This approach is advantageous when the risks outnumber the likely gains in a situation (for example, avoiding a fight in a bar); when the issue is of minor significance (for example, arguing over which sports team is the best); when other people can likely solve the problem better than you can; and when you need to buy time to gather more information, think through your strategies and options, or let emotion cool off.

On the downside, this approach is likely to be only a temporary solution in many instances—the confrontation is merely postponed. Moreover, you end up not being able to offer any input into the decision-making process that might change things in your favor. Giving people this option can also result in compliance without commitment when something has been decided in their absence.

Accommodators: Relationships are of prime importance to accommodators, who are willing to sacrifice goals for the sake of maintaining harmony (with some bosses unreasonable pressure may require submission). They want to be liked and accepted and prefer not to run the risk of damaging a relationship or seeing someone hurt.

When a goal is of little importance to you, then this is the best strategy if the goal is significant to the other person. Also on the positive side, it manages to avoid disruption and feeling of competitiveness. This approach is also useful when it is best to let others learn by their own mistakes, when you want to encourage the expression of diverse viewpoints, and when you want to appear extremely reasonable. The danger, however, is that this approach, by sacrificing one of the viewpoints, limits any creative solution from emerging. Submissiveness can backfire since people can lose respect for anyone considered a pushover, and they are more likely to underestimate how valuable the viewpoint of the accommodator may be—a problem frequently encountered by "flexibles" and "helpers."

Compromisers: When both the goals and relationships are of moderate importance, it is necessary to calculate the relative worth of one to the other. In this manner, it is possible to figure out what kind of trade-offs are acceptable so that a range of possible middle-ground solutions may prove workable. In complicated situations with short decision time frames, knowing what you can live with is important.

This strategy can help resolve matters when two opposite viewpoints are leading to a stalemate. It can represent an act of good faith since a clear attempt is being made to solve matters by giving something up. Often it is just a question of who is the first to budge.

By giving in first, you make it clear that the relationship is important and the goal is secondary. Once that consideration is evident, the other side is likely to try to show its respect for the relationship as well by now seriously trying to work toward a mutually beneficial compromise.

The shortcomings of this approach lie in not probing for underlying causes that might lead to solutions that do not require a compromise on either side. Moving towards a solution quickly may eliminate many options based on information not yet revealed in the discussion. The focus can also shift to manipulation, which does not promote relationship preservation so much as grudging acceptance.

Most important of all, this method is unlikely to be successful when principles or ethics are involved, since people are extremely reluctant to budge where their values are concerned. Yet in situations where someone with power over you is asking you to compromise your principles, it may become important to preserve both your relationship and your principles, so the collaborative approach becomes essential. For "innovators," "self-developers," and "hierarchics," this can pose difficulties.

Collaborators: When a high value is placed on both the goal and the relationship, it is necessary to work fully through a problem in order to find the common ground essential to preserving both intact—something "integratives" believe in. As a general style, it assumes the attitude that most problems naturally lend themselves to creative problem solving and that resolving conflicts represents a welcome opportunity to reduce tension in relationships by getting to know and understand one another a lot better.

It is vital that all tensions and negative feelings are fully resolved before concluding discussion on any topic. For this strategy to work, neither party can enter into the discussion with a firm view of how an agreement will be reached. Implicit within the approach is a kin of mutual respect that normally comes from any relationship that is considered important. By having two brains working together in ways that preserve another's principles and respect the importance of what is being sought, the parties involved hope that such a pooling of intellectual resources will discover numerous focus shifts to innovative problem solving as opposed to brinkmanship and gamesmanship in arriving at a solution.

Anytime you are going to have to live for a long time with what is agreed to or when commitment on both sides is important, you should definitely encourage this approach. Newlyweds often are surprised by how much closer they become after arguments, because their new context—where commitment is now embedded in the relationship—naturally leads them into this conflict-resolution style. Obviously this approach can be very time-consuming and definitely requires the full participation of everyone involved; however, long-lasting solutions are most likely to be arrived at by this means.

Table 7.9 Conflict Resolution Styles

Type	*Orientations*
Forcers *High task* *Low relationship*	Goals are more important than relationships. Overwhelming, overpowering, or intimidating opponents are seen as legitimate tactics since winning at all costs is the objective. Losing may suggest inadequacy, weakness, or failure, so there is a tendency to overcompensate to ensure victory. When fast action is crucial or when encountering a ruthless or untrustworthy opponent, this style may be effective. Disadvantages are that it precludes investigation of other possible solutions, does not engender commitment to the agreement, and causes alienation that will likely carry into the future.
Avoiders *Low task* *Low relationship*	Preference is to avoid confrontation at all costs so that giving up the goal and the relationship is preferable to engaging in conflict. This approach is advantageous when the risks outnumber the likely gains in a situation, when the issue is not important, when other people can solve the problem instead, and when you need to buy time to gather more information. Disadvantages are that in many instances confrontation is merely postponed and you may end up not being able to offer any input into the decision-making process. May gain compliance but not commitment.
Accommodators *Low task* *High relationship*	Relationships are of prime importance to accommodators who are willing to sacrifice goals for the sake of maintaining harmony. This may be a good strategy when the goal is not important to you but significant to the other person. It avoids disruption and a feeling of competitiveness, and it allows others to learn by their own mistakes. Disadvantages are that it limits any creative

	solution from emerging since it sacrifices one side's input. Submissiveness can also backfire since people may lose respect for "pushovers," and may underestimate the importance of their future contributions.
Compromisers *Moderate task* *Moderate relationship*	When both the goals and relationships are of moderate importance, trade-offs can be arranged so that workable middle-ground solutions emerge. This strategy may help to clear up a stalemate and engender respect for both sides, but is not likely to be successful when values or ethics are concerned. Disadvantages are that compromises may eliminate further investigation of different options. If the focus shifts to manipulation, only grudging acceptance can be expected.
Collaborators *High task* *High relationship*	When high value is placed on both the goal and the relationship, working through the problem and finding common ground leads to creative solutions. Engenders better understanding among both parties and releases tensions and negative feelings. Based on mutual respect and a pooling of intellectual resources as opposed to brinkmanship and gamesmanship. When commitment on both sides is crucial and decision will have to be lived with a long time, this style is preferable. Disadvantages are that it may be time-consuming, and it definitely requires the full participation of all parties.

Doing Business on the Basis of Relationships

In many countries that do business on the basis of relationships (Asia, many European nations, Latin America), the collaborative method is the only way to succeed. People working in teams usually need to go through this process before any real bonding takes place.

Since we are heading into a 360-degree world of customer service where relationships are vital investments in the future, this style despite its time-consuming nature is proving to be the true sign of both commitment to the relationships and a desire for a foundation of trust, mutual respect, and clear understanding. It is in keeping with the old-new philosophy of doing things right the first time around. By establishing solid communication up front, many conflicts, problems, and misunderstandings down the road are avoided.

As many North Americans are only beginning to learn, the outcome is a natural extension of the process of getting there. There are no real shortcuts. All shortcuts mean someone loses. In a 360-degree customer-service world, we all live in glass houses, and whatever we do is bound to return to haunt us. And in a highly networked world it usually doesn't pay to burn bridges.

The art of negotiation requires that conflict be considered both healthy and natural. It is definitely not a contest. The natural functional strategies include classifying perceptions, interests, and positions. As many options as possible within a reasonable time frame need to be generated so that premature decisions can be avoided. Emotions must be explicitly taken into consideration, and both sides need to check in with each other to monitor the level of comfort. Expectations regarding the future need to be clarified to ensure that the full implications of every option are adequately addressed. Any approach that does express the authenticity of the negotiators is failing to take advantage of the opportunity to use conflict to solidify relationships.

Dysfunctional strategies (such as brinkmanship or gamesmanship) result in unhealthy relationships and lack of commitment to any agreed-upon solution. In an age that requires joint ventures, alliances, and partnerships for survival, communication skills are of paramount importance. Unless creative solutions are sought that lead to mutual respect and mutual benefit, no relationship can last for long, especially in a world of turbulent change. Remember, no one can go it alone anymore.

Trust is the price of admission into any relationship. An open and honest willingness to try to communicate will often garner the initial respect that eventually leads to trust. Beyond trust, however, is the need to understand the crucial differences that we human beings are heir to. Even identical twins end up living different lives and having different problems.

Dealing with Difficult People

From the foregoing, it should be clear that many factors need to be taken into account when dealing with others. Some of the methods of viewing people outlined can act as starting points for understanding why the nature of problems is likely to vary according to the corporate context and the personality dimensions that make us all unique. Objectivity or "immaculate perception" simply cannot exist so long as there is a context. And all of us live in a large number of contexts at once (often an overwhelming number). It is from these contexts that we make sense out of our lives and chart our course for the future.

Successful conflict resolution thus requires that we clearly understand both our own dynamic worlds and those of others who cross our path, if we want to avoid worlds in collision either now or in the future. There is no one right answer to any problems.

Dealing with people who are beyond the pale, so to speak, often requires techniques that differ from those that assume you are dealing with someone who is directly approachable. Two excellent books I recommend you consult when the former is the case are *Dealing with People You Can't Stand,* by

Rick Brinkman and Rick Kirschner, and *Dinosaur Brains* by Albert Bernstein.

Ironically, the most difficult people in our lives are likely to be ourselves. We usually are able to see everyone's shortcomings but not our own. In the past, this was a luxury we could afford because we operated inside organizational structures that effectively made decisions and resolved conflicts on our behalf. You could open up a policy and procedure manual and find the information or precedent necessary to bring most matters to a close. Failing that, you could pass the buck up to the next corporate level. While we may not have entirely escaped third-party arbitration as a problem solver, it is nonetheless better to customize your own solutions with others in ways that keep them as allies, instead of having to live with a decision no one is happy with and which has engendered hard feelings into the bargain. No wonder unions and companies try at all costs to avoid compulsory arbitration.

Dealing with Yourself

The place to begin is by understanding how others perceive you, since that is the point of reference they are negotiating from. By the same token, they need to know how you see them, so that everyone can begin to establish a level playing field. When upper and lower managers are asked in surveys to disclose their perceptions of one another and of how they think others perceive them, the reactions of the participants, once the results are tallied and distributed, are usually responses of profound shock in most cases. The level of disparity that exists is directly proportional to the lack of communication taking place inside an organization. Unless communication improves, you can be sure that these companies are on their way out of business.

In a complex, competitive world, communication is more important than just about anything else you can think of. If the message being sent out is not the same as the message being received, we all need to know it as soon as possible. For that reason, always get as much feedback during negotiations as you possibly can.

Most problems and conflicts can be avoided so long as many opportunities for feedback are established in our working relationships. In a world of change and loose organizational structures, each communication opportunity is a chance to share information that may prove to be vital at a later date. Since information is power, we will all need to keep as many lines of communication open as we can possibly manage.

Communication often requires that we learn to understand and relate to different perspectives and points of view. Like a jigsaw puzzle, each negotiation style has its place; however, if a style is used in the wrong place or inappropriately, the result is unsatisfactory, and conflicts and misunderstandings are bound to flourish.

Not only must we learn what others think of us, we must also understand why they perceive us in the ways they do if the desired changes are to be successfully negotiated. Naturally, the same applies to ourselves and our own perceptions of others. In a world where diversity is unavoidable and expanding, and where networking is the key to survival and success, we all must learn as many communication-bridging techniques as we possibly can.

Since we are all one another's customer, perhaps focusing on mutual respect and mutual benefit will help us better communicate the kind of customer service we would prefer if given a choice. The more we focus on improving our relationships, the more choices we are likely to be given. Ideally, the best customer service assists everyone in the realization of personal vision by expanding the scope of what is possible. Moreover, it minimizes the time and effort needed to achieve it and the frustration likely to be encountered along the way. Indeed, most of us would devise grander personal visions in a more "user-friendly" world where we facilitate and honor one another's unique attempts to make the world a better place to live.

CHAPTER 8

Developing Your Own Vision

When it comes to the future, there are three kinds of people: those who let it happen, those who make it happen, and those who wonder what happened.

—John M. Richardson, Jr.

Just as visionary companies endeavor to build enduring organizations, so must each career planner aim for the same kinds of lasting qualities. Many people think that the power to influence their future is in the hands of external circumstances to a far greater extent than is actually the case.

To shape your future is not to set yourself against the prevailing forces of change but to use them to advantage. But they must be shaped in your likeness. In other words, preserve your sense of identity despite all interactions with the outside world.

Visions act like the genetic code of both companies and individuals. The vision doesn't change, but its application and what it means in any situation pose challenges that require you to renew and redefine the vision continually. Each technological change presents an opportunity to experiment further and perfect its realization. Yet you should not pursue the new growth options that emerge unless they are appropriate to or in keeping with the vision, for the idea of progress is intrinsic to the realization of all visions.

Failure is perceived as the necessary companion of all risk taking, or learning. Since visions are by their very nature at odds with the way things are, they demand change and improvement. However, all untried approaches pose unavoidable risks. For visionaries, failures and mistakes are therefore necessary and extremely valuable learning opportunities. As the former CEO of Johnson & Johnson, R. W. Johnson, Jr., proclaimed in 1954, "Failure is our most important product." Indirectly failure points you in the direction you need to go. This is why almost all visionary companies are willing to forgive failure much more readily than a lapse of faith in the abiding vision. The same applies to visionary individuals.

Experimentation is a vital part of getting strategic feedback from the environment, especially when it is constantly evolving. Artists are always experimenting with new styles of expression—in fact, all creativity involves trying out something new and taking a risk. During an age driven largely by innovation, failure to seek out creative solutions and to take calculated risks absolutely ensures failure—and the worst kind of failure, since very little has been learned other than the severe penalties for not taking risks.

Because visions are broadly defined (for example, to make a customer's hotel stay as pleasantly memorable as possible), they are multifaceted in nature. The number of ways in which they can manifest themselves are endless. The unending possibilities associated with a vision makes its fulfillment an ongoing process, yet the vision itself can usually be summed up in just a few sentences. Whether it was President Kennedy promising to send a man to the moon and back safely before the end of the decade, Martin Luther King, Jr., having a dream, or a country trying to position itself in the new global economy, visions must be both simple and easy to understand if they are to have a large following that is reading from the same page in the hymn book.

Examine Yourself

Although a simple process in one sense, developing a vision requires considerable self-examination. You've already started to do so if you've answered the two questionnaires in the previous chapter and thought about the results.

Since any vision, if it is to be compelling and motivating over the long term, must completely reflect who you are and what you want in life, these questions are the first issues that must be addressed. Prioritizing and sorting out conflicting goals requires considerable clarity and self-knowledge. Moreover, it becomes necessary to distinguish between short- and long-range goals and how they are aligned with closely held values. By determining the interconnections among the various elements of your vision, it is easier to see the role played by each and its relative importance.

Belief and the commitment that comes from a deeply held belief are necessary before a vision is capable of having the power required to bring everything else into line behind it for the long journey that always lies ahead. Having too many competing or poorly thought-out goals only slows you down and distracts you from the true purpose of your mission.

Once a clearer picture emerges about the underlying relevance of most goals, it is easier to prioritize and evaluate alternatives when it comes time to make hard decisions. Many of the objectives attached to goals can be realized in other ways, so it is best to assess the general nature of what is desired than to restrict the number of options available in achieving your ultimate goal or vision. Nonetheless, it is equally essential to have a clear sense of where you are headed so that you can easily determine how close you are to getting there and when you have reached important destinations along the way.

Why People Fail to Reach Their Goals

Many people set goals and develop visions but never manage to achieve them. What is it that gets in the way? Most resolutions often go the way of most political promises because they are not truly in keeping with what people actually want, or people are not focused enough on the final results they are hoping to realize. Getting in touch with one's fundamental aspirations is not as easy as it may sound.

Why do many attempts to change behavior or accomplish a valued goal frequently fail? There are three main reasons: failure to change the structure of one's lives to reflect their goal orientation, lack of commitment because the goals are not truly desired at a fundamental level, and discouragement in not making progress fast enough.

Many people set off in earnest toward an inspiring vision or goal but give up the journey somewhere along the way. The main reasons for dropping out stem from a poor understanding of the change or creative process, which is organic in nature. There is an almost irresistible tendency for many people to apply rational, left-brain standards to what is predominately a holistic, right-brained, intuitive process. Desired change does not come about in a neatly ordered manner so that its progress can be predicted according to schedule.

Similarly, developing a vision is not a matter of using a cookbook approach that requires only visionary ingredients. All change, just like the death of a loved one or the end of a marriage, the loss of a job, or a new marriage or job, has a developmental timetable that can be influenced but not controlled. So developing a vision and nurturing it to fruition is more like giving birth to a child and then raising it attentively as opposed to merely implementing a strategic plan. If that is the case, how does one go about creating a vision? Most people are unaware of the actual underlying principles, structures, and dynamics that operate in their lives. Lacking a clear sense of the interpersonal or internal forces they have allowed to shape their decisions, they have a feeling of powerlessness in watching their lives head in directions they did not consciously choose. Confusion sets in as to both how and why they've ended up where they are. Choices often end up being made as a reaction to the various forces buffeting them at any moment in time. By constantly putting out fires, one has little time to actually dwell on the appropriateness of such choices over the long term, let alone the short term.

Starting to Develop a Vision

Before you develop a vision, it is absolutely essential to take time out from the daily whirlwind. Corporate retreats sometimes fulfill this function; for individuals, vacations or weekends may be the only time available. In either instance, getting away is needed. If you are going to reassess the major aspects of your life, you will need both time and distance from the very things that seem so urgent if they are to be viewed more impartially.

If developing a vision requires all of this time and effort, why even bother in the first place? Aside from seeing how powerful a force it is in the enduring success of many well-known companies, it is important to understand the role having a vision plays in organizing one's life. The lives of many people do not add up to any kind of meaningful whole.

In many cases, they are a collection of attributes or events that get strewn about a bit like items in a garage sale. The more external circumstances are allowed to control one's life, the less one can lay claim to a life that contains something constant, developmental, or timeless. Having an inspiring vision brings the rest of one's life together so that the parts align to form a powerful whole over which one has considerable control. Just as companies quickly eject employees who don't fit in or share the commitment to the vision, people with a profound sense of what they are trying to accomplish quickly discard those aspects of their life that get in the way or don't contribute to the realization of their cherished goals.

Even more importantly, having a vision can get you beyond the trap of just reacting to changing circumstances, because, by simply reacting to situations, you allow them to define you rather than the other way around. Instead, you end up creating the environment and strategies conducive to succeeding.

Although everyone will naturally develop his or her own vision, there are certain fundamental choices that successful people usually have in common. First and foremost, they chose to be the primary creative force in their lives and avoid merely reacting to life's changing circumstances. Second, they believe in always being true to themselves. Third, they seek a kind of freedom by not being tied to past, present, or future circumstances—they are tied to their vision, not to the limitations of situations. Last, they have made a firm commitment to their emotional, physical, mental, and spiritual well-being. With these building blocks, any personal vision is highly likely to materialize.

Gaining Control of Your Life

People who are caught up in merely responding and reacting to the barrage of events that accompany a more passive approach to life are primarily concerned with security, survival, and salvation in any form. Much like the employees in bureaucracies that downsize or restructure, retrenchment takes the place of any former complacency. Higher-order psychological needs and values are sacrificed as the bunker mentality sets in. Weathering the storm or enduring the battle consumes all thinking and strategizing. As all sense of control is abdicated, a growing sense of powerlessness ends up further undermining whatever ability to initiate change may have formerly existed. The downward spiral to bankruptcy, failure, unemployment, or election loss takes it natural course.

How does a vision initiate change and increase the sense of personal control? As Stephen Covey, Robert Fritz, Peter Senge, and Maxwell Maltz have stressed for years, the key is focusing on the end result. By having a clear idea of where you want to end up and by being firmly and honestly committed to getting there, you will set your mind naturally to finding the means necessary to realize the vision. It is the way most scientific and other innovative breakthroughs take place. Usually the answer appears when you are thinking about something else or after sleeping on a problem.

Why doesn't thinking about how to solve a problem eventually lead to its solution? Because rational thinking is usually too limiting when dealing with complex problems, much the same way that serial or linear logic is not as effective as synchronous or parallel processing. Our minds handle complexity by using rich symbols that can contain the paradoxical aspects of situations or events. Thus dreams are frequently where we discover the solution to problems that have been nagging at us during our waking hours.

Psychologists have made a lot of money out of this simple realization. As Peter Senge notes,

> It is through the subconscious that *all of* us deal with complexity. What distinguishes people with high levels of personal mastery is they have developed a higher level of rapport between their normal awareness and their subconscious.... The subconscious seems especially receptive to goals in line with our deeper aspirations and values. According to some spiritual disciplines, this is because these deeper aspirations input directly to, or are part of, the subconscious mind.

How do they accomplish this feat? While the subconscious is very helpful in coming up with creative solutions to life's problems, it does require sufficient raw material to get the job done. A clearly defined result is essential, which is why visualization techniques are often recommended in the goal setting or "visioning" process. If the subconscious uses symbols, stories, and pictures to solve problems, it is useful to frame our visions or goals as much as possible in the appropriate format. This is not to say that considerable rational or analytical thought is not part of the establishing of goals or visions, but these reductionistic or fragmenting activities can act only as precursors to the synthesizing power of the imagination, which brings together the various pieces of the mental, emotional, and spiritual jigsaw puzzle into a meaningful and workable whole. As Einstein once said, "I have never discovered anything with my rational mind."

If our lives are like a story or journey, then they need to make sense. But where does the sense come from? From the learning process. All stories have explicit or implicit themes, lessons, or morals that we take away. Plot lines, as Aristotle insisted, should largely be the natural outcome of character development. In other words, character is destiny. Peak performers feel a sense of destiny or calling that drives them on to greatness. Peak performers feel part of some larger purpose than the mere gratification of their ego and natural appetites. As George Bernard Shaw said,

> This is the true joy in life, being used for a purpose recognized by yourself as a mighty one ... being a force in nature instead of a feverish, selfish little clod of ailments and grievances complaining that the world will not devote itself to making you happy.

Instead of fighting against the oncoming course of events, peak performers see themselves as blending in with and taking advantage of all of the natural opportunities that arise.

As Shakespeare had Brutus so eloquently put it, in *Julius Caesar:*

> There is a tide in the affairs of men,
> Which taken at the flood, leads on to fortune;
> Omitted, all the voyage of their life
> Is bound in shallows and in miseries.
> On such a full sea are we now afloat,
> And we must take the current when it serves,
> Or lose our ventures. (4.3.218-24)

The Japanese have long held this seizing the moment as the key to success. Their profound respect for nature and its cycles or seasons has taught them to figure out how to take advantage of external forces. All of the Asian martial arts are premised on the notion of leveraging forces in motion in your favor.

Going with the flow, in a sense, is not about conforming, but about becoming a part of a shared creative process. As Peter Senge notes in connection with institutional settings,

> The idea that everybody has to be in agreement about "the vision" is complete nonsense ... Building shared vision is not about people surrendering their individual visions. It is about deepening each person's unique sense of vision and establishing harmony among the diverse visions so that we can move forward together.

Keeping on Course

Noticing changes provides the feedback necessary to adjust course when required. Launched missiles or torpedoes are off course almost 90 percent of the time, yet they usually reach their destination. How? By continually readjusting each time they wander from their true course. By remembering always to focus on the end result, it is easier to see what needs altering and in which direction. Thus constant negotiation with oneself or others based on recent developments is a natural part of staying on course.

Because events can easily throw one off course temporarily, it is wise not to focus too much on the methods used in achieving the vision. Like successful visionary companies, only the mission is sacred; the strategies, policies, regulations, and tactics adopted are worth keeping so long as they continue to represent the most effective means of moving closer to goal realization. Focusing on methods too much can obscure the reasons for their utilization and often precludes the consideration of a wider range of creative alternative means that is almost always available. Continuous improvement means constantly looking for better ways of achieving goals.

Despite the best of intentions, often there is no appropriate change in individuals. There is a conspicuous inertial tendency for people to seek a return to their old habits. People on diets and exercise programs frequently yo-yo in their commitment because they have not taken into account the relationship of these goals to other facets of their lives.

By leaving out the big picture, they are trying to modify only one aspect of a homeostatic system that is naturally oriented to reestablishing whatever equilibrium formerly existed. For example, the more you diet, the hungrier you get, so eventually you binge rather than having working at a healthier lifestyle that would bring together other crucial aspects of life that play a reinforcing role in maintaining reasonable weight and adopting regular exercise habits.

In other words, the vision does not resonate at a fundamental level, so attempts at partial changes for cosmetic reasons rarely have any lasting power. Until you understand how other areas of your life play a cross-functional role in the realization of the goals sought, success is likely to be limited and short-lived.

In many instances, the vision or goal does not strike a true chord within the individual. What is desired is not really a true goal in any long-term sense so much as a reduction of tension brought on by recent events (for example, trying to do something about the weight gained over Christmas). Once the tension is reduced somewhat, the goal disappears and the underlying issues go largely unexamined. No true change was actually sought, just a change in appearances. Governed as we are by appearances in so many ways, this approach is extremely common. Unfortunately, we often apply this same approach to crucial areas of our lives where quick fixes are ineffective over the long haul, for example, marriage, raising children, education, health, and career planning.

The main reason for developing a vision is to try to take advantage of untapped emotional and spiritual energy since visions are things you care deeply about—that is, they are the values you cherish the most. All enduring motivation is based on values. Moreover, the things you feel passionate towards are those things you always have an abundance of energy for and an endless curiosity about. Discovering one's values or passions is like being born again, for finding something to believe in is truly liberating and uplifting. People are willing to commit themselves to something that gives their lives genuine meaning and purpose. Indeed, they usually want to embrace it with open arms.

In many instances, parents focused on promoting practical values and monetary reward systems. Tangible results and rewards became the measure of everything. Beliefs became tied to the effectiveness of daily conspicuous efforts in achieving reward and recognition. All cause and effect, then, was situated in the world outside. Faith was contingent on the fulfillment of explicit promises and favorable circumstances. Failure was the result of factors beyond one's control—usually others that were depended upon.

Because there was a tendency to look for causes in an external world that one can believe in, many have grown cynical or at least slightly jaded as far as trusting politicians, business leaders, and institutions, given their performance of late. The failure of others in power to provide leadership, guidance, or reassurance has fostered a victim mentality.

It is as though President Kennedy's inaugural words, "Ask not what your country can do for you; ask what you can do for your country," had become reversed. Just like avid TV addicts, the so-called victims just passively watch their lives unfold according to the plans dictated by others or circumstances. At best they merely sift through the choices thrust upon them.

All their motivation is purely extrinsic or external in nature. The values held are equally superficial and prized only for their instrumentality—that is, if working harder isn't going lead to a raise or promotion, why bother? Resignedly, they drag themselves to the office since working has become an ordeal to be endured now that many of the external rewards have disappeared. With the forsaking of the age-old employment bargain, the extrinsic motivation and the well-defined career paths are no longer "carrots" that are being dangled temptingly. For these workers, even mission statements seem like manipulative tools devoid of substance.

The difference between someone trying to get you to believe in platitudes and developing an authentic vision is that the latter depends solely on the honesty and integrity of the person undertaking the challenge—which are the fundamental values allowing you to be "principle-centered," to use Stephen Covey's term, in the first place. If you are not principle-centered, you cannot have a vision.

Another fundamental assumption underlying this endeavor is that to develop a personal vision, you must believe you are capable of being the prime creative force in your life; otherwise, there is no escaping a victim mentality. Once you believe that you can take charge of your life, the question naturally becomes what should you do with your life? What do you truly believe in? What brings you great happiness? What would you like others to honestly say about you after you die? What accomplishments in your life are you proudest of? Questions such as these begin to illuminate the task of identifying what are the genuinely core beliefs and values that motivate you. As Robert Frost said, "All great things are done for their own sake." So the question to ask yourself is: what things would you want to do even if no one would pay you to do them? If you won a state lottery, how would it change your life? The answers to these questions point to what your true values and interests are.

Values

For values to be highly motivating and energizing, they must be not only deeply felt but also integrated into our lives. Unless we structure our lives around our beliefs, our efforts will be piecemeal and scattered, with disappointing results. By looking at our lives as puzzles and determining how all of the pieces fit together and interact, we get a sense of how aligned we are with our values and the goals or purposes that grow out of them.

As Buckminster Fuller asserted, "You're not a thing, you are a patterned integrity." Understanding the relationships in our lives and within ourselves tells us if we are remaining true to our values and if we have sorted out the relative importance of each.

We must create a decision-making structure in our lives to which we hold ourselves accountable. By determining the relative importance of each of our values, we create a means by which we can govern ourselves and maintain a clear focus. So ask yourself, how do you make decisions? How do you decide among conflicting values?

Pose yourself difficult questions: for instance, would you be willing to move outside the United States in order to get a job or promotion? What if your spouse's career was taking off and required you to make some career sacrifices—how far would you be willing to go? If you had to give up most of the things in your life, what would you refuse to give up and why?

The way we spend our time usually reveals either our values or the strategies we adopt to meet life's demands. As most experts in time management are quick to point out, most people spend their time on urgent but unimportant matters and not on important matters that are not urgent, yet it is the latter that determine the entire course of your life.

Thus most people are completely unaware of how one decision is likely to have a subsequent domino effect on other decisions in their life. By focusing just on what is immediate and urgent, their future is completely sacrificed to the distracting concerns of the present.

A Sense of Urgency

While a sense of urgency is important, it can nevertheless prevent us from working smarter rather than harder. The fires we tend to be putting out today are largely a result of poor, unintegrated decisions and strategies made in the past. By getting so caught up in the moment, we never get a chance to form an identity that is actually separate from the environment. Yet it is only by forming an independent identity that you can actually begin to alter the surrounding environment and claim some control over your life.

Urgency is a natural part of life. Indeed, a powerful sense of urgency is absolutely essential for any major change initiative to succeed. The key to success, however, lies in making sure that the sense of urgency is internal and not governed solely by external events.

As Dr. Larry Dossey in his book *Space, Time and Medicine* notes, "The perceptions of passing time that we observe from our external clocks cause our internal clocks to run faster." The stress, rush, and constant pressure brought on by external events take quite a toll on the health of those who allow themselves to give in to these harrying demands. When they catch a bad cold, they will likely blame an external virus and not the fact that their inner immune system might have become compromised through the stress their lifestyle encourages.

An internal sense of urgency comes from having a powerful vision of what you would like to accomplish in life and comparing that goal with the present reality on an ongoing basis. The key lesson that must be learned is that it is necessary both to consciously reaffirm the relevance of the goal and acknowledge the distance yet to go. Urgency created in this way never disappears, yet it is not stressful healthwise since you are always moving in the direction you want to go in, unlike people who suffer from the added depressing stress of allowing external events to eclipse their values and true goals in life.

The Boiled-Frog Syndrome

Ironically, people without a vision and who lack much power over their lives frequently abuse themselves through drugs, alcohol, food, and other addictions to compensate for their lack of control. Rather than acquire the discipline necessary to face up to what may be an unpleasant and undesirable current reality, they would rather resolve the tension that exists between any vision of their future they might possess and their current circumstances by compromising or lowering the vision so that the two line up better. A vicious cycle of vision-lowering and increasing helplessness leads to permanent depression.

Dislodging this structure and replacing it with a new one is something that takes years for the tearing down of the old structure and the rebuilding of the new one to take place.

Shortcuts are really just forms of addiction: they are the result of an unwillingness or inability to face up to difficult problems combined with having access to a quick fix that will make the problems go away temporarily. Gimmicky solutions are the ways in which we sell ourselves short and encourage dishonesty. Inevitably the problems worsen, and our ability to deal with them diminishes accordingly.

The "boiled-frog" syndrome overtakes us since the undermining process is slow but sure. Like frogs placed in warm water where the temperature is gradually increased to boiling, through adaptation they lose their ability to discern any change and flee the situation. Thus focusing on the comprehensive vision or the end result and noticing incremental changes are safeguards against landing in hot water. Otherwise, our lives resemble suspense movies with a number of false endings: just when we think we are out of the woods, thanks to some Band-Aid solution, the underlying factors emerge in completely unanticipated ways to overwhelm us.

Clarity and Coherence—and Flexibility

As Carl Rogers has emphasized, we can change only those things that we accept as being true about ourselves—something that can be a painful realization. However, when we get to the point at which we can laugh at ourselves, at least we have come to accept our shortcomings for what they are. Most of us are in no danger of running out of material so long as we manage to retain a high degree of self-awareness, for our visions will always remind us of the work that remains to be done.

After finding words one can live by and self-acceptance, make sure you can explain it to someone else in less than five minutes and have him or her indicate whether it makes sense. If it isn't easily understood by others, it is most likely lacking in the clarity and coherence that are vital to all visions. Visions that are more in keeping with the way the world is evolving obviously stand a greater chance of success. In addition, if the vision builds on the strengths of your current reality, it is much easier to believe in and find a suitable starting point to get it moving forward.

Similarly, only by noticing the effects of your actions can you make the necessary readjustments, but you often need to act without knowing whether something is going to work according to plan. Experimenting or testing possibilities before committing to them is often desirable. Eileen Shapiro describes a 1966 study showing that better chess players took longer to make a move after their opponents, in *Fad Surfing in the Boardroom:*

> The opponent's moves provides an opportunity to reconsider the options on the board, an opportunity that the better players capitalized on fully. Similarly, organizations with great ambitions and overall schemes for achieving them still need to delineate the building blocks, plan the order of top priorities, and then be willing to revise their bets according to the new set of circumstances.

In many instances, there is not even enough time to devise and implement a plan before the situation alters. Instead, it is necessary to rely on one's clearly defined and prioritized values or spiritual intuition to see which strategies are most likely to further one's goals. Intuition should always be the final arbiter.

The need for flexibility is such that our values and missions may sometimes have to be revised—but not abandoned. Although our values may change over time, their alteration is usually more of a reshuffling of the value hierarchy in light of new circumstances or additional considerations than a forsaking of what is truly a part of one's identity.

In some cases, we do need to unlearn certain values or beliefs when we come to realize that the assumptions they were based on are no longer valid, if they ever were. For example, nineteenth-century statisticians calculated that New

York City would be six feet deep in horse manure by 1940. Each significant shift in the environment provides us with an opportunity to revise our plans and reexamine the assumptions we are operating under. But it is only by closely monitoring our internal and external environments daily that we can note any change.

All growth processes are slow in getting off the ground but eventually gather momentum over time, so it is important not to expect too much at the beginning. Many people give up too soon out of impatience, and others mistakenly believe they can relax once some of the changes begin to bear fruit. The results are developmental and cumulative and not tied to quarterly projections. Many career changers run into this problem, since it can take three to six months longer for them to find work than those still looking in their area of expertise. Eventually, however, though it usually seems as if they are getting nowhere in the interim, all of their efforts begin to pay off.

Be Honest with Yourself

Finding the right path to take usually means heading up a lot of wrong ones first and eliminating them as options. Eventually the search becomes more focused as much is learned in the school of hard knocks. Focusing on the end result keeps you pointed in the right direction, while learning from your mistakes makes you more efficient in the search process. The more honest you are about your mistakes, the faster you learn; the quicker you refocus and restructure your efforts based on what you have learned, the sooner the goal is realized.

The key is openness to learning, which means listening: to yourself, to others, and to the world around you. To develop a multiple learning perspective on yourself, consider using the 360-degree performance style of evaluation or holographic inquiry technique. Ask a good friend to send out an evaluative questionnaire (which you have personally scored yourself against) to everyone who plays a major role in your life, and have your friend collect the responses anonymously so that a truer picture is forthcoming.

Keeping Opposing Values in Tension

The main sign of creative genius is the ability to balance two opposing viewpoints simultaneously, appreciate the inherent value of each at the same time, and resolve what appears to be contradictory in a mutually satisfactory manner. People who are creative are not frightened by ambiguity; rather, they thrive on it, for the fundamental basis of all innovation is conflict.

In today's world, almost everyone is expected to meet paradoxical challenges of one kind or another: reduce expenditures and accomplish more; take care of people and downsize; develop core competencies and diversify into new markets; compete against other teams, companies, or countries and cooperate with them; or be both a specialist and a generalist.

Now competition is keener and market feedback comes faster. The scope of the consequences of any particular action is increasing, while the time lapse between actions and consequences is decreasing.

It is essential that family members sit down together to come to a clearer understanding of assumptions each is operating under and the implications of everyone's career plans for each other. The sooner difficulties can be resolved, the quicker the focus can shift to realizing commonly shared visions and actively helping one another achieve his or her goals.

Unless everyone has a clear understanding of the evolutionary direction the family wishes to head in, unnecessary conflict and misunderstanding will pull it in opposing directions and undermine the goodwill necessary for the success of all complicated endeavors.

Dealing with paradox requires a mind-set that moves beyond the either-or perspective. It was this mentality that allowed the Japanese to steal market share in many manufacturing areas during the 1980s. Whereas the Japanese combined high quality with low price, U.S. manufacturers assumed they had to focus on one or the other.

Similarly, it is not necessary to decide between becoming a specialist and a generalist in all instances. Each is a matter of degree, and the desirable combination is likely to vary according to circumstance and environmental developments. It would be better to focus on keeping both options open as much as possible, rather than blindly committing to one or the other without considering the strategic possibilities available by combining both. Being able to sell oneself to an employer in a multifaceted manner gives one more flexible career options, including creating a position that doesn't even currently exist.

The lesson to be learned here is that the solution to resolving most contradictions is not readily apparent, or they wouldn't appear as contradictions in the first place. Only by immersing oneself in the apparent polarities can one discover vital links to a solution that combines the options in a way that achieves the desired result.

Jerry Fletcher, in *Patterns of High Performance: Discovering the Way People Work Best,* has found that people and organizations excel when they combine the best of two contradictory aspects. High-performance oxymora are used to capture the two ends of the contradiction; for example, the Japanese became well known as "innovative imitators," and some sports coaches might be viewed as "benevolent dictators." By using an oxymoron, we can draw attention to the contradiction as a means of enhancing the creative structural tension—a strategy also recommended by Robert Fritz. By examining the pros and cons of each polar opposite, it becomes possible to focus more on the pros and minimize the cons. Ideal oxymora are encouraged for comparison purposes so that a sense of direction and progress is more self-evident.

In Polarity Management, Barry Johnson argues that people have a tendency to focus on the pros of one pole and the cons of the opposing pole as a means of resolving the conflict clearly in favor of one choice over the other. This strategy is extremely limiting and is often not a viable alternative when both sides need to be accommodated. In these instances, we resist choosing both because of the clearly perceived negative consequences on the one side. As a result, we may become paralyzed or fail to choose. The recommended solution involves bearing the ultimate goal in mind and then reviewing both the pros and cons of each option in connection with this goal. Beginning with the favorable option is one way of getting the process under way faster. Ultimately some sort of synthesis is hoped for that combines the best of both worlds. What career options do you see only in a negative light? What is the upside of each? Can some of the options be bridged in ways that minimize the unattractive aspects?

It is worth asking yourself what structures and processes describe your life. Which dominates, structure or process? Do you have entrepreneurial, competence-building, and renewal-oriented processes built into your life? Does each area of your life help out the other areas in some sense? Is vital information readily shared by all people who play a critical role in your life? Are your relationships based on trust, fairness, common purpose, and mutual understanding?

Peter Hersey and Kenneth Blanchard use situational leadership to overcome the task-versus-relationship approach to management. Initially, they recommend focusing on structuring the task; then they suggest building the relationship and offering task support, and eventually maintaining the relationship but letting the task component progressively diminish as people develop better task-related competence.

Developing a Career Strategy

From a career perspective, using networking and information interviews initially to develop a career plan might make sense. Once the plan is designed, focusing primarily on those contracts that will give you the desired skills and on those contacts who are most likely to help you to get a job in your next career developmental phase is desirable. Once most of the key skills are in place, the emphasis shifts back to broader-based networking as a means of maximizing career opportunities.

Charles Hampden-Turner has devised a number of strategies based on time and geography. The first step is to examine both sides of the paradox to see if parts of one are in any way included in the other, such as reducing price but gaining volume or market share to make up for the profits that might have been lost. The second step is to look for a developmental link between the variables and order them appropriately. A third approach is to alternate between the variables in a reinforcing manner over time. And the last step is to check to see if the first three steps are likely to produce the desired synthesis.

From a career-planning point of view, one might become a kind of generalist yet seek a more specialized focus in the next contract, then broaden out in the one after that. Changes in the industry hiring environment would likely suggest a particular alternative sequence as far as the scope of each is concerned. The same approach might figure into alternating career opportunities geographically in multinational or multistate settings.

Perhaps the most sophisticated approach to dealing with paradoxes would be to use a systems approach that maps the interactions between alternative possibilities geographically and over time. Looking for obvious and not-so-obvious reinforcing or leveraging patterns can help you understand what is preserving the status quo and what changes might reinforce more desirable behaviors or option selection.

For instance, if the opportunities for networking are limited in one geographic location or the informal information flow is much better in another setting, then moving closer to the action is more likely to put you into the kind of "feedback loop" vital to your career at the moment. Similarly, your personal life operates as a system that can either help or hinder the career development process for everyone connected.

Trying to optimize the tasks and relationships within your life requires a careful evaluation of how they currently work in an interactive manner and how they might be made to work in more desirable ways. Much like the restructuring of businesses and governments, individuals should consult with everyone regarding both how the current system actually works and what the likely effects of initiating a change might be before restructuring one's own personal life.

Before you quit your job and start your own business, you would want to make sure that all systems are go in all relevant areas of your life and to have a good idea of what the immediate and far-reaching ramifications are likely to be. All support systems should be in place. Moreover, you would want to have at least one agreed-upon backup plan and clearly delineated decision-to-abort-the-mission criteria. Everything could change down the road, but you would want to come to an agreement then in much the same manner.

All learning systems require "coordination functions, development functions, planning and strategic functions, and monitoring and evaluation functions." What aspects of your life fulfill each of these roles? If you are part of a family system, is everyone involved in each system area? Does each of these functions play an active role in your strategic career planning process?

Navigating one's way around or through paradoxes involves continuous negotiation, marketing, and new-and-improved creative solutions despite all of the strategic planning you might undertake. Sometimes the best way to deal with what appears to be a paradox is by choosing neither option or the potential synthesis.

Learning to think "outside the box" can sometimes solve both problems at once. Often there is a third possibility that has just not been entertained. For instance, deciding to lay off staff and risk low morale may not be the only solution. Changing strategic focus might lead to growth possibilities. Perhaps changing careers is not necessary in some cases. Looking for an entirely different setting in which the same function is needed may provide a possible solution.

Using metaphorical names for the polarities or players involved, making drawings, or writing stories or vignettes can often be the best way to begin an innovative problem-solving process. It is much easier for those involved to elaborate the frame or context they are working in by using humorous creative depictions that poke fun at the problems.

Key assumptions are bound to emerge without conscious realization. Since *looking* into the future is a *visionary* process, the better we are able to *see* the problem, the more likely we are to *visualize* potential solutions. By staying close to the artistic storytelling model, we can preserve the frame or context more easily while we look for a solution. We retain the sense of wholeness or integrity that is lost by extensive analysis. After all, it should be remembered that solving paradoxes is an art form.

The solutions to paradoxes and contradictions come from our subconscious. As every artist who has ever waited for inspiration can tell you, you can influence the creative process by gathering together all the necessary raw material in a careful fashion and practicing diligently, but you cannot control what is naturally a spontaneous process. Creativity is by its very nature synchronous—it is the simultaneous combining of a number of disparate ingredients into a jigsaw puzzle that makes complete sense. It is the ultimate self-organizing principle underlying all growth processes. Because we naturally seek wholeness, our creative processes never stop in their efforts to resolve what appear to be contradictions. Thus the more fully we embrace the contradictions, the greater the eventual synthesis that emerges. The greatness of a work of art is usually proportional to the scope of the challenge undertaken.

The key to finding personal solutions to the paradoxical demands pulling us in so many directions is to clarify our assumptions regarding what quality of life, success, happiness, and job satisfaction mean to us and incorporate them into our visions and goals. The balancing of these values is the juggling act or creative challenge facing us in a world slightly out of control. There is a need to resolve the issues surrounding continuity, stability, and growth. What aspects of your past are essential to you and must accompany you wherever you go, remembering that you must travel lightly in a world of change? If you consider the times in your life that you grew most as a person or professional, is there an alternating rhythm between stability and growth that seems to work best for you? Can you see your career growing in phases—what would they be? Can you create a time and place for the important things in your life? Can you make time your friend through a synchronous juggling of values in tension? What do you want out of your career? How are you preparing for changes that are bound to occur? How are you laying the groundwork for your next job and the one after that?

Questions such as these are the ones everyone needs to ask, particularly those regarding quality of life, which probably is your bottom-line comprehensive vision. Where do you want to live? Somewhere where there are few social problems? Culturally interesting amenities? Geographical diversity? How much money do you need to be comfortable? What options regarding friends and family do you seek? What kinds of companies and responsibilities are attractive to you? Where would you never want to live or work?

Remember, you are your own best customer. Are you anticipating your future needs? Do you know yourself well? Are you taking good care of yourself? Are you willing to go out of your way to give yourself heroic customer service? Have you educated yourself well as to all of the choices or options available to you? How do you measure quality, value, and service in your life with respect to how you treat yourself? If you rated yourself according to these ideas, what would your score in each category be? What kinds of continuous improvement programs do you have in place for each of these dimensions? Could you reengineer your life to improve some of the processes in your life or provide better customer service to yourself? What alliances or networks could provide you with better information and more career opportunities?

As you can see, the scope of the challenge is almost boundless, but the answer to each question is aimed at improving the quality of your life both now and in the future. Having everything in your life serve a common purpose makes living a richer and more meaningful experience. More energy is available to you to accomplish the Herculean chores that lie before us all, and the world seems a much less chaotic place when you develop a genuine sense of getting closer to your vision.

Remember that you will reap the benefits that accumulate with time, which increasingly facilitates the entire process. Before you can build up this kind of momentum, however, it is necessary to ask the appropriate questions and listen diligently for the best solutions that will emerge naturally as a result of all your exploratory immersion in the soul-searching, brainstorming, transitional processes.

The key is maintaining an openness to change so that all of the possibilities needed to solve the diverse problems will be available to you. By preparing for and accepting change, you will find that variety becomes the spice of life and uncertainty gives it a piquant zest.

It is only when you embrace the challenge fully that true, workable solutions and strategies will emerge—often in unexpected ways. As in all organic processes, it is only by planting the appropriate seeds (questions) in friendly soil (your subconscious mind) and carefully nurturing them (continually checking in with yourself and monitoring progress) that the flowers (visions and goals) will flourish (be realized).

Rational structures can act as the spark to get the process started, but in the end most of the solutions will come through creative processes with reason acting as the handmaiden. After all, even the left and right sides of the brain are a paradox that needs to be resolved. As you might expect the answer lies in both sides working together and not in one side dominating the other.

The rational side often is useful in spelling out some of the various system dimensions of the problem and in designing implementation strategies that make sense. As Peter Vaill, author of *Managing as a Performance Art: New Ideas for a World of Chaotic Change,* notes,

> "Systems thinking" is about the nearest thing we have in the management field to a direct embrace and confrontation with paradox. Systems thinking does not flinch from complexity and is willing to be surprised by the "counterintuitive" character of many organizational events and processes.... [However], permanent white water defies all models, and indeed, the more comprehensive we attempt to make our organizational models, the more we can detect phenomena outside the model that are influencing the organization. The horizon of what we know accelerates away from us.... The leader or

> manager is always part of the system being acted upon; this individual is certainly no more fixed an element than any other and, indeed, may be more variable *just because* of possessing action responsibility.... This means that "understanding the system" (comprehension) at any moment and "action in the system" (control) at any moment cannot be known.

Only by holistically marrying both sides of the brain when we tackle paradoxes can we hope to prevent Murphy's law from gaining momentum. To rely solely on reason or objectivity—that is, treating people as objects—fails because people refuse to act as preprogrammed robots in a static environment. Objectivity and rational analysis are concerned with gaining distance from matters, yet creative solutions come only from immersion in all aspects of the environment. It is a bottom-up and a top-down process—the result of directly and actively engaging the paradoxical environment.

Committing Yourself to a Solution

Developing a vision takes you beyond the mere reacting or responding to life's endless challenges. It gives you a choice as to which challenges you want to master. By accepting the contradictions that characterize all challenges in some shape or form, we have a clearer sense of what work lies before us. By then committing ourselves to finding a solution, we have already placed faith in our ability to do so. That, as they say, is half the battle. The rest will naturally take care of itself so long as we continue to renew our faith in the vision itself.

In a world where many forces are beyond our control, you must see a strategy that blends control plus continuous learning in connection with aspects of life beyond your immediate influence. As Henry Mintzberg, in *The Rise and Fall of Strategic Planning*, notes,

> Strategic learning is an inductive process; it cannot take place in the absence of detailed, intimate

> knowledge of the situation. And strategic *vision* depends on an ability to *see* and feel; it cannot be developed by people who deal with little more than words and numbers on pieces of paper.... We believe the strategy making process is better characterized as a process of learning—formation in place of formulation, if you like.

The messy hustle and bustle of daily life in a complex world forces us to learn how to make more intuitive decisions based on the information we have on hand. The ability to learn as best we can continually is the only way we can negotiate our way in the white-water rapids that we are always caught up in.

Whether our reactions take the form of "paralysis by analysis" (to use Tom Peters' phrase), denial, bargaining, anger, depression, or shock, we often hold ourselves back from embracing the changes that are undeniable. All of the willpower in the world cannot make the Information Age disappear.

Instead of mustering more willpower, we need to trust our creative entrepreneurial powers to resolve most of the problems we are currently facing. It is the same kind of pioneering mentality that made America great in the first place that will continue to show it the way into the future and each of us the paths we must take. All you need to do is commit yourself to starting the journey. By remaining an open system that engages the changing environment, you will able to learn whatever you need to know to make decisions.

Just remember that America still embraces the spirit of progress toward some vision even if much squabbling over both the means and ends often make for much tension, dissension, and conflict. As Joel Garreau asserts in *Edge City,*

> An optimist has been defined as someone who is still engaged in the problem. By that standard, it would appear self-evident that America remains a

> nation of optimists. We are battling like demons over the most basic ways we should organize our lives. This is not the behavior of people who are resigned to their fate; it is the behavior of people with a touching faith in their enduring ability to change the world—for the better. I think that our most knock-down, drag-out, hair-pulling fights are those over competing visions of the Promised Land. That is why the noise is so loud.

The secret to America's revitalizing resilience lies in its constitution, which enshrines the freedom of its citizens to pursue their own visions of happiness. By allowing everyone this privilege, the U.S. has made diversity a centerpiece of its identity and vision of the future. By doing so, America embraces the paradoxical challenge of containing contradictory visions—-something that can only lead on to greatness so long as it preserves freedom and inclusiveness as core parts of the American identity. For freedom allows us to create and change our identity as we wish to or need to and inclusiveness gives us an identity that is as powerful as the visions we allow to flourish. Why is a powerful sense of identity important? As Stephanie Marshall notes in *The Organization of the Future,* "Identity is the principle that is most fundamental to all self-organizing systems. It encompasses the organization's meaning, purpose, and intentionality and provides the coherence around which system stability emerges. Identity facilitates order and transformation even in turbulent environments because it provides a constant frame of reference for organizational integrity and renewal."

In the next chapter we will turn our attention to building the kind of relationship infrastructure that can help expedite the realization of our personal visions.

CHAPTER 9

Leverage Your Relationships

There are no Robinson Crusoes in modern society; each of us is a point in a vast network of interdependent relationships. We also create relationships to multiply our efforts. We can do more together than apart.

—WAYNE BAKER, *NETWORKING SMART*

The 1990s are characterized by a complete transformation in how business is conducted. The 1980s championed the "art of the deal" and promoted rampant takeover speculation that ended up slicing and dicing companies to exploit the book value of various corporate assets. With countless poison pills in place, most companies are now safe from hostile takeovers. Nonetheless, mergers and acquisitions are proceeding at a record clip, as are joint ventures and alliances of one kind or another.

As we head into the globally competitive marketplace, whoever has the most close friends or the broadest reach will likely win in any showdown. As a result, most companies are trying to fill their dance cards with as many suitable partners as possible. IBM, for instance, now has over four hundred strategic alliances worldwide. The art of the deal is giving way to the art of networking.

As GE's CEO Jack Welch suggested in a 1989 speech entitled "Soft Values for a Hard Decade: A View of Winning in the '90s,"

> We've spent the majority of our energy in the '80s working, appropriately, on the hardware of American business because that hardware had to be fixed. The Japanese, on the other hand, have the software, the culture which ties productivity to the human spirit—which has practically no limits. That's where we have to turn in the '90s—to the software of our companies—to the culture that drives them. The structure of most large corporations—overly bloated, diversified bureaucracies—needed to be shaken up. Downsizing, restructuring, and reengineering rushed in to provide this evolutionary wake-up call.

Once that was accomplished, the new challenge becomes how to foster communication, coordination, and collaboration processes since this is the software needed once the mortar and bricks of the old bureaucratic structures give way to the modular, flexible networked organization. Because rigid structures that acted as the whips and chains of control were eliminated, something equally powerful needed to take its place. As it turns out, networks, like spider webs, are extremely strong and resilient replacements for the simple machine bureaucracies of the past.

Unlike chains that have weak links, networks resemble the Internet—if one part of the communication system is eliminated, there are always other routes since redundant supports or connections are an intrinsic part of their weblike structure. In a machine, however, if one part fails, the entire operation can grind to a halt, much like getting a pink slip and having no inside track on other job possibilities.

Replacing Career Paths

Now that we are making great strides in tearing down the rigid corporation of the past with its built-in career paths, individuals are being left to their own devices to find employment. The appropriate communication, coordination, and collaboration networks are necessary not only for companies but also for job seekers who require a safety net for their careers.

During the 1980s, Drake Beam Morin, the world's largest outplacement firm, found that almost 70 percent of all those who found new employment did so through personal contacts. Not only did this prove to be the best way to find employment, but people also found better, longer-lasting, and more-satisfying jobs by this means. Why? The people who knew them served as a two-way screening system, fully aware of all the aspects of the person and the job that don't get mentioned in interviews.

As it turns out, managers with large personal networks end up with higher-paying positions than those with smaller ones. Moreover, the larger and more diversified the network, the faster the rate of promotion regardless of age. To top it off, these managers also live longer, enjoy greater mental and physical health, are more resilient, and are usually far happier overall.

Employment Agencies

What about those who lack an extensive network or the requisite networking abilities? They are finding their way to employment agencies. Temporary personnel agencies are growing rapidly in both the United States and in Western Europe. In 1994, Miami's Vincam Group, a personnel firm, had the fastest revenue growth of all private companies in the state; four other such agencies weren't far behind, according to *Florida Trend*. In fact, Miami's Creative Staffing is now listed on the Inc. 500 (which features the 500 fastest-growing companies in America). According to the U.S. Department of Labor, the temporary labor market will increase by 57 percent by the year 2005. The professional and technical fields now make up 20 percent of the temp market and are the fastest-growing areas. In Silicon Valley's Santa Clara County, temporary forms of employment accounted for all new job growth since 1984.

Manpower, the largest private-sector employer in the United States, employs almost twice as many people as does GM. A number of firms, such as Powersoft, even maintain an in-house temp pool. The good news is that 42 percent of those applying for work through an agency eventually find full-time employment by this means.

What do employment agencies have in common with those who are more resourceful in finding more satisfying employment on their own? Both reflect the growing trend of avoiding hiring mistakes. If people are now becoming a company's most important asset, accounting for up to 75 percent of a company's expenses, there is little room to hire inappropriately in a globally competitive market.

Through networking, most companies know who they are getting in advance; with employment agencies, at least they get to see the person in action before making a more permanent decision. Given that the number of people working for employment agencies grew by 50 percent between 1992 and 1995 compared to the 8 percent job growth for the period, many people and firms are obviously "outsourcing" their networking or recruiting needs.

"Try before you buy" is replacing the quick-and-dirty interview process. Companies now expect the agencies to do most of the screening for them as part of the outsourcing trend. The most successful companies will often interview people for months when hiring temps isn't a reasonable alternative.

Using Networks

The ultimate team-building skills needed in a shrinking world where brokerage functions multiply constantly, however, are networking skills. As Fritjof Capra notes in *The Tao of Physics,*

> Gradually physicists began to realize that nature, at the atomic level, does not appear as a mechanical universe composed of fundamental building blocks, but rather as a *network of relationships*.

Margaret Wheatley echoes this viewpoint in *Leadership and the New Science* when she says,

> Now I look carefully at how a workplace organizes its relationships; not its tasks, functions, and hierarchies, but the pattern of relationships and the capacities to form them. I cannot describe a person's role, or his or her contribution, without understanding the network of relationships and the energy that is required to create the work transformations that I am asking from that person.

As this new awareness sets in, most hiring decisions regarding managers will be based primarily on each applicant's existing network assets or connections and perceived networking capabilities for making new contacts within the industry.

The logic behind building bridges is to increase the number of connections with the outside world. The greater the number of connections, the greater the number of possible business opportunities that exist and ways available to resolve any conflict between the producer and customer logic approaches—that is, efficiency versus customer satisfaction.

With the number and quality of relationships becoming the fundamental business building blocks, it is only natural that the new assets that determine business success are not the easy-to-measure ones, such as capital, plant, and equipment, but the less tangible ones, such as concepts, competence, and connections, which bring together innovation and quality throughout the entire business process—starting with raw materials and continuing through the supply chains to the end user.

As more people continue to change jobs more frequently as a result of less permanent forms of employment flourishing, it is imperative that companies learn to take advantage of the network connections of their employees. Given that the average professional knows 3,500 contacts and these contacts know an additional 3,500 people, just two levels deep adds up to 12,250,000 contacts if there are no overlaps. It doesn't take too many employees before almost everyone is in some way connected with almost everyone in the U.S. From a business standpoint, it represents a potential gold mine of possibilities that every employer will end up trying to exploit to the fullest. Looking at it from a career development perspective, there are an incredible number of available information sources that can help you strategically to manage your career effectively.

Networking provides the best education and opportunity insurance policy that is possible to get in the world. The major criticism of MBA programs is their inability to teach people how to work effectively with others inside and outside organizations to achieve desired results—something psychologist David Coleman has termed "emotional intelligence." Theoretical knowledge has its place, but the most important kind of knowledge is tacit knowledge. Tacit knowledge is the accumulated wisdom that comes from experience and contact with others who have been through similar situations and getting the benefit of their input as well. Apprenticeship programs are built on this kind of on-the-job sharing of knowledge. For managers, mentors provide a similar function. Lateral moves and work on various teams inside companies increase the number of learning, networking, and mentorship opportunities.

Peer Relationships

Now that corporations have eliminated many vertical structural layers in favor of teams and horizontal integration, success depends far more on managing peer relationships.

Peers can provide much needed advice, political backing, information, technical expertise, and moral support. Reciprocity, IOUs, and mutual support are the implicit forms of bargaining characterizing these and most other relationships in society. Leveraging key peer relationships has always been the secret to getting things done despite what seem like insurmountable internal obstacles that thwart normal efforts. By outlining the processes or workflow inside the organization, you can identify the key peer interdependencies and resources so as to establish relationships that can prevent career-damaging cooperation or coordination bottlenecks from occurring in the daily carrying out of company business.

Mentoring

With many of the layers of middle management disappearing, there are fewer mentorship possibilities inside organizations; nonetheless, the age-old custom of managing upward is just as critical as ever. As John Kotter and John Gabarro declared in their classic *Harvard Business Review* article, "Managing Your Boss," career success depends on "the process of consciously working with your superior to obtain the best possible results for you, your boss, and the company." If you help your boss's career or anyone else's, you are helping your own. This applies equally to subordinates and peers as well. When someone consciously tries to compensate for the weaknesses (for instance, marketing) of his superior, the complementary nature of the relationship is usually much appreciated, and favors are ultimately reciprocated in most instances as dependency increases.

Honesty

The number-one personal relationship quality sought in all studies undertaken is honesty—more so now than ever. Honesty means accurate information, the one thing everyone needs to survive in a changing world. Remember the inability of upper management to get accurate information in bureaucracies despite open invitations for workers to discuss their concerns. In the boundaryless company that CEO Jack Welch is trying to create at GE, the key values are respect for honesty, candor, reality, and openness.

Remember, negative information is devastating when moving downward because subordinates take criticism far more seriously than do those giving it. On the other hand, negative information almost never manages to move upward or is extremely sanitized and reformatted in the process. As Kenneth Blanchard suggests in *The One Minute Manager*, every effort must be made to catch people doing something right as opposed to something wrong, so that they will feel more comfortable about providing more realistic negative feedback when necessary.

The coach model at least has everyone playing on the same team. Even better is the learner model within an organization. Viewed in this context, all appraisals are an important part of personal and professional development.

Effective Networking

From a purely practical point of view, it makes little sense to network only with the people in your profession or industry. If there is a downturn in your area, you could find yourself in a network of people all looking for the same kind of work as you. The broader your networks, the more opportunities are potentially available if you need to make a career transition.

—Barbara Moses, *Career Intelligence*

Aside from seeking opportunities to broaden your internal corporate network, strategically, there are some fundamental principles governing the way networking works. As already mentioned, mutual benefit and natural understanding are required for any long-term relationship if one side is to avoid exploiting the other.

The first principle in effective networking is that *the greater the number of interactions that take place between two people, the greater the amount of mutual understanding and cooperation that is likely to emerge naturally in the relationship.* Frequent interactions must be structured into the relationships. In a fast-changing world, information, competence, and concepts are perishable or can decrease in value quickly. You need to keep up with latest developments. Even sending along FYI copies of pertinent newspaper clippings, magazine articles, book reviews, etc., maintain contact with little effort and are much appreciated.

The second principle is that *most people prefer to associate with others like themselves, because it is socially easier to interact more frequently and reach common understandings.* Although these relationships are important, they run the risk of becoming incestuous—very little information from outside the like-minded group of people ever finds its way in, and there is likely to be excessive overlap or redundancy in the networking connections. Thus spending considerable time with people like yourself in an organization likely limits the number of your networking connections and their combined effectiveness. Knowing well everyone in the accounting department limits your scope and influence.

The third principle is that *diverse connections broaden your reach and are cross-functional or holistic in nature.* Diverse connections require more effort to establish and maintain but have far greater integrating or leveraging effectiveness. Because there is less overlap among everyone involved, there is also less redundancy among all of the people who make up your network. Remember that in order to have the first two levels of your network reach 12,500,000 people, you cannot have any overlap. Thus network diversity is the source of incredible reach and power as we will see in the global opportunity chapter. As with stocks, holding a diversified portfolio of relationships provides a safety net against most forms of career-related risks.

The fourth principle is that *relationships develop according to expectations*. If you expect a relationship to last, you are more likely to engage in the kind of behavior necessary for its maintenance. Unless you expect the relationship to last, deal making and exploitation are more likely to characterize the negotiation process, and little leeway is likely to be granted by either party. The litigious nature of Americans is evidence of this approach to relationships in the country. Focusing on making most relationships last longer is a worthwhile investment.

The fifth and last principle of effective networking is *knowing which relationships you want to develop, maintain, or let go*. Like poker, it is knowing when to hold, fold, discard, or ask for another card. You cannot effectively maintain an infinite number of relationships any more than a company can deal with an infinite number of suppliers or customers.

Mutual understanding takes considerable time and effort, particularly in a global context. Age, gender, culture, ethnicity, status, seniority, and education make formidable barriers in many instances. The problem is compounded by the time necessary for such understanding to emerge. Downsizings, teams restructuring, and mobile assignments can disrupt the relationship-building process. The only way to shorten the process is to emphasize the mutual benefits and increase the number of interactions taking place in the time available. The same immersion process that resolves paradoxes can equally benefit the challenge of diversity when time is of the essence. Recognition of mutual interdependence—your fates and fortunes are tied together—can often expedite matters. In other words, whoever has excellent team-building skills, diversity training, and cross-group integration skills will excel inside companies as a result.

Many relationships, however, are more long-term in importance and need to be developed and cultivated slowly. Intensity is not even desirable because you don't want to be bothering people unnecessarily or too often. Thus it is possible to manage a larger number of relationships, which may prove strategic over time. In this way, you are creating a larger number of options down the road. In most cases, you don't know when you will need to ask for assistance from your network, but you should cover all the bases for each likely eventuality.

Using Networks to Build Your Career

Although we have focused primarily on networks inside the companies where you work, the real career-enhancing relationships are much more likely to be found elsewhere. With fewer middle managers, a company's informal ties to other companies and the industry as a whole are reduced in number—which translates into weaker association involvement; lower attendance at trade fairs or industry conventions; and fewer club, board, supplier, customer, community, or political linkages or connections. Companies are having to create positions or designate teams to fulfill these functions.

These are the best areas for career advancement—providing the company's external focus. They also will help you get your next job—likely a promotion inside or outside the firm—in no time at all. Those responsible for international coordination and cooperation will enjoy the highest salaries, fastest career tracks, and unrivaled job security—as the global opportunity chapter will show. Tom Peters and Robert Waterman's "Management by Walking Around" has moved into its next evolutionary level—management by wandering around the world.

All employment positions that have an external orientation can increase your career luck enormously. Why? Because external connections are invariably diverse in nature—they bring together many people who have different ideas, experiences, and outlooks. By doing so, they enlarge the number of creative possibilities available and are the best source of trend information of all kinds, not just for the company, but also for whoever is playing an active facilitation role. You become equally well known or visible both inside the company and instrumental to the success of everyone involved.

The downside is of course the enormous challenge such positions can entail. If you are responsible for managing a joint venture or business alliance, there are often factors at work beyond your control. However, if managing relationships were easy, virtually all managers would be out of a job. Those who limit themselves to less diverse challenges risk the fate of GM and Sears, which were proud of replicating generations of like-minded, inward-looking managers.

Thus the leading and managing of relationships, which poses the greatest challenge, is the source of greatest career opportunity and success. Since external relationships are often more challenging than their internal equivalents, the career rewards are naturally commensurate with the risks involved. From a professional and personal development perspective, the growth opportunities are unrivaled.

Remember that the number of potential mentors within organizations has dwindled along with the downsizing of middle management, so most of the mentors you will likely need are to be found outside your organization. Indeed, the shortage of such relationship opportunities can become a glass ceiling for many inside any organization, particularly for women and minorities. For that reason, both groups should seek out companies that employ sufficient numbers in positions of responsibilities; otherwise, their career networking opportunities will be severely constrained unless there is an external orientation to their job.

The "ghetto-ization" of inner city businesses comes from their inability to become suppliers to companies outside the city cores. The same problem can affect the careers of those trapped inside less progressively diverse or internationally oriented companies. They are forced to maintain networks outside their work setting in order to get ahead.

Your connections outside a company increase in importance with age. The majority of those over thirty-four years of age find work through their personal contacts, whereas fewer than half of those under thirty-four find work by this means. Of those finding work this way, the weaker contacts are more important than the stronger ones. Why? Because you likely already know the same information as your stronger contacts. In addition, your stronger contacts are less willing to provide references for you unless they know you extremely well, since their own reputations are at stake. Weak ties, on the other hand, are not providing you with a reference, just as a referral, which is much more innocuous. They also represent the larger part of your network at your disposal.

Building Your Network

Remember that you are more likely to cultivate people who are like you than to choose those who differ markedly, so the widest net is actually cast by those you know less well, who possess knowledge or information you are unfamiliar with. Many of them you may have forgotten, but yearbooks, directories, and rosters of various kinds can act as excellent reminders.

Qualify your network prospects the way sales people qualify buyers—that is, are they likely to know a wide variety of people from different companies, and are they relationship-oriented? Obviously customer service, purchasing, sales, and marketing people have broad external contacts. But don't forget the less obvious ones, such as barbers and hairdressers, doctors, dentists, church leaders, insurance or real estate agents, lawyers, accountants, nurses, former teachers or classmates, bankers, brokers, civic or community leaders, association representatives, health or social club managers, charity or political fund-raisers, directors of boards, etc. All of these people are part of your networking infrastructure. But remember that just as 80 percent of all sales are made by 20 percent of the sales force, only about 20 percent of your network qualifies fully and has reliable information source credibility.

Some of the key people to target are those who are early adopters and opinion leaders. These people pride themselves on staying up with leading-edge developments, and those working to promote new products and services usually seek them out. So check out where the most up-to-date information about up-and-coming companies is likely to converge: the opinion leaders. Why opinion leaders? In the past ten years, advertising persuasiveness fell by 30 percent among consumers. As Regis McKenna has stressed, the greater the complexity of products and the more intense and numerous the competition, the more consumers seek out the advice of opinion leaders to simplify the decision-making process. Nowadays poor reviews can quickly sink a product regardless of marketing expenditures.

Magazines such as *Inc., Success,* and *Entrepreneur* feature the hottest and fastest-growing companies in America and thereby act as opinion leaders, as do other industry-specific magazines. Large domestic companies in most cases tend to be late adopters, so paying attention to newer firms and multinationals makes more sense.

It is important to remember that networking requires persistence. According to the National Research Bureau, Inc., "Eighty percent of all sales are made after the fifth call." The same is likely to be true with networking. The relationships have to be developed. Some opinion leaders in industries who are often asked to refer appropriate job candidates admit that they expect those hoping for referrals to have networked with them for at least two years since they too worry about their reputations as referral sources.

Suppliers are a good networking source since they supply many companies with essential components and often know quite a bit about each company, especially now that there is greater integration taking place between everyone in the supply chain. The closer relationships that are being formed with fewer suppliers linked with EDI, or electronic data interchange, helps to diffuse important industry information rapidly throughout the chain, right from the end-use down to the lowest supply level.

Customers are obviously an additional source of networking information and connection now that they too are playing a larger role in product design and prototype evaluation. Companies that have formed close partnerships with their customers are likely to prosper more than those that don't. In addition, customers are likely to be less biased in terms of the information offered, since they have the least invested in the relationship.

Because randomness and diversity produce the broadest network possible, starting up or joining diverse networking clubs can serve as a wonderful way of prequalifying everyone involved. Many differ according to rules, procedures, interest, and membership composition and rules and procedures are geared to maximizing networking energy; for example, two referrals are required per week and must be recorded monthly. As long as they are approached with a clear-cut strategy in mind, networking clubs are an excellent means of making connections.

The best way to network is to increase your visibility. That can mean becoming an industry association representative, hosting conventions, giving community speeches or seminars, joining high profile committees or community organizations, starting your own network club, or writing articles or books. The higher your profile, the more you are perceived as an opinion leader. Since people want to supply opinion leaders with information to pass on or contact them regarding their views, you end up at the vital information and networking crossroads that almost ensures your success. After all, you will have more options available to you than anyone else.

Using the Internet

The information highway will eventually be used as a temp agency service and a place for locating professionals and specialists. In a try-before-you-buy world, the initial sort can be done over the Internet, even a preliminary computer-based screening interview. Videoconference interviewing is in the process of taking off. Already some companies advertise positions only on the net, based on the assumption that if you are not using the information highway, you do not meet a critical baseline requirement.

Books that provide you with most of the information you will need regarding gaining corporate information and finding employment on-line include the *Resumes in Cyberspace* by Pat Criscito, *Electronic Job Search Revolution* by Joyce Lain Kennedy and Thomas J. Morrow, *Finding a Job on the Internet* by Alfred and Emily Glossbreiner, *Hook Up, Get Hired* by Joyce Lain Kennedy, *Be Your Own Headhunter Online* by Pam Dixon and Sylvia Tiersten, and *The Online Jobsearch Companion* by James Gonyea. Many services are free, and companies looking for specific employees often list positions on their Web home pages (see the Appendix).

To get the jump on everyone else, following the newspapers to learn who has recently won a large contract is the most obvious tip-off regarding companies soon to be hiring.

Any company listed as among the fastest growing by any of the various business magazines or papers are likely to be in a hiring mode—employee number changes are frequently mentioned. The lists come out frequently, and libraries store back issues of most sources. All are usually available on-line. Easier still is using daily stock quotes to find a job. You can search on-line any of the stock exchanges. Look for companies with a big 52-week high and low spread. If the stock closed near the high, the company is doing well and likely hiring.

On-line employment will not entirely replace word-of-mouth referrals or references but will often be used as a supplement. Hiring through newspapers was too expensive and inefficient. Fax machines would go crazy with resumes, phone lines would get jammed, people would show up in large numbers at reception desks, and thousands of resumes would have to be sorted through. Now search engines on the Internet can scan fifty thousand resumes in less than two seconds, looking for five key hiring criteria. If a company wishes to remain anonymous, there are on-line job listing places that will electronically file the resumes for you. Eventually everyone will be expected to include a five-minute self-presentation video on-line as well.

Networking on-line is becoming a wonderful way to tap into diverse and unexpected sources of connection and information both inside and outside companies. Now that it is possible to talk on the telephone over the net, written exchanges in forums are bound to spill over into telephone conversations and eventually videoconferencing. On-line networking is risk-free since you can decide to remain anonymous or just to follow discussions others are having. The fact that the discussions are kept on file for about a week makes it easier to jump in and out at your convenience. Increasingly, people will find jobs by this means.

Other Uses of the Network

The value of networking extends well beyond facilitating career success. It leads to more appropriate jobs, faster promotion, greater job security—but more importantly, it leads to lower levels of stress, a longer life, and greater happiness.

Networking acts both as a means of getting you into the kinds of jobs you truly want and as a psychological safety net. It allows you to benchmark yourself and the companies you are involved with so that you can make decisions that are in your best interest. People who are happiest in life are self-monitoring in nature. They are continually noticing the degree of fit between themselves and their circumstances. They adjust their behavior to meet the needs of the situation, but they also try to navigate themselves closer to more suitable environments.

These people have always moved from one job to another, either to seek a new challenge or to find a more appropriate position for someone with their talents. Through this process, they end up in the kinds of positions they have always wanted. In contrast, those people who have worried the most about job security have proved to be the most unhappy people of all, because they will stick with an inappropriate job until retirement.

No one has job security anymore, so we are forced to be self-monitoring. Networking is the best way in which to monitor yourself because it alone is capable of providing continual feedback from many diverse sources both inside and outside an organization. Coupled with your values, goals, and vision, it keeps you on target by always letting you know the lay of the land and how much progress you are making toward your destination. It also provides you with the leveraging power of teams, since everyone in your network is part of your team.

Doris Lee McCoy in her book *Megatraits* identifies the following as the key traits of successful people: they are persistent; enjoy their work; have high-self esteem and a positive attitude; use negative experiences to discover their strengths; are decisive, disciplined goal-setters; have integrity and help others to succeed; take risks; have developed good communication and problem-solving skills; surround themselves with competent, responsible, supportive people; are healthy, have high energy, and schedule time to renew; believe in God, a higher power, and sometimes plain luck; have a sense of purpose and a desire to contribute to society; often challenge traditional concepts; are constantly coming up with innovative, fresh ideas; are able to shift gears easily; begin companies at any age; often chose not to retire at sixty-five; and schedule time for education though they are always learning.

Charles Garfield in his book *Peak Performers* adds to the success attribute roster: self-management through self-mastery, change management, team building and playing, results in real time, and missions that motivate. Rosabeth Moss Kanter in her book *World Class* stresses the importance of concepts, competence, and connection as the necessary ingredients for world-class competition. All of the foregoing characteristics are based on learning, inspiration, and mutual support.

Networking provides the environment for all of these traits to develop, especially the ability to shift gears quickly and manage change, which will often be required in the future. People you know can help you learn whatever it is you need to acquire in order to make the necessary transitions.

Ultimately it is people who inspire one another through a sense of common purpose. By supporting one another, we make the world a more welcoming and comforting place to compete in. Fortunately competition is not a zero-sum game—that is, one person need not win at another's expense.

So long as we continue to learn from one another, we naturally increase the amount of wealth to be shared by all. Perhaps one of the best and unexpected benefits of networking is the number of genuine friendships that end up emerging given the common interests and purposes eventually uncovered. It is a much less stressful world when we know that there are many people in our network who are willing to help in whatever way they can.

Marketing Yourself

Your primary loyalty is not to any particular job or company but to your career, which can end up being a snakes-and-ladders affair. Both you and your career are your business, and your network is your market. The more you network, the greater the likelihood that your career will have many ladders and few snakes.

Career entrepreneurship involves learning how to position yourself much the same way a company positions itself or its products or services in keeping with future trends. Just as products have life cycles that must be renewed for continued success, so must you engage in continuous improvement so that you can always claim to be "new and improved."

Regardless of how wonderful your achievements are, they are of little consequence unless the rest of the hiring world (your network) knows of them as well. Marketing yourself and networking effectively are the ultimate customer service challenge. In both cases, you need to engage in soft selling since these are long-range strategies. As such, the sale is more of an intangible one based on honesty, integrity, concept, competence, and connections.

In addition, such a sale is always exploratory or experimental in nature because it is somewhat unclear who will be the eventual buyers. The focus needs to be on human bonding and friendship, with the hope that taking a keen interest in others and making them aware of your hopes and aspirations on behalf of yourself or your company will lead you to those who can be of most assistance. Everything is done in the spirit of trying to help out one another. Almost everyone is receptive to people who take this approach to marketing themselves or networking.

Marketing and networking are matchmaking activities much like dating or life itself. They are sorting-out processes helping you get closer to where you or your company want to go, as long as you monitor the proper fit at all times. It is in trying to see if there is some common ground that the creative renewal process takes place.

All people become a potential solution to a problem since they may know someone you need to meet even if they themselves cannot help you directly. If you ask for enough directions, you can usually find out how to get somewhere. Like trying to solve a jigsaw puzzle, each person plays an important role in helping you try to grasp the dimensions of the problem overall and the most likely people, companies, ways or places where solutions are to be found. In other words, it is through your immersion in the search process that multiple solutions present themselves.

There are many ways to network and market yourself. Perhaps the most creative ways will emerge through the information highway; however, for now, it is worth remembering that successful marketing and networking are "wide-band" activities. They must be fully interactive in order to succeed. Just like excellent customer service, both sides need to feel that they trust one another and will mutually benefit from investing some time and energy in the relationship. Although many people may be willing to pass on to you the weak ties, you still need to establish some sense of rapport before they genuinely try to think of acquaintances who may be able to help you.

If you do spend the time and energy to develop key relationships, you will find yourself in the situation of most successful real estate agents and opinion leaders—everybody calls them for advice and business. Managing your career means creating and maintaining strategic relationships. To succeed in the future, most people will need to spend as much time managing their relationships as they do upgrading their skills. Both are continuous improvement processes that eventually lead to quantum career leaps once the appropriate connections or settings are found.

Just as all major innovations come from a combination of complementary developments, career success is tied to finding the right places to be in given the marketable skills you have. Marketing yourself through networking will help you find those places faster, especially if you have a vision you are trying to attain. Remember, luck always favors the prepared and the persistent. By tapping into just the first two layers of your network, you can possibly reach up to 12,500,000 people indirectly. Imagine if you were to go a few layers deeper than that. At that point, almost everyone in the United States would likely be included.

The connections are there, so just figure out how to access them and make use of them. After all, that is the true challenge facing us all—and it is what career entrepreneurism and continuous learning are all about.

In a world where people will alternate between different forms of employment (self-employment or contract, full-time or part-time, employment agency or direct response to an ad, etc.), it pays to increase the number of options available to you so that you have a true choice as to how you would prefer to be employed. Freedom is the ability to choose.

By improving your networking and marketing skills, you are giving yourself the broadest possible reach in making choices and finding new undiscovered options. You are also ensuring that your choices are based on more complete information regarding positions sought—something vital to upping the odds of succeeding in any new assignment undertaken.

By using your connections to the fullest, you will be able to deliver heroic customer service both inside and outside your organization without considerable effort. In a value-added era, where exceeding customer expectations determines the competitive edge, having the networking resources to do so at your disposal can make you a prized employee. It can also pave the way for promotion or more interesting and challenging personal and professional development opportunities that will help realize your vision far faster than merely improving your technical abilities.

The creative and entrepreneurial challenge is to leverage your relationships so that everyone expects to comes out ahead. By doing so, you are making the future a more welcome place. Choices tied to positive expectations are usually self-fulfilling, so success is actually something you have every right to expect if you do all of the groundwork. Just focus on making and maintaining the necessary connections and communicating the mutually beneficial opportunities that you would like to explore, and the rest will take care of itself.

As we will see in the next chapter, entrepreneurs are in fact the most effective orchestrators of relationships and interdependencies because they fashion and grow them into new "wholes" or enterprises. They are the gardeners of the economy who sow the seeds of all our future visions and interrelationships.

CHAPTER 10

Meeting the Entrepreneurial Challenge

Uncertainty is an invitation to innovate, to create; uncertainty is the blank page in the author's typewriter, the granite block before the sculptor, the capital in the hands of the investor, or the problem challenging the inventive mind of a scientist or an engineer. In short, uncertainty is the opportunity to make the world a better place.

—Walter Wriston, former CEO, Citicorp Bank

Work Satisfaction in a Changing Environment

During any time of change or uncertainty, every action—including the decision not to act—assumes a greater amount of risk. At least before, you could always wait to see which side was likely to win before jumping on a bandwagon, but nowadays you would probably be too late if you waited that long. Things just change too quickly. Given that we are likely to be immersed in various synchronous change processes over the next fifteen to twenty years, all people, but particularly managers and entrepreneurs, will need to be able to include risk management in their resume or skill portfolio.

The increasing uncertainty and unpredictability is scaring many managers in corporations who became successful by hedging their bets. As James Emshoff claims in his book, *The*

New Rules of the Game, "The global challenges of the 1990s are scary for companies stuck in the 1980s culture and staffed with terrified, permanent fence sitters. And they are hardly encouraged by the fact that many people who opted to play it safe in the 1980s today sit in senior management positions. They were rewarded for running the business smoothly, for not taking chances." Larger, mature corporations, in particular, are prey to this kind of play-it-safe mentality.

As it turns out, most people do not actually enjoy working in environments that are overly predictable. In 1987, *Inc.* magazine, in conjunction with the Hay Group consulting company, did a comparison between the employees of the large Fortune 500 companies with those of the much smaller Inc. 500. Despite suffering from lower pay, fewer benefits, and fewer opportunities for advancement, most people working for smaller companies reported extremely higher overall job satisfaction. Why? Smaller company employees felt as though they mattered more and their company was doing something of significance. They also found the work to be more challenging, their ideas more readily listened to and accepted, and a greater sense of accomplishment and mutual respect. Moreover, they tended to identify more with the smaller companies and used inclusive terms such as "we" or "us" in referring to the organizations.

Employees of smaller companies also felt that they gave their customers better service. According to a Forum Corporation study in 1988, if employees felt that their company treated their customers well, they were much less likely to plan on leaving the company within the next year, unlike those in less customer-caring environments. Not surprisingly, the way most companies treat their customers is an excellent indicator of how they treat their employees as well.

The common disaffection with finding career success in larger corporations is the central theme of John Kotter's book, *The New Rules,* in which he traces what has happened with the

Harvard graduating MBA class of 1974. By 1991, only 23 percent were still in big business. But 62 percent were in small businesses by 1992 with over 40 percent actually having become entrepreneurs. If engaging in entrepreneurial-like activities—for example, leading business growth or negotiating large business deals—were included, roughly 70 percent of the 1974 class would qualify. Only 8 percent were involved as executives in manufacturing by 1992, although roughly half of those were in entrepreneurial ventures. Most of them pursued the service sector, where the opportunities were greater and barriers to start up were lower. The graduates who stuck with the more traditional big businesses earned substantially less money, had less authority or power, had more work difficulties, and reported less job satisfaction. They merely inherited the difficulties and lack of promotional opportunities that accompanied the loss of over 2.5 million jobs at Fortune 500 companies between 1973 and 1991.

Indeed, the percentage of the population working for Fortune 500 companies fell from 19.4 percent in 1974 to 10.9 percent in 1992. Those in smaller businesses were three times as likely to have real positions of power and far higher compensations levels, with the top 10 percent likely to make over one hundred times what the bottom 10 percent will over their lifetimes. Whereas, only 13 percent were general managers in 1975, over 50 percent were managers by 1992, reflecting their new entrepreneurial leadership roles.

According to Kotter's study, people who go to Harvard Business School are typically very talented, ambitious, and competitive. Most of them soon realized that climbing up an ever-narrowing ladder was going to take forever and that most of their talents would be wasted in the meantime. Smaller firms gave them wider latitude in using their own judgment, seeing projects through from beginning to end, and learning more through greater experimentation and immediate feedback. Thus, graduates who went on to pursue entrepreneurial activities cared less about security but much more about autonomy than those who confined themselves to the traditional career paths.

Their counterparts in the larger companies lacked authority, generally found their roles too ambiguous, and complained of too many conflicting demands. Their lack of ambition and preoccupation with security played a major role in undermining their level of work satisfaction by encouraging them to remain in undesirable situations.

Determinants of Success

What were the key determinants of success among the class of '74? According to Kotter, they included an ability to turn adversity into learning experiences:

> By not running away from tough times, and by reflecting seriously on their experiences, they grow. Low standards, a weak drive, and a lack of self-confidence in competitive situations undermine lifelong learning. Without real ambition, painful episodes from which one can learn so much are avoided both on and off the job. And with avoidance comes stagnation.

Attitude toward risk and learning opportunities seem to be the major factors in the decision-making process for those who cling to unsatisfactory jobs and those who carve out their own future. The biblical parable of the servant who buries the master's talents in the ground versus the servant who takes a risk and invests the master's money seems apt. Burying one's talent in exchange for holding onto a job leads only to a false sense of security. Such people are becoming more unemployable when the day of reckoning arrives. Many downsized middle managers are quite surprised to learn that their talents no longer command a handsome salary.

According to University of Toronto professor Anil Verma, 50 percent of the existing work force will be downsized over the next ten years. Postponing the inevitable is the most career-limiting option of all. Just as people who do not strategically network and market themselves in diverse ways end up creating their own glass ceiling, those who fail to constantly improve their talents or marketable skills will run up against a brick wall.

Growth or evolution, on the other hand, depends more on experimentation and error management. As Kevin Kelly notes, "Even the most brilliant act of genius, in the final analysis, is an act of trial and error. 'To be an Error and to be Cast out is a part of God's Design,' wrote the visionary poet William Blake. Evolution can be thought of as systematic error management."

Using Risk

Deciding which action to take or road to head down involves risk because risk is nothing more than some uncertainty regarding the outcome of events. During periods of change, all outcomes are to varying degrees uncertain, so there is no way of avoiding risk. Minimizing uncertainty, where possible, is actually less desirable than ensuring that at least the potential rewards are commensurate with the level of risk. Joint ventures and alliances are often undertaken as a means of spreading out risk and speeding up the experimentation process—which amounts to managing but not avoiding risk. When the rewards of undertaking a joint venture far outweigh the risks of doing so, then not to enter into some kind of collaborative activity is far riskier.

As Matthew Kiernan asserts in *Get Innovative or Get Dead,*

> The emerging rigors of the twenty-first century hyper-competition leave us little choice. We must experiment, and experimentation inherently carries with it the near certainty of at least occasional failure. In a truly entrepreneurial culture, failure tends to be regarded as a learning opportunity, a necessary precondition to eventual success. Entrepreneurs instinctively understand the

> importance of real-world experimentation, trial and error and speed. Get the new concept out into the real world, test it, refine it and then get the next iteration out—fast. Experimentation, feedback, failure, learning, adjustment, action. That's what successful entrepreneurship is all about.

Life has a messiness about it that is unavoidable, but as long as we keep trying to muddle through as best we can and continue to try out new approaches that seem to make sense in terms of our vision, we probably will get to where we want to go. Even natural evolution does not lead to neat solutions. Most evolved species are not models of elegant design and function, but they nevertheless work quite effectively. As Laura Henderson, a successful entrepreneur and CEO, elaborates, "The biggest risk I take is managing my own way. A lot of what I've done contradicts popular management thinking. To manage this organization well, I needed to manage in a way consistent with who I am. When you're truly an entrepreneur, you don't always know what you're doing. If you're willing to make mistakes doing it 'your way' and learning from them, then I say, go for it!"

Grow with Your Intuition

Going with your intuition does not mean always taking a flier on every hunch; instead, it implies that after you have done all of your homework, you may be wiser to base your final decision on intuition, rather than strictly on the numbers or the facts on hand. Why?

When dealing with the complex situations that characterize modern times, you can never get sufficient information in time to make a fully informed decision. You are forced to do the best you can with whatever resources you have at your disposal in the time frame allotted. So, in one sense, we are all being forced to fly by the seat of our pants, or as Richard Branson, CEO of the Virgin Group boldly states, "Everything is experimental." This is why Lawrence Bossidy, CEO of Allied Signal, insists that, "At the end of the day, you bet on people, not on strategies."

Every venture capitalist will tell you the same thing: if an idea makes good investment sense, you are really just betting on the ability and commitment of the person to deliver, despite the unavoidable birth pains and difficulties that lie ahead.

The ability to monitor the effects of your actions and make corresponding adjustments is more important than the decision to act. Continuous learning ends up taking the place of formal planning. Overall direction is determined by our vision of what we are trying to accomplish.

Remember that successful visionary companies are always willing to revise strategies as necessary to meet current and developing situations—both Wal-Mart and GE have weekly, open-forum meetings precisely for this purpose.

Perhaps a helpful analogy is the one about people who fish for a living. They are not just fair-weather fishers. They head out in rough weather and trust in their ability to cope with whatever surprises nature has in store. Implicitly, they know that they will be able to figure out what needs to be done when the time comes. In other words, they rely on the accumulated knowledge derived from their experience to avoid unnecessary risks and to take measures to reduce unanticipated uncertainty. The key ingredient is the accumulation of previous risk-taking experience.

Entrepreneurs do not see themselves as risk-takers; indeed, in surveys they come out as being risk-averse, or the opposite of gamblers. They minimize risk in their minds by placing greater faith in their competence and ability to learn as they go. Obviously, they love the creative challenge of successfully taking advantage of what seems like golden opportunities. The more faith they have in the opportunity, the less risk there appears to be involved.

Learn from Your Failures

Failure, to entrepreneurs, means only that the risk associated with any new venture will be reduced by what they have learned through past mistakes. No wonder that the average successful entrepreneur has failed two or three times prior to eventually succeeding. Bill Clinton claims he learned the political lessons he needed to win the presidency when he lost in a previous bid to become governor of Arkansas. Abraham Lincoln was no different since he finished eighth in a field of thirteen candidates in his first run for political office.

Each new innovation is an example of a dynamic risk since it breaks with the status quo. Failure is almost inevitable since methods or products are unproven. The key to success is to speed up the rate of failure so that enough can be learned to quickly capture the market with a more appropriate version. Both Toshiba and Sony are well-known for their rapid evolutionary strategy of releasing a wide array of products continually in Japan and keeping only those that meet with customer approval.

All forms of continuous improvement involve continuous risk-taking. The Baldridge award-winning Ritz-Carlton hotel chain found that both quality and employee satisfaction increased when a newly introduced continuous quality improvement program encouraged staff to take greater risks in an effort to improve service.

With continuous risk-taking on a daily level comes the need for continuous learning. In an era of innovation, the person who is the fastest up the learning curve wins. In his book *The Peter Principle,* Laurence Peter noted: "There are two kinds of failures, those who thought and never did, and those who did and never thought." True failure, in other words, is failure to act and failure to learn from your actions.

Failure must act as the whack on the side of the head needed to stimulate the learning process. As Gene Calvert mentions in *Highwire Management*, "Find a manager with excellent judgment, and you will meet one who made many mistakes." As we head into periods of uncertainty, more people will be hired for their judgment abilities regarding risk management. If you don't know how to take risks, how are you going to be able to manage them?

The Importance of Timing

Obviously, no one would recommend that you take on tasks guaranteed to fail, but it is important to be stretching yourself continually in each assignment. Everyone must learn how to fail selectively—that is, to fail in ways that are acceptable and that will be viewed in the context of your previous successes. So timing plays an important role as does how you fail. You need to be asking yourself if you can afford to fail in certain ways at the moment. Al Neuharth, who created *USA Today*, believes that you should take larger risks earlier in your career (before reaching forty) since you will then have a chance to learn more, yet still have time left to recover—an evolutionary strategy similar to that of Sony and Toshiba in their product development.

As it turns out, people tend to have more sympathy for people who fail in big ways. Larger undertakings are seen as being riskier and more liable to failure, so it is not entirely unexpected. But people admire anyone who tries to climb Mount Everest. If Jack Welch had failed in his attempt to turn GE from a rigid bureaucracy into a boundaryless company, most would end up blaming GE and not Jack Welch.

You tend to learn more lessons from failure on a larger scale. For example, if you do your utmost to achieve an ambitious goal and humbly explain to others what valuable lessons you learned in the process, they will appreciate the redeeming aspects of the failure. Rarely is there such thing as a total failure. There are almost always secondary gains. In many cases, these secondary gains lay the groundwork for a large subsequent success.

One fast track IMBer made a rather big mistake costing the company many millions of dollars. When reporting to his superior, he was sure that he was going to be fired; however, his boss said, "Fire you? We can't afford to fire you. We just spent millions of dollars educating you." When people who possess creativity, competence, integrity, and commitment fail, the ultimate blame is rarely placed on their shoulders. Honest mistakes are allowed to happen, since it is assumed that the same thing could have happened to anyone else as well.

Coping with Fear

Perhaps the biggest obstacle to risk-taking comes from the emotions we feel in connection with uncertainty. As Dr. Lawrence Peters observes, "Success goes to the head, failure to your heart." It is necessary to get beyond ego considerations in order both to take risks and to learn from mistakes. If the pain of making mistakes blocks the ability to learn from them because of the humiliation felt, you are obviously personalizing failure too much—something women have a strong tendency to do.

Most men blame failure on bad luck and things beyond their control, whereas many women assume they are to blame when things go wrong. (Conversely, most men take all the credit for any successes, yet many women assume that circumstances favored their efforts.) Many people also assume that they should have known what in hindsight may be more obvious, but that is simply the way life is. Everything is obvious once you have learned to recognize the ultimate meaning of what originally were only partially-formed signs.

Dealing with fear by acting always ends up reducing fear. Waiting for fear to disappear is the equivalent of waiting until you die. Stress and fear are part of life's vitality—unfortunately, we still possess some of the vestigial qualities associated with our cave-dwelling past.

In the past, fears were exaggerated because there were many real threats to life and limb. Nowadays, many people still possess the same powerful emotional responses, even though these fight-or-flight reactions are completely out of proportion to the kinds of risks we are discussing. Furthermore, these risks can be minimized only by acting in ways that provide us with a reality check that puts them back into a manageable perspective. Children are plagued by nightmares because they lack the firm grasp of reality that older people possess, so there is little to curtail their imagination or fears.

Failure to act has the same magnifying power in the mind of adults because no sense of proportion has been established.

As Susan Jeffers suggests in *Feel the Fear and Do It Anyway*, "People who refuse to take risks live with a feeling of dread that is far more severe than what they would feel if they took the risks necessary to make them less helpless—only they don't do it."

Many people are afraid that their incompetence will be revealed if they take risks, so they would rather harbor feelings of inferiority than risk exposure. Ironically, this fear is even shared by many successful people who often feel as if they are impostors who ended up where they are by luck.

If you can't be honest about your weaknesses, you won't take the necessary steps to improve upon them, which only makes matters worse. Ironically, many people feel they need permission just to be human beings—something revealed by the extraordinary power that confession can play in people's lives.

Start Small

As with most things in life, it is usually best to begin by taking smaller risks before graduating to the big league. Building on many small successes creates the resilience needed for the setbacks that inevitably occur. But it is also possible to minimize risk, even in larger undertakings.

It is possible to manage risk better by becoming fully informed; soliciting opinions from a number of experts and asking them about their confidence in their own projections; bringing key players on board; outlining the risks completely in advance to everyone; assessing the likely impact on different areas of the company or your life; and clarifying and prioritizing goals, problems, potential solutions, resources available, steps along the way, time frames, and commitments. Even decision-to-abort-the-mission criteria should exist along with contingency plans that you can fall back on.

Aside from these common-sense strategic planning approaches, it is also a good idea to become better at understanding the dynamics of the forces that are rewriting the rules and changing the playing field on an ongoing basis. It is important to examine our assumptions regarding the changes taking place and to gain a better understanding of exactly what rules have changed.

Entrepreneurial Opportunities

> *Nothing is as important to the state of small business—or to the health of the U.S. economy—as the rate at which entrepreneurs are creating new companies.*
>
> —*Inc.* Magazine

In the 1960s, almost half of all men in corporations succeeded by moving up the corporate ladder, but in the 1990s only one-third will find success by this means. Along with a growing number of women, they are starting their own businesses instead as a way of taking control over their careers and lives.

Each year in America, 800,000 to 900,000 new companies with employees are created. In fact, 4 percent of the population say that they are in the process of starting a company—one-third of whom are women. Among college students, 38 percent said that owning their own business was the best route to success versus only 24 percent who expressed a preference for working in a large company. Indeed, 80 percent of all new jobs come from small companies with fewer than 100 employees—only 70,000 companies employ more than 100 people and only 14,000 employ more than 500. Between now and 2005, health and business services are expected to account for one-quarter of all new jobs created—most in the small-business sector.

In 1970, only sixteen business schools offered small-business entrepreneurship programs, while today there are over four hundred such programs. By the end of the decade, franchises are expected to triple in number.

There are many myths concerning the risks of starting a new business. It is commonly assumed that over the long run most small businesses fail; however, this notion is misleading. As it turns out, the companies that were most likely to go out of business did not employ anyone other than the owner. In many cases, the owner folded one company to start another (for instance, closing a typewriter repair shop to start up a laser-jet printer toner-cartridge recycling business) or take a business elsewhere (for example, closing down a restaurant in one location to start up another in a different location).

According to David Kirchhoff, author of *Entrepreneurship and Dynamic Capitalism*, only 18 percent of all new businesses actually end up failing. Most of the others going out of business merely closed up shop voluntarily and did not leave creditors in the lurch. In 1994, Joseph Duncan and Doug Handler of Dun & Bradstreet found that roughly 70 percent of all companies created in 1985 were still in business in 1994, with smaller companies having a higher survival rate than the larger ones with their 50 percent failure rate. So starting a business is not such a risky proposition as is commonly perceived.

Outsourcing

The major trend driving the resurgence in small business growth is outsourcing. Since it is not possible to be the best at every aspect of an operation anymore, it makes more sense to hire whoever is the best to handle that area of expertise. In addition, trying to do everything in-house is becoming something of a management nightmare. Even staff functions that fail to earn one-third of their revenues externally are not likely to be world competitive and should be outsourced.

Moreover, in a just-in-time era, outsourcing allows companies to acquire the services they need when they need them without delay—and dispense with them should business move in other directions or take a momentary downturn. It also spreads out the risk and frees up resources to be used for other strategic purposes that are more in line with a company's core competitive advantage.

A 1993 Coopers & Lybrand study of 392 companies found that 65 percent of the fastest growing firms outsourced. In addition, their revenues were 22 percent higher, capital investment was higher, and their growth rate was 5.2 percent greater—all despite having the same number of employees. Their relationships with their suppliers were also predictably much closer.

As Van Honeycut, president and CEO of Computer Sciences Corporation, notes, "Outsourcing is being looked at more in the context of a corporation's effort to restructure itself."

The Computer Sciences Corporation has found that 63 percent of American and 72 percent of European companies either outsource or are planning to do so. Over $38 billion was spent in 1995 in America on information technology outsourcing, according to an Outsourcing Institute/Frost & Sullivan Market Intelligence survey.

With product delivery becoming the next area of competitive advantage after quality, we are seeing a huge growth in full-service logistics outsourcing—which in 1993 accounted for $16 billion of the $390 billion in freight expense by U.S. companies, according to Case Information Systems.

Large institutions, such as hospitals, now outsource many business, support, and health care services. According to a 1995 study by MATRIXX marketing Inc., customer service—that is, complaint handling, sales and order taking, sample fulfillment, and product information—is now being outsourced by 44 percent of companies, with 5 percent completely outsourcing these functions.

Spin-Offs

Even large companies have caught the entrepreneurial spirit and use "intrapreneurship" to obtain the same advantages as outsourcing. Bell Atlantic, once part of AT&T's stodgy machine bureaucracy, now requires that training, accounting, and business research market charge for their services, allowing those it serves inside the company to purchase these services outside the organization if desired. Bell Atlantic also has its Champion program, which provides employees with capital, mentoring, and training to develop new services and products. Since 1988, there have been 250 champions whose activities are now contributing over $100 million to the company.

Xerox has taken its organization to the next evolutionary stage. In 1989, it launched its Xerox Technology Ventures (XTV) program, which acts as a venture capital fund for its employees to start up businesses, which are subsequently spun-off on their own. If the venture is successful, those primarily involved on the boards and management teams are eligible for a 20 percent equity position. Outside investors are welcome, although Xerox maintains a majority shareholder position. So far, eight out of the twelve start-ups are quite profitable, with three on the verge of going public. There are no second chances allowed, and those out on a limb do not necessarily have a warm spot waiting for them back inside the company should things not pan out. Those who are enterprising enough to recognize what an incredible opportunity this represents end up with a company that has instant status through its association with Xerox and access to Xerox's customers, managerial talent, and additional capital. Xerox, for its part, retains an ownership position in the commercialization of many of its innovations—something that other companies in the past did better than Xerox (for example, Canon with its photocopiers, which were originally invented by Xerox).

New England-based Thermo Electron has even taken the spin-off concept to the limit—it has spun off the R&D division, which is the major source of intellectual capital in this science-based company. As an entity, it now consists of a number of individual companies that are publicly traded with a parent company that acts solely as a venture capitalist. In much the same spirit, Brazil's Semco had already spun off 50 percent of its manufacturing to former employees by 1994 and plans to increase that to 70 percent very shortly. As CEO Ricardo Semler states, "I just own the capital, not the company." To date, only one spin-off has failed.

Venture Capital

Even the venture capital game has taken a new twist with companies such as Teknekron Corp., a Berkeley, California firm that has had an annual revenue growth rate of 40 percent since 1968. Teknekron acts as both a venture capitalist and an entrepreneurial incubator for innovations developed in universities and company research labs. It provides the linkup with customers, leading—edge experts, and marketing channels. The company's 50 percent success rate is 400 to 500 percent higher than the industry average for high-tech start-ups.

As with Xerox, having a guardian angel certainly reduces the risks of starting up a new business considerably. Or as the company's founder and CEO, Harvey Wagner, notes, "Identifying and nurturing entrepreneurs and connecting them to sources and users of innovation are the open corporation's raison d'être and the main driving force of corporate growth."

Taking Advantage of the Trends

But how can the average person take advantage of these trends in a risk-averse way? Simply copy a successful franchise or business that has not moved into your area, assuming that the market conditions are appropriate. Copying proven success makes the most sense for those who are not capable of coming up with some completely new, innovative solution to a current consumer need or competitive business issue.

As more people leave big cities, thanks to the ability to work remotely, many business opportunities will arise to allow a transferal of what has worked successfully in larger cities to growing smaller towns. However, you will need to thoroughly research an opportunity's feasibility. Whereas, franchises have head offices that specialize in researching ideal locations for their outlets, you will have to provide this function for yourself. If the conditions are appropriate for a cloning strategy, then you only need the venture capital to get yourself started. Fortunately, the U.S. has easily the world's largest, most liquid source of venture capital (see Appendix).

The most risk-free entrepreneurial option would have to be multilevel marketing or networking, since most of these opportunities require only initial investments of between $100 to $300, and they no longer require that you fill up your basement with product or retail their products directly—you can succeed just by getting more people involved.

Amway is by far the most successful among a growing number of companies trying to bypass conventional distribution channels as a means of passing on savings to its own distributors. Although definitely not for everyone, this kind of marketing is risk-free and can allow those who buy into the program fully to retire within five to ten years. To make it work, however, you need to have even more missionary zeal than is characteristic of the most visionary companies. This is achieved by playing upon the egalitarian notion that you can succeed only if you help others you bring on board to succeed. This communitarian form of capitalism has a strong populist or grass-roots appeal to many who view it as merging of capitalism and Christian values.

The ability to retire after five years or so of living, breathing, and sleeping, "the plan," regardless of your current state of employment, holds great attraction for those who want a sense of running their own business without the risk normally associated with any start-up operation. Essentially, it is a low-budget franchising concept that is ideal for anyone with sufficient drive and the willingness to become completely immersed in both its culture and marketing approach (see Appendix). Indeed, most businesses these days require a kind of evangelism, as Guy Kawasaki notes in *Selling the Dream,* "Evangelism means convincing people to believe in your product or ideas as much as you do, by using fervor, zeal, guts, and cunning to mobilize your customers and staff into becoming as passionate about a cause as you are."

The most important question you need to ask yourself before taking the plunge is whether you have the endurance to run a marathon—the average entrepreneur puts in a 58-hour week—since the key determining factors in the success of most new ventures are dedication and persistence. As Harry S. Dent observes in his book, *Job Shock*, "Success is going enthusiastically from failure to failure. Giving up too soon is perhaps the biggest single reason I have seen entrepreneurs fail, even those who had promising products or innovations."

Just remember that Colonel Sanders received 1,008 rejections for his famous chicken recipe before finally striking a deal.

Building Your Business Skills

Obviously, anyone deciding to start up a business needs to have a broad spectrum of business skills; however, before long this will be expected of everyone in the workplace.

For those who prefer the turnkey approach, buying a franchise helps solve many of the questions of how to run a business. For others, working out of their homes is becoming a viable option.

As companies try to reduce their real estate overhead costs, more and more they will be asking people to work out of their homes, on the road, or directly with customers. American Express increased its productivity from 25 to 30 percent by having its phone travel agents work out of their homes to reduce office politics and other distractions.

As companies become more virtual in this sense, they may also become virtual altogether—hiring a larger portion of their staff on a project basis. For many, then, working for themselves may not even be an option but an inevitability—at least for some parts of their working life. So be prepared to become a one-person, cross-functional team.

After all, all companies will be looking for well-rounded entrepreneurial qualities in their outsourcing relationships and in their employees. In a sense, you are being asked to become a consultant or contractor: either you are fulfilling an outsourcing function, or you are involved in the managing of those who are. For instance, over 25 percent of the Harvard MBA '74 class ended up consulting alone.

One of the most important things to bear in mind if you are trying to start your own business is the full effect of the information highway in about five years when it is likely to begin to become the main means by which most commerce is conducted. At that point, all previous assumptions regarding business as usual will disappear, so be sure to position yourself appropriately to take advantage of a just-in-time world where shelf-space is unlimited and everything is interactive. Avoid becoming roadkill on the information highway.

Last, but not least, make sure that you take into account the increasing globalization of trade and careers, the subject of the next chapter. Going into business is likely to mean setting up shop in the global village. You may never even see the people or companies you will actually be competing against.

The idea of becoming a big fish in a little pond is rapidly disappearing. To survive, you are going to have to join a bigger school of fish. In the age of the networked organization, you had better be prepared to look for those who can help your business or career, regardless of where they might be in the world.

As Rosabeth Moss Kanter notes in *World Class,*

> Competitiveness is network embedded, a matter of connections across companies. For innovation, an entrepreneur must create, manage, and recombine sets of relationships with suppliers. The ability to glue together external expertise and capabilities in original and unique ways is a key factor for innovation. Entrepreneurs act as "orchestrators of inter-firm linkages."

For example, Rhoda Makoff, founder of R&D Laboratories, spotted a niche too small for big pharmaceutical companies to go after—vitamin and nutrition supplements for dialysis patients. Nonetheless, she convinced pharmaceutical companies to manufacture and package her eighteen products, which she then sold to 200 drug wholesalers for warehousing and distribution. By being able to leverage these relationships, the company was able to increase sales in 1994 by 84 percent with the introduction of two new products.

So rather than sticking close to the shore looking for shelter, we are all going to have to make ourselves more seaworthy and then head out to the open seas—often as part of an armada of like-minded companies or individuals—if we hope to remain competitive and in business.

Fortunately, the rewards will likely far exceed the risks if you go with trends and use your best judgment. Even better, if you are part of an innovative process of creating trends and linkages, you will be able to carve out your niche in a world that is in the process of reshaping itself. As MIT economist Lester Thurow said, "Wealth is created by the capitalization of innovation."

Time is of the essence, however. A study by McKinsey & Co. found that companies that met their product development target dates outperformed those that were six months late by eight times. Even products delivered 50 percent over budget

— but on time—enjoyed this competitive advantage. So begin your entrepreneurial journey today.

But don't forget to consider global opportunities. The Internet allows access to an unlimited number of market niches that previously were too hard to identify or serve. Now is the time to take advantage of these global opportunities since entrepreneurs are the ones who benefit the most from the opening up of new frontiers. Stake your claim before everyone else does—even if it means taking advantage of global career opportunities by working for someone else. For we all need to acquire a global mindset along with an entrepreneurial spirit.

PART IV

Going Global

CHAPTER 11

The Transcultural Imperative

Transnational corporations view the world as one vast, essentially seamless market in which all major decisions are grounded solely in the desire to gain a global competitive advantage.

—Henry Wendt, CEO of SmithKline Beecham

In the twenty-first century, going global will not be a choice but an imperative because almost all companies will be part of global supply or distribution chains and partnerships. Companies will have no choice but to follow growth opportunities wherever they may be, and in most cases, they are likely to be outside the U.S.

The World Bank predicts that by the year 2020, nine of the fifteen top economies in the world will be industrialized countries such as Indonesia, India, and China. India, for instance, despite its poverty, has a middle class equivalent to the size of the entire U.S. population. And more people in China receive Star TV than the population of Canada.

World trade, according to DRI/McGraw-Hill, is expanding by over 6 percent per year, which is more than twice the growth rate of the world's GNP. The United Nations found that there are over 37,000 transnational firms deriving from the world's fourteen wealthiest countries. According to the U.N.'s 1993 *World Investment Report,* the top one percent of multinational corporations own 50 percent of the 206,000 foreign-owned subsidiaries and affiliates worldwide. The biggest ones currently control roughly one-third of the world's private sector assets. In 1992, they controlled foreign direct investments worth $2 trillion, had annual sales worth $4.8 trillion, and employed 20 percent of all non-farm workers in developed countries and 10 percent of workers worldwide.

Already it is becoming difficult to tell the difference between domestic and foreign companies. Digital Equipment, Cray Research, Gillette, Motorola, Coca-Cola, and Exxon now generate over two-thirds of their revenues outside the U.S. The Ford 2000 project required that Ford merge its European and North American operations with its Asian and Latin American operations to follow suit shortly. In Asea Brown Boveri, a Swedish-Swiss firm, 80 percent of its managers communicate in English. Unilever presently is made up of over 500 companies in 75 countries.

It's even difficult to determine which country owns a company because most corporations' shares are held by people from around the world. Products themselves are researched, developed, designed, produced, assembled, and marketed throughout the world. As Labor Secretary Robert Reich suggests, it is getting harder to tell "who are they, and who are us."

Indeed, there is no longer really any domestic company of any importance, since any successful domestic company immediately catches the eye of foreign competitors who are quick to challenge its market position or enter its market. As domestic markets become more specialized and segmented, it is necessary to seek business abroad in order to expand or grow or earn. The U.S. now achieves 40 percent of its productivity growth by taking advantage of foreign innovations.

Becoming world class entails finding the best global sources for capital, technology, materials, and people. All companies must be continually surveying the global market place if they hope to offer the most innovative products with the highest quality and lowest price. Consequently, the wealth of a country is, as Reich insists, determined by its ability to add value to global economic services, processes, or products.

The Individual in a Global Environment

Individuals hoping to succeed and thrive in such a dynamic environment must develop a global mindset. According to Glen Fisher, author of *Mindsets: The Role of Culture and Perception in International Relations,* mindsets are "differing ways that the subject at hand is perceived, understood, and reasoned about."

Peter Senge in *The Fifth Discipline* talks about it as part of the need for a larger view of how things influence one another interdependently. In a global context, it requires having a big-picture outlook with respect to trends, both in the past and in the future. As indicated earlier, attitudes toward time can play an enormous role, both in the way situations are approached and how change is welcomed.

The need for such a global mindset is rapidly expanding now that exports are becoming the fastest growing and most profitable part of the economy. In 1996, the *Wall Street Journal* noted that, "Major corporations required candidates with international experience in 28 percent of senior-level searches last year, up from 4 percent in 1990."

The Global Personality

The personal characteristics of such individuals include knowledge (both specialized and in general regarding geopolitical, competitive, and market information) and high right- and left-brain conceptualization ability.

Flexibility is also essential—process must be trusted over structure, which tends to bias one in favor of one world view or one business or personal philosophy. Process is the means by which value is added and the way in which people are cross-functionally integrated around a business activity, such as the manufacturing process, customer service process, or strategic planning process. The nature of the work or process and not the job or structure defines what needs to happen in order to have everything flow together.

The challenge is to integrate the various processes synchronously and synergistically so that all interdependent aspects of a company are part of one's territory, thereby making structural boundaries irrelevant. In addition, one must possess sensitivity to cross-cultural issues—something that requires considerable ego strength and a solid sense of one's identity that respectfully takes into account the values and beliefs of others.

A well-developed intuitive ability to make judgments despite lacking adequate information is a natural requirement in a world built on shifting sands. Broad experience in a wide variety of organizational, cultural, and international business environments lays the foundation for such holistic, intuitive judgment ability—especially when ethical dilemmas inevitably arise.

When there is no one right answer to a problem, wisdom based on extensive experience is needed to make the best call.

The final personal characteristic is reflection, or the ability to learn continuously, since it is never possible to know enough in a changing world. Such learning requires "thinking outside the box" or getting enough distance to begin to see the overall pattern of relationships that is emerging. Partnerships and alliances with other companies and with the various surrounding communities are the best ways of gaining this kind of insight.

Gold-Collar Workers

Openness, playfulness, a trust and belief in human ingenuity or the creative process, a multidimensional perspective, an acceptance of an unlimited rangc of possibilities, plus a desire to transform the world by leveraging even apparently contradictory interdependencies are really the defining characteristics of the global mindset. As Stephen Rhinesmith, author of *A Managers's Guide to* Globalization, explains:

> A global manager needs to learn how to live with conflict management rather than resolution, must look for opportunity from diversity.... Ideally, a global mind does not coerce resolutions from opposite forces in life. Priorities may be set, but the concept of balance requires continued nurturing even for the interests not chosen. This is central for a global mindset, because it entails the simultaneous appreciation of contradictory ideas, [feelings and interests] in a way that energizes rather than paralyzes.... A global mindset recognizes and acknowledges that process is more powerful than structure and that organizational processes such as information and decision-making systems, not structure, are the key to organizational adaptability.... Teamwork and interdependence on others is a basic tenet of global management.... People with global mindsets flow with change as opportunity and are comfortable with surprises, ambiguity, and change. Global managers have experienced enough of the world to know that it is unpredictable because it is too complex; sometimes because it is simple, but different; and sometimes because it is unknowable.... People with global mindsets continuously seek to be open to themselves and others by rethinking boundaries, finding new meanings, and changing

> their directions and behavior. They are constantly searching for improvement in their own lives—not against surprises, but for surprises.... Global mindsets are not exclusive, but inclusive.... These are people who live life on many levels—physical, intellectual, emotional, and spiritual. The world is their playground and their school.

Global management truly involves managing on the edge of chaos, or white-water management. Kevin Kelly observes, "In brief, the universe and life as we know it are poised on the edge of chaos.... This evolutionary rich environment produces [people] that also learn to tune their internal connectivity to keep the system at optimal evolvability. Each step extends the stance at the edge of chaos, poised on the thin path of optimal flexibility, which pumps up complexity. As long as the system rides this upswelling crest of evolvability, it surfs along."

The hardest part for most managers is learning how to flow with change, since it involves a kind of letting go. Navigation becomes the management of uncertainty, diversity, and risk—-especially when there are no simple answers, no obvious clarity, and no clear means of unifying diverse people, cultures, or business practices.

Like an artist, the challenge is to strive to create synergistic relationships among as many people and processes as possible so as to optimize the evolution of an organization. During times of change, the natural selection criteria are tied to the ability of one to evolve, given the various changes taking place. Chris Langdon, in his book *Complexity,* emphasizes the importance of trying to gain some control over as many forces influencing evolvability as possible in order to remain safely on the edge of chaos.

In a global setting, that means learning to understand, value, and manage differences strategically. For instance, Unilever operates with a regional structure by using local managers in East Asia and the Pacific, Latin America, and Africa and the Middle East because significant consumer differences exist in these markets, but in North America and Europe a worldwide products approach is employed since consumers in these areas are more similar in taste.

How do people differ? Charles Hampden-Turner and Alfons Trompenaars, in *The Seven Cultures of Capitalism,* found six basic dimensions along which people from various cultures tend to differ:

- Behavior based on universal principles or specific circumstances and relationships;
- Group versus individual behavior as the most important element;
- Neutral (closed) versus expressive (open) emotional manners and attitudes;
- Achievement (individual or personal) versus affiliation (rank and peer group) in connection with status;
- Synchronous versus sequential view of time and attitude toward the future and change; and
- Shaping the environment versus going along with it.

The challenge for global managers is to realize that no cultural viewpoint is necessarily any better or worse than any other in any absolute sense. Each has its merits and failings. The goal is to leverage the advantages and minimize the shortcomings as much as possible; in other words, diplomacy and negotiation skills are needed most. Parochialism and ethnocentrism must be avoided at all cost—a difficult lesson for many American multinationals.

Since America is largely cut off from the rest of the world geographically, many U.S. firms have a limited appreciation of other cultures—something clearly reflected in the reluctance to allow foreigners to become members of the board of directors. An Accord Group study found that fewer than 40 percent of the 50 biggest U.S. companies had a single foreign board member. Less than 14 percent of 348 U.S. companies had a foreign director in a 1993 Korn/Ferry study. Elsewhere in the world, foreign board members often comprise roughly 3 to 15 percent of the board of the directors.

Obviously many American firms will pay a steep price for this kind of chauvinism, although the Japanese (who are even more xenophobic in outlook) will suffer even more. Now that two generations of American economic dominance are coming to an end, few U.S. companies can afford to maintain a colonial attitude toward the rest of the world. The new era is one where no country is capable of economically dominating the rest of the world.

Many American managers end up failing in foreign assignments as a result of a lazy attitude toward learning foreign languages and customs—something left over from the Ugly American days when everyone else in the rest of the world was expected to kowtow to Americans in order to do business.

According to the Center for International Briefing, 25 percent of U.S. managers fail abroad, which is three to four times the failure rate of transplanted Asian and European managers. The inability of many organizations to develop a global mindset is extremely widespread.

According to Doug Ready, founder and CEO of the International Consortium for Executive Development Research (an alliance among twenty top business schools and thirty global companies) in Lexington, Massachusetts, 1,500 executives from twelve large global companies each recently rated themselves last on 34 dimensions dealing with developing a global mindset in their organization.

According to Floris Maljers, co-chair of Unilever, the key limitation in the globalization effort is in human resources and not unreliable or insufficient sources of capital.

Unilever, since the 1980s, has had a policy of rotating managers around the world at an early age and has 25,000 employees using Lotus Notes in order to exchange information through its global PC network.

Given the shortage in global managers, graduates from well-known international business schools, such as the American Graduate School of International Management in Glendale, Arizona; IMD in Lausanne, Switzerland; and Insead, in Fontainebleau, France, are eagerly sought by such global companies.

Since anyone with international experience is now more marketable in the job market, the American Graduate School of International Management, Wharton's Lauder Institute, Connecticut College, Notre Dame, and University of Cincinnati, among others, now offer and encourage overseas internships. Upon their return, many participants end up leapfrogging their classmates who remained behind when it comes to career opportunities. For instance, one intern sent to Nepal by the U.S. Agency for International Development to work in a new bank was hired upon return by Tenneco to analyze opportunities in Chile, Argentina, and the South Pacific. Fortunately, many organizations now exist to help anyone wishing to take this route.

Rosabeth Moss Kanter in *World Class* refers to the new class of international managers as cosmopolitans and sees them as truly inheriting the earth from a job perspective: "The global economy threatens to create a class divide between cosmopolitans and locals.... Cosmopolitans are better positioned to cope with change because their linkage to wider networks also links them to wider opportunities. Workplaces in companies that are world-ready offer a new form of security, employability security."

The new "gold-collar" workers are highly paid professionals and executives with international connections. Job security once again depends upon networking assets and networking capabilities. Cosmopolitans, with their diverse connections, therefore enjoy the greatest security and opportunity.

In order to encourage better networking within global companies, job and assignment rotations are commonly used. Alternative viewpoints from elsewhere also serve to improve the quality of the decision making. Global town-hall meetings and best-practice benchmarking sessions are held frequently. As Ron Ashkenas, Dave Ulrich, Todd Jick, and Steve Kerr explain in their book, *The Boundaryless Organization:*

> Global Launchers need to develop a *liquefied* work force, so that they can pour it into whatever vessel they must fill. The rationale for resources liquefaction is that, in a completely globalized market, companies need to move people with flexible sets of skills from location to location or task to task to respond to customer needs with speed and innovation.... Another technique to foster continual training and learning is twinning, the process of assigning one local and one foreign person to the same job for a time.

Survival Criteria

Many social and task situations are created for the sole purpose of fostering socialization, trust, and common practices. As Paul Evans notes, by this means a global organization's "network becomes the nervous system of the organization. [However] a network does not require everyone to know everyone else.... Network theory and research show that a relatively small number of strong ties (strong relationships) among appropriate 'gatekeepers' ... can provide a vast set of potential linkages."

The same is equally true of companies. As Kanter asserts, "Quality is a matter not of internal processes only, but of excellence in relationships with suppliers, distributors, venture partners, and end users as well as with employees. And as linkages across boundaries become more important to success, influencing the quality of what occurs with an organization itself, leaders must build, manage, and nurture their organizations' networks of relationships to ensure that they have the best concepts, competence, and connections."

Even countries' futures are subject to the same survival criteria. When America was young, it could afford to be isolationist because of the unlimited opportunities that existed within her borders. Upon reaching middle age, her limits to growth are becoming evident, and self-sufficiency is no longer an option. America is only one of an ever-growing number of nations with highly competitive economies, and the gap is quickly closing between the former front runners and those trying to catch up as quickly as possible—and become part of trade agreements such as NAFTA.

Just as no country can dominate the world any longer, neither can any company. As Fumio Sato, president and CEO of Toshiba, explains, "It is no longer an era in which a single company can dominate any technology or business by itself. The technology has become so advanced, and the markets so complex, that you simply can't expect to be the best at the whole process any longer."

As the market place begins to become crowded everyone will find they need "friends" of one kind or another—often in ways that defy the traditional idea of friendship or partnership. Even multinationals find their relationships somewhat convoluted. As noted in the *Wall Street Journal,* "Competitors cooperate in one digital arena while banging heads in another.... 'You very much have to accept that you are going to compete against a company in some places and cooperate in others,' says Chuck Lilly, the US West executive."

Transnational Marketplaces

The idea of a national economy in any straightforward sense is also being called into question. Some cities—such as Tokyo, Paris, London, Zurich, São Paulo, Hong Kong, Sydney, Amsterdam, Toronto, Miami, and New York—have clearly evolved into transnational marketplaces with more in common with one another than their own nation-states.

The National League of Cities claims that America is a "common market" of local economic regions. In many cases the economic regions spill over national borders, such as Cascadia, which contains Washington, Oregon, Alberta, and British Columbia. Not surprisingly, Kenichi Ohmae in *Borderless World* and *The End of the Nation State: The Rise of Regional Economies* focuses on the regions or cities as the "natural business units" of economic competitiveness. Or as George Yeo, Singapore's information minister, observes, "In the next century, the most relevant unit of economic production, social organization, and knowledge generation will be the city."

But don't be surprised to see inter-city collaboration become the next evolutionary step that begins to take hold. Newcastle, in the UK, for instance, has foreign offices in Chicago, San Francisco, Brussels, Bergen, Seoul, Hong Kong, Osaka, Taipei, and Tokyo.

Rosabeth Moss Kanter in *World Class* shows how five American city regions (for example, Boston: high tech, medicine, and biotech; and Spartanburg and Greenville, South Carolina: manufacturing) have managed to become global competitors because of the clustering effect of a number of mutually supportive initiatives by local governments, business, and the community.

In each case, becoming world class has meant encouraging foreign companies to set up shop locally—a game almost all cities or regions are having to get involved in around the globe.

For instance, in the United Kingdom, the Newcastle region was deemed the number one new plant location by the *World Economic Forum* magazine in 1993. There are over 380 foreign companies situated here—of which 130 U.S. and 50 Japanese firms use the area as a jumping-off point for serving the rest of Europe. Indeed, 45 percent of Newcastle's output is exported, which is higher than anywhere else in the UK. In the last nine years, foreign companies have invested more than $7 billion on almost 400 projects in the region. The area has become one of the fastest growing job markets in the UK, with over 50,000 jobs having been created by foreign companies setting up shop. The Newcastle Development Company, in addition to having foreign offices throughout the globe, networks together over 10,000 companies within the region for the purposes of matching customers and suppliers and exchanging information. Over 300 executives are involved in trying to attract new companies to the region, and its Fit for Europe export program is geared to helping companies gain access to other European markets.

In a benchmarking world, cities and regions are beginning to model themselves to some extent on one another. Sydney, Australia, and Glasgow, UK, have both tried to copy the success of the Boston area, while Cheltenham, UK, is imitating Spartanburg and Greenville, South Carolina.

The growth of foreign-owned companies located in the U.S. is evident from the fact that 5 million Americans work for these foreign companies or their affiliates. Needless to say, this is a two-way street; for instance, 75 percent of Gillette's 31,000 employees are located in other countries.

The need for companies and regions to become global is part of a chain reaction or domino effect. When global consolidation takes place in one industry, all of its suppliers are encouraged to do likewise if they hope to remain a preferred supplier. Global integration then proceeds through to the next layers of the chain so that before long everyone in the supply chain has been forced to become a global entity.

The reinforcing nature of this process also affects communities since where the various suppliers choose to set up shop in each country is determined by the location of others in the chain. The end result is a clustering of international companies in cities that have ideal networked infrastructures for supporting each industry's needs.

Miami, with its large number of well-integrated Cuban and Latin American businesses with abundant connections in Latin American countries, is a natural go-between or jumping-off point for companies wishing to do business in these parts of the world—much like Hong Kong is for China. *World Trade* magazine put Miami in second place in its "Top 10 U.S. Cities for Global Companies" in 1994.

Since many futurists predict that Spanish will be widely spoken throughout the U.S. by 2050, if not before, Miami is well positioned to take advantage of all of the international business that will be generated by this inevitable long term north-south integration process, which will bring into focus the enormously expanding South American markets. By the early 1980s, South Florida was already handling well over 40 percent of our trade with Latin America. By 1994, there were 98 international financial institutions located in Miami, making it the fourth in the U.S. in international bank concentration. Integration across industries extends even to tourism with Latin Americans spending over twice as much as New Yorkers in Miami ($1.5 billion in 1981). Given this city's obvious natural competitive advantages, anyone looking to find work in Latin American countries would be advised to seek employment in an exporting Miami company.

The San Francisco area, including San Jose, is another huge international growth area. *Fortune's* 1995 "Top Global Cities" survey ranked it second in the world but number one in the "Best U.S. Cities for Business." Silicon Valley alone exports $25 billion per year, which is more than all states except for Texas, Washington, Michigan, and New York. It received over $1 billion in venture capital, and the San Jose area obtained 2,359 patents in 1994. Biotech companies, such as Genentech, Chiron, and Scios Nova, and multimedia companies, such as Macromedia, Ikonic International, and P. F. Magic, were spawned by the rich university environment in the area. Asian banks and companies are also moving in to take advantage of these technological developments and the fact that one-third of San Francisco's population has connections in the East. Over 175 Pacific Rim companies currently employ 19,000 people in the Bay area. Thus San Francisco is poised to become the gateway to the Asian market.

Silicon Valley is perhaps one of the purest examples of the new knowledge-based economy. Given the fact that high technology has become the driving force in the economy since 1993, the region is likely a harbinger of future economic development. In 1996, one-third of the U.S.'s GDP growth came from information technology with Silicon Valley's GDP now equaling Chile's. Forty percent of every U.S. dollar spent on capital investment now goes to information technology of one kind or another. No wonder the market capitalization of Intel, Microsoft, and Cisco together is about three times that of Detroit's Big Three.

Jobs in the valley now pay double the United States average and wages are rising 5 percent per year. Competition for bright, young techies is such that Cisco rents billboards and touts stock options and spin-off possibilities to attract the 400 people it hires each month. The secret to the area's success has been an entrepreneurial culture and equal opportunity employment.

The venture capitalists in just one street in Silicon Valley control around one-third of America's independently raised venture capital and roughly a sixth of the world's total. Everyone in the valley has at least one friend who has made it big. Even bankruptcy is merely thought of as getting your feet wet.

Women, immigrants, and anyone else who is highly talented have no trouble finding employment. New recruits, however, are expected to be creative problem solvers, highly articulate, personally effective, mentally agile and alert, and totally dedicated to overcoming major challenges. In a meritocracy, only the ability to create, perform, or deliver counts. Thus, as the world moves increasingly on-line or high tech in focus, we are likely to see that whoever is involved with such fast-paced companies can succeed as well. For instance, there are many long-standing secretaries working for Microsoft who are millionaires, given their stock options. Welcome to the world of high-risk, high-return, or low-risk, low-return. Or as Palo Alto entrepreneur Michael Skok notes, "You are either one of the people in the middle spinning the wheel, or one of those on the outside being spun."

What is it about the region that has made it a high-tech magnet? Aside from the entrepreneurial excitement generated in conversations in bars and restaurants, Silicon Valley, according to the *Economist*, benefits from "the size and flexibility of its labor pool, the breadth of its network of suppliers, its access to venture capital, and the excellence of its education facilities and research institutions—notably the universities of Stanford and Berkeley, and Xerox's Palo Alto Research Center (PARC).... One way or another around 1,000 companies have spun out of Stanford University."

Other parts of America and the rest of the world are trying to copy Silicon Valley's winning formula. Silicon Desert (Utah), Silicon Alley (New York), Silicon Hills (Austin), Irvine (California), and Silicon Forest (Seattle and Portland) are other U.S. clones, while Taiwan (Hsinchu Science Park in Taipei), Britain (Silicon Glen in Scotland, Cambridge, and the Thames Valley), India (Bangalore), France (Cote d'

Azure), Egypt (Pyramid Technology Park), and Israel are busy creating their own. Malaysia is currently spending $40 billion to create its own version just south of Kuala Lumpur that will accommodate 100,000 people. You can expect to see more regions adopting similar economic or industry thematic approaches, such as Hollywood or Silicon Valley, as a means of creating an economically competitive identity. Fortunately, it's an excellent way of creating jobs.

Atlanta has one of the fastest growing economies in the U.S. and is edging its way toward global elite status. Twenty-five years of technological development are beginning to pay off. Home of Bell South, the biggest of the Baby Bells, Atlanta now has more fiber-optic cable than any other U.S. city. Foreign telecommunication companies are flocking there to take advantage of the excellent coordination that exists between private and public sector research, such as the incubator program run by the Georgia Center for Advanced Telecommunication Technology.

Georgia is also the first state to provide research funding for high-tech companies. Other Fortune 500 companies, such as UPS Inc., Coca-Cola, Delta Airlines, Home Depot, and Turner Broadcasting Systems Inc., have their headquarters there. *World Trade* magazine put Atlanta in the number one spot for the "Top U.S. Cities for Global Companies" in 1994; *Fortune* listed it in seventh place in its 1995 "World's Best Cities for Business," which is only the second time Atlanta has failed to make it into the top-five rank (it was number two in the 1995 "Best U.S. Cities for Business"). It also tied for first place with Washington, D.C. in the 1994 Association of Foreign Investors survey of the "Top U.S. Cities for Foreign Investment."

New York City ranked fourth in the 1995 *Fortune* "Top Global Cities" and "Best U.S. Cities for Business." The headquarters of 49 Fortune 500 companies are located there, as are 350 foreign banks. Multimedia is well represented by 500 companies, many of them young and growing quickly in places such as the Information Technology Center and Silicon Alley. Its abundant professional services and diverse blend of cultures make it a natural for global trade.

Outside the U.S., the usual round of suspects or foreign capitals are overrepresented in the 1995 "Top Global Cities"—Singapore, London, Frankfurt, Hong Kong, Toronto, Paris, and Tokyo. Singapore—number one among the "Top Global Cities"—is preparing itself to become the gateway to the Asian market outside China.

A self-proclaimed English-speaking "learning nation," Singapore plans to double its number of software programmers in the next five years to help it become a software center. Special tax breaks exist to encourage companies to set up their regional headquarters here. Moreover, Singapore is involved in setting up industrial parks in lower wage countries (such as Indonesia, China, India, and Vietnam) for multinational manufacturers, such as AT&T and Siemens, as an added bonus.

Most top global cities, such as the ones mentioned above, have excellent business support infrastructures and a clustering of world-class companies or headquarters. For example, Hong Kong is home to 2,000 multinationals; London's lead in foreign exchange trading and international bank lending is reflected in the 520 foreign banks located there and the 700,000 people employed in financial, business, and professional services; and Toronto and nearby Ottawa control the lion's share of Canada's $44.5 billion information technology market. The clustering effect represents a solid core competitive competence.

Despite the technological possibilities of working remotely from rural locations, big cities will continue to prosper in the future, particularly those with a global bent. Why? As Jane Jacobs makes clear in *The Economy of Cities,* cities with great diversity are able to renew themselves because of the cross-fertilization of ideas that naturally takes place. They also tend to be leading-edge adopters of new technology. In other words, diversity intrinsically is a form of experimentation that is more likely to reveal new possibilities. Like paradoxes, the provocative challenge of trying to reconcile opposites seems to afford countless entrepreneurial bridging or linking opportunities. Large cities, ever since Pericles of Athens proclaimed his city open to the world, have always been inviting, complex, democratic places that have avoided the undermining feudal parochialism or insularity of smaller towns. Large, global cities are also much more productive than the rest of a country. A 1980 University of Paris study found that Paris was 35 percent more productive than anywhere else in France. The enormous variety of skills to be found in cities gives them a natural advantage over smaller locations. As noted in *the Economist,* "When the European Bank for Reconstruction and Development set up in London in 1991.... three-quarters of those it eventually recruited were already living in London...."

Close ties with suppliers and customers in a just-in-time world are also important advantages. And even though the information highway will make telecommuting worldwide more feasible and desirable—telecommuters are expected to triple within the next 15 years to 20 percent of the U.S. work force—quality of life considerations and the optimizing of chance encounters with people you would like to meet will continue to foster a herding instinct among like-minded knowledge workers.

While the cities just mentioned represent the tried and true global economies that have been developing their infrastructures for long periods of time, there are other smaller, more entrepreneurial cities that are growing rapidly in some important respects. Auckland, New Zealand represents an English-speaking global entrepreneur's dream come true. At the moment, New Zealand's economy is among the world's least regulated and most openly competitive. Inflation is legally held at less than two percent, the federal budget is running a 2.8 percent GDP surplus, which is expected to rise to seven percent by 1998, and the economy is growing at six percent per year. Exports have significantly shifted away from the European Community to Asia: exports to the European Community have fallen from 62 percent in 1966 to 15 percent in 1994. Roughly 20 government-run companies and agencies have been sold between 1988 and 1994 (for example, Ameritech, a U.S. consortium of telecommunication companies, purchased New Zealand Telecom Corp.). But perhaps most surprising of all, manufacturing, which accounted for only 2.6 percent of GDP in 1966, now is responsible for 25 percent. Now that Asia accounts for over 50 percent of New Zealand's trade, H. J. Heinz Co., which recently purchased food processor Watties Industries Ltd., plans to use it as the mainstay of its Asia-Pacific operations. Many Asian companies have purchased or are looking to purchase New Zealand companies as well. Here is definitely an entrepreneurial crossroads where East will meet West.

Subic Bay in the Philippines also represents an English-speaking entrepreneurial growth opportunity now that the U.S. Navy has pulled out and the area has been designated a free-trade zone. Growth is running at six percent, the stock market rose by 322 percent in 1995, and the minimum wage is roughly $6 per day. Acer, the world's seventh-largest computer maker, is anticipating hiring 19,000 people at a global manufacturing and repair center that is expected to have $1 billion in sales within five years. One Taiwanese company is creating a 750-acre industrial park that will manufacture everything from food to clothing. Hosting the Asia-Pacific Economic Cooperation forum in 1996 along with Hong Kong's reversion to China in 1997 should provide an additional boost to Subic Bay's economy over the next couple of years.

Other global entrepreneurial hot spots include Oulu, Finland (which has over 1,000 start-ups in software, sensors, opto-electronics, and lasers, accounting for more than $1 billion annually); Bombay, India (its "Bollywood," which is now starting to move into high-tech filmmaking, produces almost twice as many movies each year as Hollywood, generating $1 billion in sales); and Soweto, South Africa (which now has its first "mixed" shopping mall with plans for casinos, industrial parks, more shopping centers, and hotels on the horizon).

Tianjin, just outside Beijing, which has had over 140 American, European, and Asian multinationals invest $2.5 billion in the city, has China's largest container port, excellent industrial parks, and a growing financial district. Bangalore, which is India's Silicon Valley, is filled with high-tech companies including Apple, DEC, AT&T, IBM, Hewlett-Packard, Intel, Texas Instruments, and Motorola. Jerusalem's high-tech advantage includes Hebrew University, plus significant Intel Corp. and Digital Equipment operations.

Bratislava, Slovakia is expected to become one of the most desirable production locations with its two excellent universities and low-priced, highly-trained workforce—something Volkswagen is already taking advantage of. Nizhni Novgorod has always led Russian cities in its privatization efforts and has entered the securities market. São Paulo, Brazil's capital, is the center of the Mercosur free trade zone, which includes Argentina, Brazil, Chile, Paraguay, and Uruguay. Over 1,300 U.S. companies are now located there.

The Transcultural Imperative

We are witnessing the emergence of a mutually interrelational and integral world. The world's economy is becoming a single organism.

—Mikhail Gorbachev

The reality now facing everyone is the inescapability of having to come to terms with cultural diversity. By 2000, 80 percent of the work force will be made up of minorities, immigrants, and women. Women will account for two-thirds of labor market growth, with native non-whites and immigrants contributing most of the remainder.

The challenge of cultural difference has always existed, but now it is beginning to play a much larger role in all aspects of the business world. Inside organizations distinctly different cultures exist among departments, for example, R&D focuses on the long term, but marketing and sales is devoted to the short term. Other such differences exist among divisions and subsidiaries.

Every time a cross-functional team is created, each member's subculture and methods of solving problems that are unique to each person's profession or specialty are subject to challenge from opposing viewpoints that are embedded in entirely different contexts. As it becomes more competitively important to hire the best person for the job, regardless of his or her race, color, creed, or place of origin in the world, and border crossing becomes easier, the amount of diversity encountered is magnified accordingly. For example, industrial parks everywhere hire people based on their scientific abilities, not their cultural backgrounds.

Joint ventures, alliances, and partnerships bring together strange bedfellows, as do consortia made up of industry, universities, and government. Macroprojects such as the creation of Airbus Industrie in Europe brought together five governments and a wide array of other public and private sector players, as did the $15 billion "Chunnel" project joining Britain and France.

Corporate Culture Clashes

In an age of mergers and acquisitions, corporate cultures are suddenly brought together overnight. Each year since 1983, there have been over 2,500 mergers and acquisitions in the U.S. American companies were part of 600 international mergers and acquisitions in 1988. The Japanese have begun to get in the game as well with an initial involvement of only 44 M&As in 1984, which increased to 315 in 1988. For all the effort involved in such transactions, stock prices and financial performances rarely improve, largely due to the failure of the two cultures to blend in a mutual reinforcing manner.

Most of us take for granted our culture, which conditions us in every way as to what is expected of us and of others. It smoothes human performance in all of our daily activities. Culture shock or clash occurs because we are unaware of our values or those of others and their subsequent influence on behavior.

Increasing Your Possibilities

Becoming more attuned to cultural differences requires that we first learn to understand ourselves more clearly—the very same thing that is required in developing a personal vision. By increasing our awareness of the values of others, we actually increase the number of possibilities available to us in the formation of our own identities.

All of us, in a sense, have just reconfigured the values we have been exposed to in ways that seem to fit our natural needs and preferences. The more values you are exposed to, the more likely you are to find a better combination of values that expresses exactly who you are.

Innovation, in other words, applies equally to ourselves. We are continually in the process of creating our identities but always within the context of those around us. Going global means enlarging the context enormously and engaging in a kind of merger-and-acquisition activity with other cultures. But how does one proceed?

Like multinationals, you begin by trailblazing. All global strategies are by definition long-range strategies, but they need to begin somewhere. It took McDonald's ten years of negotiations to set up a fast-food location in Russia, and it virtually had to build the entire food chain in the process.

Just as companies go through various phases of internationalization, it makes sense for individuals to mirror this process to some extent as well. The first step is usually exporting to other countries, which requires some familiarity with the companies and countries receiving the exports.

From a career perspective, it would make sense to vacation in areas in other parts of the U.S. or in the other promising parts of the world. Combine career interests and pleasure. Go on a cooking, wine, art, ecotourism, or historical tour of these locations, and take time to scout each place out from a job and quality of life perspective. Try learning a foreign language, subscribe to international publications (for example, the *Economist, Wall Street Journal Europe, Far Eastern Economic Review)*, get on the Internet, join an international or foreign association, or read travel literature about places with a growing economic future. It will help you stay aware of worldwide trends, and who knows—it may take ten years, but perhaps by then you will find yourself working in a new, interesting location in the U.S. or elsewhere that can play a vital role in your strategic global career development. Just imagine how diverse your network will become.

One lesson learned by multinationals is called the domino effect. Entering the first foreign market is always the hardest, just as taking on your first foreign assignment is likely to be. Before long, however, the lessons learned in one country often are applicable to another. The more countries you enter, the easier it becomes. Thus, companies or individuals moving to one Latin American country are likely to find moving on to another a much easier transition.

Both entrepreneurs and global job seekers are likely to find themselves traveling up the global cultural learning curve, just as every multinational has had to do in order to become successful.

Global Homogenization

One evolutionary megatrend is global homogenization. As the world is getting smaller, cultures are becoming more similar. Global competitiveness is demanding that all countries, companies, and individuals become more innovative, quicker to respond to change, more flexible and adaptive, more networked and interdependent, and faster to market.

The end result is a common business understanding of realities that need to be addressed. Multinationals are all developing common policies and procedures throughout the world so that it is easy to move personnel from country to country as needed, develop a global intelligence network, realize economies of scale wherever possible, and speed up the innovation process. Local conditions are taken into account, but global realities also require global solutions. All extremely complex systems benefit enormously in these highly competitive and changing conditions from standardization of information flows and processes.

Much of the heavyweight partnering among the large multinationals is all part of the effort to establish their brand of worldwide standards in information technology, telecommunication, marketing, insurance, and banking. ISO 9000 is just the beginning of global standardization in almost every realm. Eventually, even education and training will become more standardized throughout the world with certification standards widely accepted (for example, Novell LAN certification).

From a career perspective, we are beginning to witness the emergence of a class of world professionals or cosmopolitans who share more in common with one another than they do with the people in any one country—and increasingly they are becoming networked together through joint ventures, alliances, and partnerships.

Already it is probably reasonable to say that people who drive BMWs likely have more in common with one another in significant ways than they do with many others in their respective countries. Just as trade agreements end up reducing the abilities of governments to protect cultures and ways of life (for instance, rice farming in Japan), the new competitive realities are completely unforgiving of cultural myopia that gets in the way of more efficient and effective economic growth.

The message many are having to come to grips with is this: either you have the skills to compete in a global job or business market, or you are unemployable or out of business. Governments can no more stop this trend than they can stop electronic signals from traveling around the world. In fact, it would only make matters worse—imagine Russia trying to return to its former ways.

But individuals, like countries and companies, who try to take advantage of these trends end up gaining more control over their destiny in the process. This lesson, something that is naturally accepted in Asia, is one that many North Americans with their belief in indomitable willpower still need to come to terms with.

You cannot willfully turn back the clock in America to a time when foreign trade was less necessary because there was a wealth of opportunities yet to be discovered and exploited within the U.S. itself. There will be even more opportunities than have ever existed in the past; however, they will not be confined by borders, barriers, boundaries, or cultures. For the most part the opportunities will lie outside most Western countries.

In the future we will all need to learn to travel lightly. Before long, all of us will be asked to become mobile "road warriors" capable of working from any location. French futurist Jaques Atally refers to these "liberated nomads" as the new knowledgeable elite who only need their electronic gear, their knowledge, and their imagination in order to work anywhere. According to Edward Castleton, "The world has transformed itself into a place without space, where time zones are more important than trade zones, and where an address on-line is a thousand times more significant than any petty street coordinate. Busying themselves with faxes, voice mail, e-mail, and the Internet, this new class (cyber-elite) couldn't care less where they physically happen to be....There is, for example, no difference between Sunday and Monday in [high tech author Nicholas] Negroponte's workweek. Work follows him everywhere, and he follows it, jacking in with his laptop wherever he happens to be." As Peter Bamevik, CEO of Asea Brown Boveri, indicates, his office headquarters are "where my mail arrives before the important letters are faxed to wherever I happen to be." Fortunately, employability security, which comes from developing a global mindset and world-class skills, is something you can always take with you anywhere.

The final remaining challenge involves seeking opportunities to constantly refresh your vision, your entrepreneurial spirit, your global mindset, and your world class skills. Luckily, the life of a "liberated nomad" is one of constant renewal.

CHAPTER 12

Renewal

When people have the freedom to express the full range of their human talent, a job ceases to be just work. It is a place of growth, of belonging, of contribution, and of meaning. So begins the cycle of genuine productivity improvement. From a heightened intellectual and emotional harmony flows the commitment for more innovation.

—John Dalla Costa, *Working Wisdom*

Charting a career course amidst the inevitable chaos and confusion that attend each new wave of automation, downsizing, restructuring, reengineering, and outsourcing requires an ability to assess which companies are likely to do well and which companies might be able to use your particular talents. Understanding the historical dynamics underlying the evolving corporate landscape will help bring these issues into better focus so that you are able to make more strategic career decisions.

As former Drake Beam Morin chairman and CEO, Bill Morin notes,

> There are three essential work force capabilities today. The ability to thrive on change, the ability to take ownership and initiative, and the ability to foster and achieve alignment between the individual's values and the firm's goals.

The question is how to find those companies that will allow you to make full use of these abilities in a way that helps your career development.

Fortunately, the evolution and change process follows well-developed patterns that repeat themselves again and again. Even if we are in the throes of epochal upheaval, the lessons of the past are likely to apply equally well both now and in the future.

Nomadic Hunter-Gatherers

Don Peppers and Martha Rogers, authors of *The One to One Future,* suggested in a recent *Wired* magazine article, the rise of the independent contractor, the self-employed consultant, and the freelancer suggests a connection to the hunter-gatherer of "primitive" cultures:

> We use silicon weapons to search out ideas and images, and we forage for services that can be sold for living. Instead of a society divided into consumers and producers, we will be participating on both sides of the economic equation: a hunter-gatherer is ... consumer and producer, buyer and seller.

Other books, such as Cliff Hakim's *We Are All Self-Employed,* William Bridges' *JobShift,* and James Cabrera and Charles Albrecht Jr.'s *The Lifetime Career Manager,* echo this theme of rootlessness now that all forms of employment are impermanent.

In a corporate setting it takes on more tribal connotations. David Hurst in *Crisis and Renewal* views history as a process of continual renewal within corporations, cultures, and tribes:

> The concept of organizational renewal assumes that in the beginning of an organization's life, at its founding, there was something of value, some shared experience that was authentic and meaningful. Over time, this original feeling of authenticity, of meaning, has either faded or been lost. Renewal involves going back to the founding

values to reconnect the past to the present, to rediscover the old in the new.

Career entrepreneurism requires this same act of renewal. In a way we are all now in the process of rediscovering our anthropological roots as hunters and gatherers. Indeed, entrepreneurism has become the new egalitarian playing field that our ancient ancestors understood instinctively given the changing situations they found themselves in.

There are some marked similarities between the Bushmen of the Kalahari desert and our current transitional economic circumstances. As nomads, they were able to adapt to highly variable environmental conditions and yet remain a very stable, coherent society. Survival depended on continuous learning. They grouped themselves in nonhierarchical, self-organizing teams of multiskilled individuals who fanned out over the landscape in search of sustenance (much like many employees who now spend more time interacting with other divisions, suppliers, and customers than with their own departments or companies).

When one party located a fruitful location worth exploiting, the entire tribe would coalesce around this area to share in the good fortune. Since survival depended on sharing, everything was shared openly with one another. Indeed, since only nineteen or so hours a week were necessary to secure food, the rest of the time was spent in constant dialogue with one another.

If any problem arose, those members of the tribe closest at hand and appropriately skilled would take care of the situation immediately, and then go back to their activities of the moment. Rarely would any problem occur that required decision-making at a higher level than by those close at hand. The mythology surrounding campfire discussions usually consisted of a retelling of the historical "best practices" of the tribe, and in this way everyone, including the children, was always aware of the strategies that had met with the greatest success.

The temporarily constructed huts were always circular with the entrances always facing one another across a small common area. There was little privacy, but communication and socialization took place almost constantly. Social condemnation consisted of shunning anyone who displayed pretensions to status or who hoarded possessions. As sharing was absolutely essential for survival and knowledge was always distributed or decentralized, hierarchical structure was unnecessary. As might be expected, everyone felt intimately involved in a highly valued way.

Eventually, however, the Bushmen entered the next phase of evolutionary development as their increased knowledge eventually allowed them to become herders who could stay in one location. Wealth accumulation became possible because their energies could be more efficiently focused on increasing productivity, and before long the hoarding of wealth became a preoccupation that ended up having the expected divisive effects.

People moved their huts further apart and faced their entrances away from everyone else's so that others would not see the wealth that they had accumulated. People talked less, so serious problems began to arise that had to be settled by a chief. Social problems began to proliferate, and outbreaks of violence and virulent disputes became common.

Corporate Evolution

Most companies or organizations go through a very similar evolutionary development. As Hurst notes,

> If an organization is to form, there have to be periodic gatherings, when the network participants come together for intense exchanges ... As the young organization begins to "gel" ... People spend more and more time together ... Communication will be free and open and

characterized by a continual sharing of individual views and opinions among all members of the organization.

Not surprisingly, many original employees of organizations such as Nike, Levi's, and Apple pine for the days when the companies were young, vibrant, and truly on the edge—that is, before systems of control began to be widely implemented and decisions moved up the corporate ladder.

The egalitarian nature of the entrepreneurial phase of development is one of intimacy, inclusion, and constant problem solving. The shared sense of purpose that characterizes these times gives work a personal meaning that is virtually unrivaled in other settings. Because of this, John Sculley, former CEO of Apple, found that roughly 40 percent of his employees quit the company after finishing a project. After devoting an incredible amount of extra time and personal energy to a project, once the dream became a reality, they found themselves not just physically exhausted but without a sense of purpose.

The companies that are capable of building a sense of entrepreneurial and personal renewal into their operations are the ones that will succeed in the future. One place that is definitely driven by this imperative is Microsoft, where it is estimated that over 10,000 employees are already multimillionaires as a result of holding stock options. These employees are referred to as "volunteers" because they are not working for financial reasons. The challenge to Microsoft is to provide them with the kinds of projects they find highly engaging.

At 3M, employees are allowed to spend 15 percent of their time on any project of personal interest, which also helps to encourage continuous renewal and commitment. The opportunity to spin off innovations into separate companies can fully inspire employees to offer their emotional energies and innovative ideas willingly since they can literally take ownership in the process, such as happens in Japan's Bunsha Group, which even encourages the spinning off of all high-performing departments.

A Better Sense of Freedom

As our Bushmen example illustrates, successful companies are likely to be those that try to eliminate status differences and create a better sense of freedom responsibility, trust, and inclusiveness—for example, profit sharing, no ridiculous salary differentials or exclusive executive perks, and self-empowered teams.

At Chaparral Steel, the thirteenth-largest steel mill in the United States, two-thirds of the employees are stockholders. Workers are allowed to be away from work for whatever reason they deem appropriate. As a result, the daily absence rate is less than one percent. Empowered teams are used, and, as one foreman indicates, "Probably ninety percent of the problems never even make it to the morning meetings held among everyone on the shift to discuss problems. They were fixed in the field." Line managers can spend large sums on experiments without higher approval. And at any one point in time, over 80 percent of the company's staff is engaged in some form of education or training. In such a supportive environment, it is understandable that the annual job turnover rate is less than two percent. The company's egalitarian nature is also reflected in the fact that there are only two levels between the shop floor and the chairman.

Successful companies must also be physically and organizationally laid out so as to maximize communication opportunities, foster multitasking, and allow for self-organization.

At Denmark's Oticon, no one has his own office desk. Everyone is given a trolley containing cabinets to wheel up to any free desk. As a result, most people working on a project congregate around desks nearby. Paper is virtually banned in the organization because it is assumed that talking about problems solves issues faster than writing about them. Employees are expected to be able to perform at least three different jobs and can initiate their own projects if they can recruit enough free and interested staff.

Chiat/Day, which Intel has used as a management-style model, also lacks separate offices and uses open, similar-sized cubicles. Job descriptions or titles are not used, and everyone is free to work from any location he or she feels like, including home.

Honda enforces communication by having only six desks in a common open area for forty-six senior executives. The rest end up using conference tables, which promotes interaction. Wal-Mart even uses high tech to bring everyone together in its company, since there is a video link connecting all parts of the organization. After networking together its electronic infrastructure, Northern Telecom found that its employee videoconference hours jumped from 2,000 in 1990 to 68,000 in 1994 and audioconferencing increased from 5,400 hours to 96,000 hours—as a result, its internal "warring tribes," as they were formerly referred to, are now well-coordinated on a global scale. Although the information highway may alter work patterns considerably, companies will still need to create situations for employees getting together in more informal ways so that more spontaneous communication is facilitated.

The extent to which companies consult and communicate with their suppliers and customers as part of a coevolving, cocreation process is also equally important—especially since the new model of competition is not one company against company but one integrated supply chain versus another that extends even beyond one's customers to their customers and so on.

The Ecocycle

While looking for telltale innovative signs such as these as a way of assessing which companies are likely to succeed, it is also important to take into account where a company or industry is in its life cycle. Like it or not, we all end up becoming herders to some extent, since most companies and individuals have a vision that transcends mere survival. The forest ecocycle development model is extremely helpful in gaining a grasp of the dynamics of the growth and renewal processes as they affect all living systems—including countries, states, cities, companies, and individuals.

After a forest fire, large numbers of small organisms immediately rush in to take advantage of the newly created growth opportunity. At this stage of development, speed plays a crucial role in the race to consume as much of the new "market opportunity" created. Once crowding begins to occur, competition intensifies and competitive advantage shifts to efficiency. The species that do best under these circumstances invest considerable energy in protecting their territory and less on replicating themselves. In the process the land begins to take on a fairly hierarchical structure as stands of trees begin to emerge. Greater specialization takes place, and the amount of diversity is diminished through a competitive shakeout process. The survivors, however, are vulnerable as a result of the specializing qualities that allowed them to edge out their rivals. Any change in the environment can wreak havoc quite quickly.

Forest fires usually prevent this specialization process from proceeding too far, therefore minimizing the potential for damage that can occur if a forest is artificially protected from forest fires too long. Why does inhibiting the natural destructive process end up in a greater level of eventual damage? In the case of a forest, the excess deadwood created by large trees choking off the smaller ones prevents the formation of natural firebreaks and drastically reduces the number of tree types left. In the case of an economy, protectionist legislation similarly allows industry dinosaurs to risk destroying the entire industry as all-new competitive developments are artificially choked off through tariffs and special-interest tax breaks.

The reason both Germany and Japan have succeeded so well is a result of the devastation wrought by the Second World War. Old habits were broken, and most industries had to rebuild from the ground up. Americans firms, such as the maturing auto industry, were untouched by the war, and so they focused more on performance at the expense of innovation. Needless to say, the forest fire started by these foreign countries has since awakened them.

The three phases of development then are growth, specialization and efficiency (performance), and renewal. The trick for everyone subject to equivalent market forces is to make the transition from one phase to the next without getting completely destroyed in the process. Many start-up companies flourish in the beginning but fail to make a successful transition to becoming larger, more performance-oriented companies as the industry becomes more crowded and competitive.

Compaq fell into this trap. It succeeded at first because it was the fastest company to offer leading-edge technology in its computers. However, once other companies caught up to it in this area, the competitive advantage shifted to price or cost. After sales fell by 9 percent in 1991, Compaq was forced to lay off 25 percent of its workforce and cut costs by over 75 percent in order to return to profitability. The next challenge that will face Compaq is how to renew itself while still focusing on performance or cost. So far, it is doing well by moving up the value-added chain by including software and peripherals in their Presario computers while controlling costs at the same time.

Visionary companies that are always challenging their assumptions and ways of operating manage to get the best of both worlds. As Harvard's Chris Argyris and Don Schon note, most companies need to shift from single- to double-loop learning. Single-loop learning involves comparing oneself to and adjusting to preestablished standards, whereas double-loop learning requires a periodic questioning of the standards themselves to see if they are still relevant. The same applies to individuals who must be both benchmarking their skills and assessing their evolving market value and relevant transferability. The more things change, the more renewal and revision become necessary. Even when change is not being forced on one by external development, it is necessary to build change into companies or careers since competitive advantage and revitalization come from continuous learning.

Everyone needs to learn enough to become a specialist of some sort initially, but he or she also needs to look for lateral moves that act as a natural bridge from the past to the future and offer renewed learning opportunities. Many companies are now looking for people with "T-shaped skills" or "deep expertise in one discipline combined with enough breadth to see its connections with others." Lateral moves provide the connections.

The Next Frontier

You might be wondering what the next frontier after knowledge is. The answer is wisdom. Since the half-life of knowledge keeps shortening—three or four years for engineers—its speed of depreciation requires that it not only be generated faster but that it also lead to richer and more fruitful areas of pursuit. This need for direction has finally even dawned on shareholders, since a recent study by Shareholders Surveys Inc. found that long-term vision was the number-one trait sought in companies for prospective investment purposes.

"Management taking a long-term view" was the top organizational requirement according to a 1994 *Industry Week* study. In a recent international study, fifteen hundred senior managers from twenty top industrialized countries indicated that "a strong sense of a vision of the future" was the most desirable trait for a CEO to have both now and in the year 2000.

Having a vision is one thing; shepherding your workforce to the promised land is quite another. The new limiting factor is human beings, not technology. Technology is growing and expanding at such a rate that it now easily surpasses our ability as human beings to keep pace with it. Companies that do the best job in facilitating learning and growth among their employees will reap the benefits of their investment in human capital. As Robert Aubrey and Paul Cohen suggest in their book, *Working Wisdom: Timeless Skills and Vanguard Strategies for Learning Organizations,*

> Wise people know what knowledge or know-how is needed in a given situation, how to circulate and renew that knowledge by working with others, and how to use it to solve problems or achieve a goal ... They find opportunities to *let learning happen* as circumstances demand.

The payoff? According to Dave Basarab, manager of evaluation at Motorola University, the average return on investment is 30 to 1. But these figures pale in comparison to what is possible if managers learn how to apprentice, sow, catalyze, mentor, and harvest knowledge and wisdom in their workforce in all their daily activities. Wisdom is needed to "lead while being led," as GE's CEO Jack Welch recommends.

Gary Hamel and C. K. Prahalad suggest, "Senior executives are not the only ones with industry foresight. In fact, their primary role is to capture and exploit the foresight which exists throughout the organization." Wisdom consists of an openness to strategy as an emergent or learning process—something that is essential in a ever-complex world. The key skill needed for this new economy is excellent personal judgment.

John Dalla Costa, in his inspiring book, *Working Wisdom: The Ultimate Value in the New Economy,* insists that,

> When we discuss a problem with the wise, we generally want context or insight, not facts. If anything, we seek a synthesis, a revelatory understanding that will free us from the burden of too many irreconcilable facts ... Value is now generated through synthesis—the merging of facts with knowledge, experience, creativity, and interactions of the workers, suppliers, and customers who customize it ... Only an advanced judgment can solve the complex problems attending this new type of value creation: only personal insight can deal with situations of pressing ambiguity.

In a world that is becoming a creative, complex web of relationships, wisdom is needed to balance the many competing concerns and inevitable conflicts that multiply exponentially. Companies will highly prize individuals who display these leadership and management abilities. But the key is self-knowledge, since all wisdom begins with an understanding of your strengths and weaknesses—particularly your limitations, for that is where all learning begins.

Self-Knowledge, Flexibility, and Quality of Life

> *Wisdom is not an achievement of intellectual rigor, but one of opening. It requires taking down those boundaries, established by what we know, to experience the connection with our deeper humanity...To unlearn means we know ourselves well enough to identify and release those aspects and attitudes of character that*

> *undermine our ability to grow. While learning requires that we look outside ourselves for new stimulus and information, unlearning starts inside. Instead of adding new knowledge, unlearning involves subtracting tired beliefs and assumptions.*
>
> —John Dalla Costa, *Working Wisdom*

In an era requiring full "broadband interactive" capabilities, the most important assets are yourself, your connections and experience, your core competencies, and your ability to learn and create innovative solutions. With technology coming and going at an accelerating rate and work content skills depreciating just as quickly, the emphasis shifts to learning, particularly just-in-time learning that builds on our transferable experience.

In an era of relationship marketing, we will all need to think of ourselves as "brands" whose relationship-building currency is reasonable knowledge value, trustworthiness, dependability, accountability, proven excellent quality and performance, adaptability, and speedy customer service. Everyone will be a consultant of sorts since we will all be part of the information or knowledge service industry in one way or another. As Eric Benhamou, CEO of 3Com Corp. claims, "Customers are less interested in technology and more in solutions." With all of the changes unfolding, we need to have our hands held by experts so that we get what we want when we need it. Often we will require help in just figuring out what it is we need or what is possible. All change requires new solutions, so we will be dependent on those with appropriate knowledge to ease the transitional pains as much as possible.

How fast customer needs can be learned and satisfactorily met will define what is meant by "real time" commerce. Indeed, learning is now the primary relationship between producers and consumers. Or as Pepsico's David Hatch says,

"Learning is the coin of the realm." Since the customer is driving the entire process, everyone ends up in the customer service "learning" business.

Because each customer is unique, creativity and innovation become the key to competitive advantage. As Don Tapscott, author of *The Digital Economy,* stresses,

> In the innovation economy, human imagination is the main source of value. The critical challenge for any company in the digital economy is to create a climate in which innovation is prized, rewarded, and encouraged ... And you need a climate in which risk is not punished, creativity can flourish, and human imagination can soar.

Creativity, by its very nature, requires breakthrough thinking or thinking outside the box we are familiar with. It means questioning our assumptions of what is true and possible. The mark of genius has always been the questioning of original assumptions. Jack Welch has always insisted that managers put their underlying assumptions on the table for open discussion during the GE's Workout sessions.

Look at Your Skills

Job seekers need to reevaluate constantly what assumptions they are making about their careers and their skill base. Ask yourself, If your job were open, would you be hired for it once again? Where will your learning likely lead you, or in what ways are you growing professionally? Do you know the value of your contribution and how it compares to others in the organization? What other jobs could you do if your job was eliminated in your company? To what extent are you being "milked" by your employer—that is, being perceived as not worth training in any new area, so the company is just having you do what you are currently capable of doing? If you eliminated the names of the companies you worked for and the job titles, could you make up an impressive resume based on your marketable skills alone? Do the want ads list skills for your occupation that you are lacking?

In an era of innovation, we all need to reinvent ourselves continually. The reality is that you cannot be good at everything, so it makes sense to focus on your most valuable adaptive or self-management skills and your most portable or transferable skills. Work content skills—that is, skills specific to an occupation—count for specialization purposes only. The importance of developing a clear strategic focus works for companies as well.

As recently noted in the *Economist*, "When firms narrowed their interests, their shares outperformed the market by an average of 11 percent in the next two years. Firms that diversified, and thus lowered their clarity score, underperformed the market as a whole by around 4 percent."

Concentrate Your Efforts

Narrowing your focus does not mean overspecializing; rather, it means strategically concentrating your efforts in ways that are most likely to be additive in nature yet do not close off lucrative career options or directions that leverage your skill base. As headhunter Gary Knisely points out,

> Never narrow your options. To the extent that technical expertise narrows your market, you've made a bad career decision. Companies may love it at the moment, but if you've got that good a crystal ball, get out of a job and into investing.

In other words, if choosing among projects or career paths that will either broaden your knowledge or deepen it, pick the option that will improve your flexibility and afford you a number of career and entrepreneurial opportunities—something called *multipreneuring*.

If you do decide to be highly specialized, you will likely find that you will be hired just for particular projects that require your skills. But if you do decide to specialize, try doing so in a "hyphenated" way. That is an area that combines two or more former areas of narrow specialization—for instance, by becoming a computer-math biologist engaged in bioinfomatics.

Every rule, of course, has an exception. Some highly specialized companies, high-tech firms in particular, require highly specialized managers just as football teams have separate coaches for individual positions (for example, quarterback, linebackers, receivers) as well as coaches for broader functions such as offense or defense.

In 1994, the National Technical Services Association found that 37 percent of contract workers preferred contract employment, while only 23 percent saw themselves as between permanent jobs. Even corporations are coming to share this "contract or project" viewpoint in connection with their full-time staff, since it is the equivalent of reengineering or restructuring according to process.

The New Career Route

The new career route to success becomes tied to the importance of the projects you manage or are involved in. Indeed, you may end up working under someone you managed in a different assignment. The new job, however, may require more of your expertise. Thus the ability to be a good team player and team leader is essential. Obviously the more projects of significance you end up managing, the greater your indispensability and promotability.

Natural selection has its analog in the vying for which projects to manage or become a part of. The best will always seek out the best talents in order to make their assignment a conspicuous success. You are unlikely to be picked to join a project unless you excel in an area of specialization, yet your prospects for becoming a team leader hinge on your ability to bridge or connect talents that will have to include a holistic understanding of all aspects of the money-making side of the company.

Those with "T-shaped" skills (the ability to grasp a variety of concepts in a given field, but with deep expertise in a specific area) are more valuable to companies than are people with just an area of expertise or broad project managing experience. Remember, however, that CEOs are ultimately generalists even though they began their careers in an area of specialization.

Managing a number of projects is the equivalent of having been an entrepreneur who started up various businesses. The same kind of mindset and skills are involved. Working with department VPs and upper management is akin to being part of a joint venture or alliance. Spin-off options, which are becoming more widely entertained, can become the launching pad for you to start your own successful business with the backing and help of a powerful partner with an extensive network.

As newer technology comes on stream at an even faster rate, companies will need to reengineer or restructure more often to take advantage of the more competitive ways of operating. The speed with which this will happen is truly astonishing. As Northern Telecom's CIO Dave Cox observes,

> In 1991, when we restructured our business, it took eighteen months to rework our organization systems—reporting, financial, systems, HR. In 1994, we did it in four months. Soon, we will be able to do it in weeks, and then days. The goal is to be able to build our systems instantly.

Be Flexible

Given this technological imperative, flexibility becomes the most important career survival factor. Employees and job seekers must constantly be in the process of reinventing themselves so as to fit in with the altering competitive landscape. To do so requires paying attention to the changes taking place and sketching out possible scenarios that might unfold for yourself, your profession, and your places of employment.

The Pentagon always is playing war games as a means of reducing the extent to which it can be caught off guard. We too need to develop "what if" scenarios in order to anticipate potential outcomes and develop appropriate contingency plans. In other words, what would you do if you lost your job today? If you already have, what are the various means by which you are marketing yourself and making yourself more employable? If employability security consists of having an extensive and diverse network as well as a resume that has been strategically built up over time, how do your networking and resume-building strategies address the concerns of the scenarios you envision?

Eternal vigilance is demanded because we are very much in the midst of change factors that are constantly interacting with one another. Whereas it is possible to get a reasonable overall sense of how many developments will unfold, at times it can be very tricky to figure out the particular ramifications in individual circumstances.

We all need to be ready for a few wildcard factors coming our way. The process is a bit like learning how to surf: you can't be daydreaming as the wave begins to curl. Depending how things are shaping up, we should to be prepared to go in a number of directions at any given moment. Since companies need to have the same kind of nimbleness, they will highly value those who can help them roll with the changes more proactively.

Perhaps the biggest challenge facing everyone will be psychological. Most people are probably not ready to go fifteen rounds with the change process; however, those who are willing to let go of or unlearn increasingly irrelevant assumptions can at least focus their energies on adjusting to change instead of fighting its inevitability.

The ability to expand the context in which one comfortably is capable of operating is the inherent wisdom of those who easily surpass those with the highest IQs or most extensive education. Not surprisingly, it those cosmopolitan professionals with a global mindset who are outdistancing everyone else. Why? Because they realize that each of the world's cultural perspectives is inherently blind to other important realities.

Howard Gardner, Harvard psychologist and author of *Creating Minds,* found that in studying the seven "creators of the modem era," all had either left their original country or had traveled extensively.

Stephen Rhinesmith, author of *A Manager's Guide to Globalization,* talks about,

> the challenge of developing the capacity to discern patterns in complex situations ... If you go far enough outside your box, you will see patterns around yourself that will give you a whole new understanding of your relationship to everything else.

Letting go of ego worries and attachments will be fundamental to success in the new global economy. We are all going to have to make many mistakes if we are to survive and thrive, so we need to focus on each experiment as a learning opportunity that is to be shared with others. Remember, the informal network of egotists usually consists of one person.

If ego concerns are irrelevant, what becomes the primary focus of all your endeavors? Quite simply, quality of life. It is quality of life that gives everything we do meaning. Meaning and our sense of ourself are largely defined by our goals and roles; and for most of us the main goal in life is to improve the quality of our lives, whatever that might mean to each of us.

This larger objective cannot be achieved, however, unless most of our subsidiary ones are well-integrated into this larger whole. The larger the context we wisely include in our quality of life scope, the more aware we become of the interdependencies that exist in the various aspects of our lives and their connections to others and the historical world we engage.

As Stephen Covey, Roger Merrill, and Rebecca Merrill stress in *First Things First,*

> The fact is that quality of life is, by nature, interdependent. Our roles are interdependent—we're husbands, wives, parents, friends' bosses, employees, co-workers, associates, community members, citizens. Quality in almost every role involves a relationship with at least one other individual. Our accomplishments are interdependent. Although we look back in history and tend to say that one particular person "invented" or "discovered" a particular thing, the reality is that most great achievements were not made in a vacuum.

Aiming for Quality of Life

Quality of life is one thing that everyone can commit to fully. Just as successful companies have clear missions, goals, rewards, and recognition processes that inspire everyone to work together and try harder, committing yourself to a quality of life requires the same kind of clarity.

Most people in Silicon Valley feel as though they work for Silicon Valley rather than for any one company. Everyone wants the option of jumping to the most exciting projects, wherever they may be. While many people would not mind leaving a particular company there, in most instances they would not want to leave the valley.

In a world where work is not confined to particular times of day, such as at Microsoft with its restaurants, gyms, and twenty-four-hour open buildings, every aspect of life—work, play, friendship, family—gets intertwined. All boundaries disappear. In such a world, everyone needs to complement one another if anything is going to work at all. And all of us will need to acquire the ability to achieve both internal, external, and interpersonal harmony if we are going to weather the competitive challenges that await us all.

Rosabeth Moss Kanter in *World Class* found that the key to success in those areas of the United States that are global economy hot spots was the high degree of integration of all aspects of business and community life. With the city or region becoming a new economic competitive entity in the global marketplace, it makes sense to move to one that has a prosperous future ahead of it and the kind of lifestyle you enjoy.

Career and competitive success are primarily the result of being able to immerse yourself completely in something that consumes your interest. The difference between those who succeed or fail in their pursuits is almost completely dependent on the extent to which they can immerse themselves in it. Fortunately, it is also the way in which all paradoxes are resolved—by creative solutions. People who can immerse themselves in their passions relish challenge, like players absorbed in a chess game. Indeed, people who learn chess enhance their math, problem-solving, and reading comprehension skills by improving their ability to think logically and concentrate better.

Most of us, however, are not caught up in finite games like chess, where there are clearly established rules, an end to the game, and a winner declared. As James Carse, author of *Finite and Infinite Games,* suggests, our lives resemble infinite games where there are no clear rules and the purpose is not to win but to continue playing the game. You want to be able to immerse yourself in a field of endeavor and locations that can sustain you over the long haul. But we must always be willing to adjust even these choices as both we and life's circumstances coevolve.

Nonetheless, we need to optimize our possibilities despite a cloudy crystal ball at times. We just need to know when it is time to move on and always remember that it is the nature of the process that defines our quality of life and not some distant goal. In other words, the means is ultimately the end, for goals must be constantly revised as part of the renewal or change process that is a natural art of life's rhythm.

Americans have always seemed to have intuitively understood this process, for as Wilf Corrigan, CEO of Silicon Valley's LSI Logic, believes,

> One of the great advantages of America is that Americans have no memory. The reason I left Europe was because there's such a long memory that you can't initiate change. But Americans have no memory at all. I'm convinced an American work force can come into work on Monday morning and find the whole production line has changed and by coffee break they're used to the new environment. Americans, unlike, say, the Japanese, are used to change. Most other countries are not. Americans are uniquely adapted to change. Change is the way we can win.

Location, Location, Location

In the larger context at any given moment, you should be trying to find a location, like Silicon Valley for high-tech workers, that will allow you to immerse yourself completely in a highly competitive business culture and lifestyle that will make you world class, increase the diversity of your career options and networking opportunities, and give you the quality of life you need. Whether it is through magazines such as *Inc., Success,* or *Entrepreneur,* which frequently feature the hottest entrepreneurial locations in America, or through industry and trade journals that benchmark the winners by place, make sure you are keeping score.

As with real estate, the fundamental rule—even for those who are doing business strictly on the information highway—is location, location, location. In a just-in-time world, being close to a well-integrated supply chain and the customer counts even more in many instances. As William Davidow and Michael Malone indicate in *The Virtual Corporation,*

> The virtual corporation ... will abhor distance. If it can find a friendly environment close to customers, it will want to locate there. Being close will enable it to be more responsive ... One likely result of this will be a repatriation to the United States of production operations moved overseas a generation ago ... Factories will be located centrally in some cases, in the distribution channel in others, and at the customer's site in other instances.

Once quality and dependability become commodities, the ultimate competitive advantage in an age of mass customization lies in speed and flexibility. Flexibility, however, is deeply dependent on a conducive location and atmosphere that provide alternative options and encourage diverse network building.

As noted in a report by the Association for Manufacturing Excellence, "Flexibility is something people do. Organizations of people may be combined or dissociated, but flexibility itself is not attained through things, financial or physical."

In a similar vein, finding a favorable location that improves the overall quality of your life in a dependable manner and that naturally brings together the kind of people you need to meet for career development purposes will give you the resilience and flexibility needed to make whatever adjustments are necessary when the time comes.

Most people will want to avoid locations that unnecessarily complicate or burden their lives with extraneous worries and concerns. In a complicated world, accommodating one-stop shopping and easy-to-navigate, friendly, relaxing environments are essential catalysts for immersion. People will therefore demand quick and customized services that help make their lives simpler and easier to manage.

Indeed, even with manufactured items it is the time to market and the responsiveness of any product that now determine their value. In other words, the overall service component has become the defining competitive advantage in most cases. Knowing the customer intimately becomes the precursor to flexible customization. But intimacy requires trust. So only in an environment where people or companies trust and understand one another and feel a kindredness of spirit can this necessary flexibility flourish—especially in the supplier, customer, company, community, or life relationships that must become more tightly interwoven to attain the world-class quality we have all come to expect.

Thus most people and companies will avidly seek out places that best serve their particular quality of relationship needs so that they too may flourish. Indeed, many entrepreneurial career and business opportunities will arise from identifying highly segmented markets that are profitable or undeserved but well understood and appropriate to one's focus.

Agile companies or individuals who take advantage of this increasing segmentation of markets and communities and tailor their offerings accordingly can even establish market leadership in these areas. Quality of life, like dating and entrepreneurial opportunity, is often a question of finding the right match—in this case, the appropriate place where things are likely to come together for you and your customers.

Synchronous synergy comes from the complete integration of all aspects of one's life just as regional competitiveness depends on a well-integrated business, municipal, and social community. So this kind of continuous collaborative improvement with everyone involved would seem to be unavoidable since global competitiveness will demand it of us all. With increased integration comes interdependency and a strong sense of co-destiny.

One trend likely to grow out of this quality-of-life movement will be industry-specific tax havens around the world in desirable locations. Large real estate development firms and well-situated countries will eventually wake up to the potential in creating a city or regional environment attractive to firms that are competitively interdependent and want to avoid social problems and the taxation associated with them. If they can create an attractive cultural climate, these industrial parks or incubators on a global scale will flourish at the expense of less desirable locations.

As many aging boomers want to retire to some location where their retirement income goes further because of friendly taxation policies, safe neighborhoods, and satisfactory health facilities, the notion of national loyalty could shift to a willingness to relocate to the place with the best quality of life, irrespective of location, in the world.

The American Dream may be in the process of becoming the Global Dream and all of the implications suggested by it. Companies wanting to stay close to paying customers will naturally follow. If such is the case, then scenario planning would make even more urgent sense since these developments force us to ask serious questions concerning the future of employment opportunities in America.

First, the Bad News

A March 1995 *Business Week*/Harris poll found that 70 percent of Americans were pessimistic about the future despite a raging bull stock market. *The New York Times* ran a front page headline announcing the "Paradox of '94: Gloomy Voters In Good Times." Even *Time* magazine's cover on one issue asked, "Boom for Whom?"

The painful reality behind the booming economy is that many people are making longer commutes, working harder but getting paid less, watching more families deteriorate as couples take on second jobs in order to get by, feeling the hollowing out of the middle class as the wealthy prosper even more, and noticing crime and congestion increasing in their neighborhoods. If things are getting worse, why are they not being reflected in the economic picture we are being given?

Just as everyone in the story came to realize that the emperor had no clothes on, it has become glaringly evident that using the Gross Domestic Product as a measure of wealth and prosperity can be misleading. Why? GDP measures economic activity but not the quality of the business generated.

For instance, between 1950 and 1990, non-wealth-creating economic activity increased at a faster rate than the GDP in the United States and was estimated to account for 10 percent of all economic growth. In other words, except for a possible increase in the quality of goods and services delivered over that time span, many Americans were economically poorer in 1990 than in 1950.

If we look behind the smoke and mirrors associated with economic growth, we find that most of the growth has taken place in things that actually decrease the quality of life. How is this possible? We have only to realize that each crime committed increases the GDP to begin to understand what has been happening (for example, each gunshot wound ups the GDP by $50,000 in medical expenses).

Even in 1980, $21.7 billion was being spent annually on private security. In shopping malls, security staff account for a larger portion of the labor costs than do sales staff. Drug abuse increases the GDP each year by an estimated $60 billion. No wonder half of the world's insurance business as measured by premiums is devoted to covering Americans.

Hamish McCrae notes in *The World in 2020,*

> Around three-quarters of the world's lawyers live in the US ... there is some evidence that the number of lawyers in a country is in inverse proportion to its economic growth rate. Too many lawyers, so it would seem, actually destroy wealth ... Another "transaction cost" is political lobbying ... The number of political lobbyists registered with the U.S. Senate soared from 365 in 1960 to 40,111 in 1992.

Depressing? Almost enough to make you turn to Prozac, which also boosts the GDP by $1.2 billion annually. Clifford Cobb, Ted Halstead, and Jonathan Rowe in an *Atlantic Monthly* article entitled, "If GDP is Up, Why is America Down," came up with what they call a "genuine progress indicator" or GPI, which compensates for these quality of life distortions masked by the GDP. As they explain, the rosy picture painted by the GDP is false:

> The GPI shows a very different picture: an upward curve from the early fifties until about 1970, but a gradual decline of roughly 45 percent since then. This strongly suggests that the costs of increased economic activity—have begun to outweigh the benefits, resulting in growth that is actually uneconomic.

No wonder politicians only talk about growth and not what it consists of since a rising GDP does not lift all boats; instead, it actually lowers many.

This tragedy is the result of failing to adopt a more holistic view of what has been happening in society. All of the foregoing problems are all interdependent in nature, yet governments and individuals have typically tried to treat each problem separately with the expected disastrous results.

It should be obvious that if society is having serious problems getting its act together, there will be individuals who are noticing these developments and taking appropriate measures to ensure the quality of their own lives. Just as the first people to leave a company that is downsizing for the sake of cutting costs are usually the most highly skilled and valued employees, it is likely that many knowledge workers will seek out more favorable locations in the United States or elsewhere.

As Christopher Lasch points out in a *Harper's Magazine* article, the "privileged classes," as he calls them, have detached themselves from the notion of national decline:

> It is not just that they see no point in paying for public services they no longer use; many of the them have ceased to think of themselves as Americans in any important sense, implicated in America's destiny for better or worse.

A recent *Forbes* magazine cover article, entitled "The New Refugees," explored how, "As their tax burdens grow, many affluent Americans are abandoning their citizenship." Wealthy people hold over $2 trillion in accounts located in places such as the Grand Caymans or Zurich. As Nassos Michas, head of Merrill Lynch's private banking division notes, "Offshore money is growing faster than any other part of the financial services industry. It's multiplying at a double-digit rate of growth." Merrill Lynch's trust bank on Grand Cayman has over $5 billion in held assets, which are growing at the rate of $100 million per month. People are obviously beginning to weigh their worldwide options very carefully.

Those locations in the United States that are significantly integrated, cosmopolitan, and self-renewing will continue to prosper. Other U.S. locations certainly have their global challenges mapped out for them. Over the long term, the U.S. government will simply have no choice but to privatize most of its functions as described by Joel Garreau in *Edge City* if taxes are to be kept within reason and jobs kept in the country.

All entitlement programs will likely be severely curtailed very soon—not through choice or design, but out of sheer economic necessity. Thus, becoming a career entrepreneur is not even an option but a forced choice: either become a career entrepreneur and take advantage of these inevitable changes, or let the world pass you by.

Hope for the Future

Fortunately, for those who choose to accept the entrepreneurship challenge, there is plenty of good news in store. America is back on its competitive feet once again. The United States has had six years of solid growth while Japan has been struggling. For the third year in a row, the World Economic Forum has ranked America as the world's most competitive economy.

In fact, in 1994 AT&T became the first American company to win Japan's coveted Deming Prize for quality control. Moreover, in 1994 America's growth rates in its standard of living, investment in plant and equipment, and manufacturing productivity were the highest in the past ten years.

In 1989, a distinguished MIT commission issued an industrial productivity report, "Made in America," which was rather unsparing in its criticism of how far America had fallen behind the best practices of the rest of the world.

Since then GM has learned from Toyota through joint ventures, Ford from Mazda, and Boeing from Toyota. Detroit owes its turnaround to putting people with significant foreign experience at the helm: Chrysler's Robert Eaton originally was in charge of GM Europe for four years, Ford's British-born Alex Trotman had run operations in East Asia and Europe, and GM's Jack Smith established his credentials by running international operations as well in Europe.

Not surprisingly other foreigners now are in charge of other American companies: German-born Eckard Pfeiffer runs Compaq, and Andy Grove, Intel's CEO, was a Hungarian immigrant. In addition, during the current export boom, most American firms are exploring how to take advantage of business opportunities in Brazil, China, India, or Russia.

Even shareholders are now taking a long-term view and are actively removing pay that is based on short-term performance, as well as getting rid of CEOs at GM, Eastman Kodak, Digital Equipment, and Westinghouse.

Manufacturing? Intel has put in $10 billion into new manufacturing facilities over the past five years and is expected to become America's most profitable company. The status of manufacturing engineers has greatly improved, and even the universities are now giving manufacturing the respect long due.

Employee training, supplier and union relations, and productivity tied to quality, reliability, and customization are all in process of dramatic improvement. Productivity has improved by 2 percent per year since 1991, over twice the 1978-1987 average.

The service sector is about to experience a productivity revolution thanks to $1 trillion that has been spent on information technology. Deregulation and free trade agreements have awakened just about everyone to the new global marketplace realities.

Outsourcing in the form of smaller firm "help supply" services (for instance, computer operators, security guards, cleaners, and accountants) have been responsible for 14 percent of all new jobs created since the last recession, an increase from 5 percent between 1982 and 1990. Roughly one-third of all companies are experimenting with various forms of teamwork or worker empowerment. Infrastructure renewal is well on its way.

Indeed, it is America's willingness to reinvent itself that will always keep it on top. As the *Economist* declares,

> No country has done a better job of mixing together personal ambition, footloose capital, and ferocious competition ... Perhaps, more than a decade after Ronald Reagan coined the phrase, it is really about to be morning in America.

Almost all managers agree that America is in the midst of a fundamental change. The rest of the world looks on with keen interest since it realizes that it too will be heading down the same road shortly.

What is hard to replicate elsewhere, however, is American culture and the experimental, Wild West frontier mentality that still lives on. In fact, the rest of the world is paying an ever-increasing fortune for its entertainment products that celebrate this maverick license to experiment that Americans seem to claim as their birthright.

In 1900, 50 percent of all Americans were self-employed, so job entitlement is only a recent transitory mass production aberration. When in January of 1992 the stock market value of Microsoft surpassed that of GM, the new knowledge economy began to hit its stride. There is no turning back now that the information technology genie has been let out of its bottle.

Thus before long everyone in America will be regaining her entrepreneurial spurs, except this time around it will be in the knowledge economy. The open-ended nature of the information highway with its unlimited number of lanes will provide an essentially free distribution system for all who realize the incredible entrepreneurial opportunity that lies at everyone's doorstep—and connects us all together.

Just as Henry Ford's mission was to democratize transportation by offering cars that everyone could afford, the new highway we are all about to head down welcomes us all as hunters, gatherers, and herders to stake our claim, however fleeting, in a world that is definitely open for business. Although it may be a bumpy ride at times, anyone who cherishes the qualities that have made America great will definitely want to be part of this pioneering wagon train. After all, the first settlers get their pick of where to put down their roots. If you can immerse yourself in the creative excitement of it all, you should have no trouble finding your way.

In order to win a lottery, you need to buy a ticket. In this case, the ticket is an unreserved commitment to carving out your destiny in this ever emerging, kaleidoscopic world of ours. The rest will take care of itself, for as the German poet Goethe so nicely put it:

> The moment one definitely commits oneself, then providence moves too. All sorts of things occur to help one that would never otherwise have

> occurred ... Whatever you can do or dream you can, begin it. Boldness has genius, power and magic in it. Begin now.

Just trust to the self-reliance celebrated by Ralph Waldo Emerson, and in one shape or form you will find many paths that lead to a number of global doorways. If you have the career resilience to keep knocking, they will surely open for you with less effort each time. Fortunately, there is much wisdom to be gained from the rhythm of life's many experiments that will help us to renew ourselves, to find new directions, and to rediscover those values that give our lives their quality, meaning, and purpose.

We just need the courage of our career convictions to venture forth. That shouldn't be hard though, since America has always applauded those who try to make things happen.

All the best to you, and may the future be kind to us all.

PART V

Internet Resource Guide

Internet Resource Guide

In an information and networking era, connections to the right information and the right people are essential for making innovative and mutually beneficial things happen. With people mobile and information dating quickly, you need a way of staying current at all times, and a means of meeting everyone you might like to meet from wherever you may be. By taking advantage of the many resources available, you are never further than a phone call or a modem line away from leveraging the rest of the world's resources to your advantage. Besides, you can also cut out all the redundant intermediaries as well. In the age of the virtual corporation, when fortunes can be made by running a business from out of your house or from any location you happen to be, the obvious secret is staying connected and keeping in touch. Remember a just-in-time era demands just-in-time resources. So either become a real-time, direct resource provider, or be the first to take advantage of all the new opportunities that each information change delivers.

How to Get Money

Loan Institutions

Get loans based on your inventory assets and accounts receivables.

Commercial Finance Association
212-594-3490

Investment Companies

Individual private investors spend from $10 to $20 billion per year bankrolling entrepreneurs for a portion of the equity or percent of the revenues, according to William Wetzel, director emeritus of the Center For Venture Research at the University of New Hampshire.

Accelerate
714-509-2990

Accel Partners
http://www.accel.com

Adams Capital Management
http://corp.tig.com/acm/index.html

Atlas Venture
http://www.tisco.com/atlas

Capital Express
http://moneyhunter.com/capex/pl.htm

Capital Network Inc.
512-305-0826

FinanceNet
http://www.financenet.gov

Financial Information Link Library (FILL)
http://www.mbnet.mb.ca/~russell

Investors's Circle
708-876-1101
(community development education, energy efficient, environment, health)

National Association of Small Business Investment Companies
703-683-1601
http://www.nsbu.org/affiliat.htm

Northwest Capital Network
503-225-2980
(Oregon)

NYU EDGAR
http://edgar.stern.nyu.edu/index.html

Olympic Venture Partners
http://product.com/olyrnpic

SEC EDGAR
http:/www-sec.gov/edgarhp.htm

Seed Capital Network Inc.
423-5734655
($225 connections fee to wealthy investors)

Technology Capital Network at MIT
617-253-7163

Overseas Ventures and Export Financing

Consider taking advantage of markets growing at a much faster clip than in the United States.

Accel Partners
609-683-4500
415-989-5656

Asia Business Directories
http://www.asia-directory.com/~bruno/

Asia Trade
http://www.asiadir.com

Amsterdam Pacific Corp.
415-421-3636

Alliance Forum
415-433-7118

Europa
http://europa.eu.int

IBEX, c/o Global Business Alliance
613-230-5371

International Trade Administration
http://www.ita.doc.gov

National Assoc. of Small Business Investment Companies
202-628-5055

U.S. International Trade Commission
http://www.usitc.gov

When You Don't Have Money

Barter

When you don't have lots of cash, but you can trade goods or services, mutual problem solving is the way to go.

International Reciprocal Trade Association
703-916-9020

BarterNet
http://www.teleport.com/~dtpdx/bnhome. htm

Credit Checks

Before you run up big accounts receivable balances, check out prospective customers to ensure that you will likely get paid.

CDB Infotek
714-708-2000

National Credit Information Network
513-522-3832
1-800-374-1400

General Resources

This is the world's largest nonprofit membership association of CEOs and entrepreneurs.

Center for Entrepreneurial Management
212-633-0060

Leasing

One way to make scarce financial resources go further and avoid committing to rapidly dating equipment.

Equipment Leasing Assoc. of America
703-527-8655

Multilevel Marketing or Networking

Say goodbye to start-up costs, accounts receivables, mounting inventories, and the need to show up for work every day. Find friends who enjoy helping everyone get ahead in a mutually supporting franchise system. Pick the company with products you would like; get people involved in it; and eliminate accounts receivables, upfront investments, inventory costs, and business loans. Retire with other people generating your income.

Career World
http://careerworld.com
http://homeshoppingunlimited.com

How to Get Information

Government

Can provide loans based on fixed assets or equity and often supply patent information, development help, market information, and industry standards application resource material.

National Assoc. of Development Companies
703-812-9000

National Institute of Standards and Technology
301-975-3058

Network Marketing Solutions Inc.
281-463-2420

The SBA Answer Desk
1-800-827-5722

SBA Investment Div.
202-205-7333

U.S. Patent & Trademark Office
http://www.uspto.gov

U.S. Small Business Administration
202-205-6600

Incubators

Contacts, group insurance and facilities, and training are available.

National Business Incubation Assoc.
614-593-4331
mperdrea
reach.com
http://ra.cs.ohiou.edu/gopher/
dept.servers/aern/homepage/nbia.html

Investment Forums

Great financial dating services and idea generators for investors and entrepreneurs.

Information Industry Assoc.'s Investor Conf.
202-639-8262

Oklahoma Investment Forum
918-587-1909

Minorities and Women

Make use of a supportive network that has solutions to some of the problems you are likely to encounter.

National Assoc. for Female Executives
212-477-2200

Office of Minority Business Development
312-814-3540

U.S. Dept. of Commerce. Minority Business Dev. Agency
202-482-1936

Women's Business Dev. Centre
312-853-3477

Women's Equity Fund
303-443-2620

Online Resources

Hookup and tune in to an unlimited world of resources.

African American Board
America Online→*keyword* communities→African American Board

African American Business Hotline
1-888-BLACK-411
http://www.scbbs.com/~unite-us

African-American and Minority Businesses
Genie→*keyword* hosb→HOSB Round-Table Bulletin Board→14 African American and Minority Business

alt.business.multi-level
Usenet

alt.make.money.fast

Association of Collegiate Entrepreneurs
http://www.csupomona.edu/ace

Better Business Bureau
http://www.bbb.org./ bbb

Big Dreams
http://www.nlc-bnc.ca/eppp.archive/bigdreams-b/bigdreams.b09/

biz.jobs.offered
Usenet

Business (echo)
Fidonet

Business-Ad.
Smartnet

Business Conference
Well→gbusiness

Capital Quest
http://www.usbusiness.com/capquest/home.html

Catalogue of Federal Domestic Assistance
Internet→*gopher* gopher.rtd.utk.edu→Federal Government

CEO ACCESS
http://entrepreneurs.com/eol/index.htm
Information→Catalogue of Federal Domestic Assistance

Chicano-Latinonet
Internet→*gopher* latino.sscnet.ucla.edu

Classifieds Software Library.
America Online→*keyword* classifieds→Classifieds Software Library

D.I.C.E. National Network BBS
(Free postings from over 80 agencies)
modem 515-280-3423
phone 515-280-1144

Disabled Businesspersons Association
http://www.catalog.com:80/rmg/dba.htm

Entrepreneur
Fidonet

Entrepreneurial and Business Funding
Compuserve→*go* ius-8679

Entrepreneurs on the Web (EOTW)
http://www.eotw.com

Entrepreneur Magazine Small Business Forum
Compuserve→*go* ent32

Entrepreneur Magazine Small Business Survey
Compuserve→go entmagazine

Entrepreneur Online
http://www.entrepreneurmag.com

Ernst & Young Business Series.
America Online→*keyword* news→Ernst & Young

Exec-PC BBS
414-789-4200

Executives.
Classified—ProfMgmt. (echo)—JOBNET
Resumes—ProfMgtmt.
(echo)—JOBNET

Federal Grant Database
Genie→*keyword* directory→Federal Grant Database

FEDIX/MOLIS—Federal Information Exchange, Inc.
http://web.fie.com

Foundation and Corporate Grants Alert
Internet→gopher gopher.enews.com→
Magazines, Periodicals and Journals→
Foundation and Corporate Grants Alert

Fourll White Page Directory
http://www.four11.com

Franchise & Business Opportunities
Compuserve→*go* ebs.4

Global Entrepreneurs Network
http://www.entrepreneurs.net/

Global Network Navigator (GNN)
http://nearnet.gnn.com

Guide to Business Credit
America Online→*keyword* business strategies→Guide to Business Credit

Home & Small Business Answer Book Excerpts
Genie→*keyword* hosb→Home & Small Business Answer Book Excerpts

Human Resources
Classified—HumResor (echo) JOBNET
http://www.ideacafe.com

http://www.inc.com

Internet Business Center
http://www.tig.com/ibc/

Internet Business Pages
http://www.ibp.com

Internet Marketing Discussion List
http://www.popco.com

InvestQuest Inc.
http://invest.quest. columbus.oh.us

IOMA Business Page
http://ioma.com/ioma

Job Listings from around globe—U. of Texas
Internet®*gopher*
bongo.cc.utexas.edu®Information About Gopher®World®Jobs

Lycos (index of over 5 million Web Pages)
http://lycos.cs.cmu.edu

Marketing
Classified—Marketing
JOBNET

Maui Small Business Development Centre
http://www.maui.com/~sbdc/

MicroPatent Patent Server
http://www.micropat.com

Microsoft Small Business Centre
America Online®*keyword* small business

Misc.entrepreneurs
Usenet

Money Hunter
http://www.lowe.org/smbiznet/sites/98.htm

National Indian Policy Centre
®*www* gopher://gwis.circ.gwu.edu/11/Academic%20Departments/National%20lndian%20Policy%20Centre/

NlightN Universal Index
http://www.nlightn.com

NYNEX Interactive Yellow Pages
http://www.niyp.com/

Office Automation Vendor Forum
Compuserve®*go* oaforum

JobHunt
http://www.rcf.usc.edu/~.haiynez/job/jobform.html

Open Market's Commercial Sites Index
Alta Vista

Professional Salaried Jobs.
America Online®*keyword* classifieds®Business & Jobs Postings®Professional Salaried Jobs

Professionals Online
http://www.prosonline.com

SBA Financing Assistance
Internet®*telnet* sbaonline.sba.gov®[2] Services Available®[3] Financing Services

Self-employment Forum
Delphi®*go* cus 276

world.gov®D®40 or 41

Small Business Advancement National Centre
http://www.sbaer.uca.edu/

Small Business Innovation Research Program—SBIR
http://www.sbaonline.sba.gov/sbir/sbir.html

Small Business Institute Program
http://wwwsbanet.uca.edu/sbi-2.html

Small Business Resources.
America Online®*keyword* small business®Small Business Resources

Small Business Software Library.
America Online®*keyword* small business®Software Library
http://www.successmagazine.com

The Business Resource Directory
sbaonline.
Genie®*keyword* directory

The Entrepreneur's Forum
Compuserve®*go* usen

The Grant Getters Guide to the Internet
Internet®*gopher* uidaho.edu®Science, Research, & Grant Information®Grant Information

U.S. Small Business Administration
http://www.sbaonline.sba.gov/

USENET Groups
http://www.execpc.com

US News Women's Forum.
Compuserve®*go* women®Messages®Working Women

Venture Connect
http://www.vencon.com

White House Conference on Small Business
America Online®*keyword* small business®Small Business Resources

White House Conference on Small Business
America Online—*keyword* whcsb

The Whole Internet for Windows 95
http://www.ora.com/catalog/twiwin/

Women and Business.
Genie®*keyword*®hosb®HOSB Round-Table Bulletin Board®Category 29 ## Women's Business ##

Women's Center
America Online®*keyword* communities®Women's Board

Working from Home Forum
Compuserve®*go* work

Working Solo
Eworld®*go* solo

World Entrepreneurs' Association
http://www.wrldea.com/

The WWW Virtual Library
http://www.w3.org/pub/DataSources/bySubject/

Yahoo!
http://www.yahoo.com/

Publications and Software

Make full use of databases and directories in finding what you need regarding financing and business connections.

Arthur Andersen North American Business Sourcebook
1-800-920-0005

Finding Money: The Small Business Guide to Financing by Kate Lister & John Hamish
John Wiley
605 Third Ave.
NY 10158-0012

Gale Research
1-800-877-4253

How to Grow Your Business on the Internet by Vince Emery
Coriolis Group Books
7339 E. Acoma Dr., Suite 7
Scottsdale, AZ 85260

International Venture Capital Institute
203-323-3143

The Internet Business Guide: Riding the Information Superhighway to Profit by Rosalind Resnick & Dave Taylor
Sams.Net
201 W. 103rd St.
Indianapolis, IN 46290

The Investment Exchange
416-512-9957

National Assoc. of State Development Agencies
202-898-1302

National Venture Capital Association
703-351-5269

Venture Economics, a Division of Securities Data Publishing Inc.
212-765-5311

Television

Good question-and-answer program for entrepreneurs.

Money Hunt Properties
203-866-2503

Finding a Job

Jobs

Use these on-line resources to get into more industry-specific categories.

Arizona—az.jobs

Atlanta
—atl.jobs
—atl.resumes

Austin.jobs

Baltimore/Wash.
balt.jobs

Biologists—bionet.jobs

Cleveland—cle.jobs

Computer—biz.jobs.offered

Chicago—chi.jobs

Connecticut—conn.jobs.offered

Contract/tech/—misc.jobs.contract

Dallas/Fort Worth
dfw.jobs

Dept. of Defense—dod.jobs

Directory of Executive Recruiters—http://www.careermag.com/careermag/

Florida—fl.jobs

Houston—houston.jobs.offered

Huntsville—hsv.jobs

Iowa—ia.jobs

Illinois
—il.jobs.misc.
—il.jobs.offered
—il.jobs.resumes

Indiana—in.jobs

Los Angeles—la.jobs

Michigan—mi.jobs

Milwaukee—milw.jobs

misc.jobs.misc.

misc.jobs.offered

misc.jobs.offered.entry

misc.jobs.resumes

NeXT hardware/software—comp.sys.next.marketplace

New England—ne.jobs

New Mexico—nm.jobs

New York City
—nyc.jobs
—nyc.jobs.contract
—nyc.jobs.misc.
—nyc.jobs.offered
—nyc.jobs.wanted

Ohio State Univ.—osu.jobs

Physics—hepnet.jobs

Pittsburgh
—pgh.jobs.offered
—pgh.jobs.wanted

Programming—prg.jobs

sci.research.careers

San Diego—sdnet.jobs

San Francisco
—ba.jobs.contract
—ba.jobs.offered

Seattle—seattle jobs.offered

St. Louis—stl.jobs

Texas—tx.jobs

Univ. of Ca
—ucb.jobs
—ucd.kiosk.jobs

Univ. of Illinois
—uiuc.cs.jobs
—uiuc.misc.jobs
—uiuc.kiosk.jobs

Univ. of Minnesota
—umn.cs.jobs
—umn.general.jobs
—umn.itlab.jobs

US
—mh.jobs
—us.jobs.contract
—us.jobs.misc.
—us.jobs.offered
—us.jobs.offered.entry
—us.jobs.resumes

Univ. of Texas—ut.jobs

vmsnet.employment

Washington—dc.jobs

World Wide Web Yellow Pages—
http://www.yellow.com

Yahoo—Business and Economy:
Organizations
http://www.yahoo.com/business and economy/organizations

Jobs—Foreign

Consider getting a global leg up on your rapidly growing competion. By going to where the best jobs are, you can find the best learning curve opportunities.

Australia
—aus.ads.jobs
—aus.jobs

Canada
—ab.jobs
—can.jobs
—kw.jobs
—ont.jobs
—ott.jobs
—tor.jobs

Chile—chile.trabajos
(Usenet)

Denmark—dk.jobs

Germany
—de.markt.jobs
—bln.jobs

Ireland—ie.jobs

Israel
—il.jobss.misc.
—il.jobs.offered
—il.jobs.resumes
(Usenet)

New Zealand
www gopher.//central.co.nz/
11Jobs%20Online%20New
%20Zealand

Russia
relcom.commerce.jobs
(Usenet)

South Africa—za.ads.jobs

Sweden—swnet.jobs

United Kingdom—uk.jobs

Internships Abroad

Leapfrog your competitors in global learning careerwise and be perceived as someone who is culturally flexible and adaptable.

Assoc. for International Practical Training (AIPT)
10400 Little Patuxent Parkway, Suite 250
Columbia, MD 21044-3510
tel: 410-997-2200 fax: 410-992-3924

Assoc. Internationale des Etudiants en Science Economiques et Commerciales (Aiesec)
135 W. 50th St., 20th fl.
New York, NY 10020
Tel: 212-757-3774 Fax: 212-757-4062

Institute of International Education
Free Market Development Advisers Program
1400 K St. NW
Washington, DC 20005-2403
Tel: 202-362-7855 Fax: 202-962-8834

International Association for the Exchange of Students for Technical Experience
10400 Little Patuxenet Parkway, Suite 250
Columbia, MD 21044-3510
Tel: 410-997-2200 Fax: 410-997-5186

MBA Enterprise Corps
CB 3440
Univ. of North Carolina
Chapel Hill, NC 27599-3440
Tel: 919-962-2682 Fax: 919-962-2784

Work Permits
Council on International Educational Exchange
Tel: 212-822-2600

Best Search Engine

http://www.hotbot.com
(Tip: Use words such as "recruiters," "entrpreneurs," "employment," "career," etc. Plus indicate your location of interest—for example, Los Angeles.)

More Good JIST & Park Avenue Books

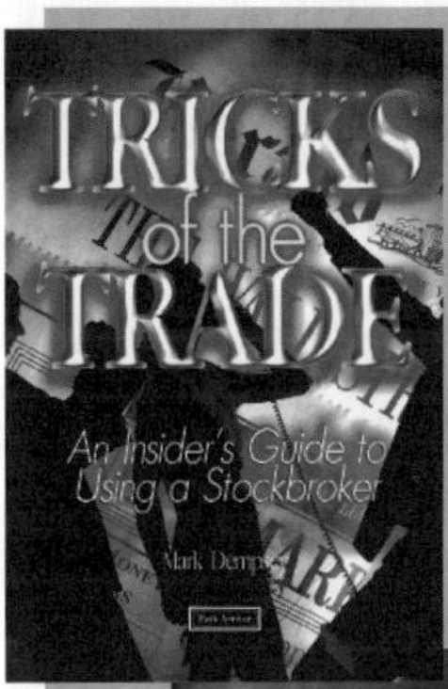

Tricks of the Trade

How to Get the Best from Your Broker Without Your Broker Getting the Best of You

by Mark Dempsey

Millions of Americans who invest their money are at the mercy of full-service brokerage firms. What exactly are they paying for and how can they avoid costly mistakes? Our Wall Street insider presents the answers in a lively, entertaining, informative style.

ISBN 1-57112-084-X • **$14.95**

SuccessAbilities!™

1,003 Practical Ways to Keep Up, Stand Out, and Move Ahead at Work

by Paula Ancona

Our noted national columnist tells readers how they can find more time in their busy days, handle conflicts, balance work and family, network, negotiate, and take charge of their careers in this thoughtful, lively book that was voted Best Business Book of the Year.

ISBN 1-56370-444-7 • **$14.95**

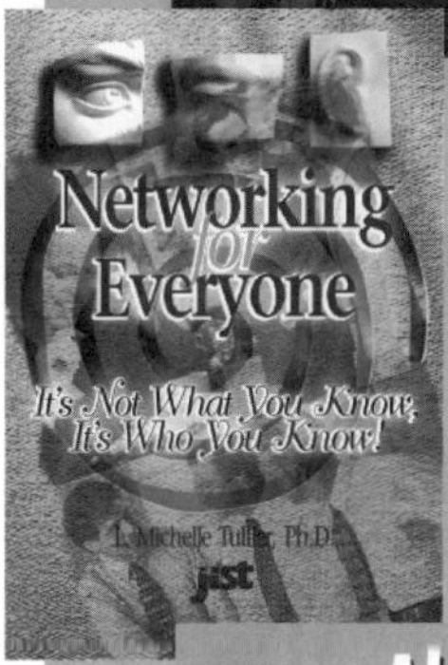

Networking for Everyone

It's Not What You Know, It's Who You Know

by L. Michelle Tullier, Ph.D.

Networking is the key to business and professional success. The know-how that people need to network effectively is here in this lively, entertaining book. It's the most comprehensive guide on how to make, maintain, and capitalize on your connections.

ISBN 1-56370-440-4 • **$12.95**

Living Abroad

Survive and Thrive in a Second Culture

by Pat Westheimer & Allison Mackey

Living and working abroad can be an adventure: difficult, surprising, challenging, and extremely rewarding. These authors tell readers from personal experience how to make the decision and the move, and explain a thousand-and-one other considerations.

ISBN 1-57112-087-4 • **$14.95**